SUPPLEMENT TO

TRIAL

ADVOCACY BEFORE JUDGES, JURORS, AND ARBITRATORS

Fifth Edition

■ ■ ■

by

Roger Haydock

Professor of Law, William Mitchell College of Law
Member, Minnesota, South Dakota, and Federal Bars
Director, FORUM International
Founder, ABA LSD Arbitration Competition
Board Member, Academy of Court-Appointed Masters

John Sonsteng

Professor of Law, William Mitchell College of Law
Member, Minnesota and Federal Bars
Regional Director, National Institute for Trial Advocacy
Director, William Mitchell Summer International Program

AMERICAN CASEBOOK SERIES®

WEST
ACADEMIC
PUBLISHING

To

All the William Mitchell College of Law Students
We Have Had the Privilege of Teaching

PREFACE

Skills without ideas are a menace, and ideas without skills are a mess. You need both to be a complete advocate.

This Supplement provides the additional, essential "idea" information to develop effective skills. Our text, *Trial Advocacy Before Judges, Jurors, and Arbitrators*, provides the basic and advanced notions of advocacy, supplemented by the materials in this book.

You learn how to be an advocate by reading about advocacy, understanding its theory and application, studying examples, reviewing entire case transcripts, reading about how others successfully act as advocates, conducting advocacy exercises, being critiqued by professionals, observing yourself on video replays, and eventually representing real clients in real cases and being an actual advocate yourself. The accompanying *Trial Advocacy* book and these materials help you complete the first five steps to becoming an advocate. References to sections in this *Supplement* refer to sections in the *Trial Advocacy* text.

This *Supplement* contains advocacy rules and case transcripts with commentary. The federal rules of evidence and selected federal rules of civil procedure provide a handy reference to those sources. There are also three case transcripts accompanied by extensive commentary:

> A jury trial, *Riley v. Garfield House Apartments*
>
> An arbitration, *Bingham v. Ecotronics*
>
> An administrative proceeding, *Scratch v. Stone*

Individually and collectively, they present examples of how advocates bring to life the strategies, tactics, and techniques necessary to win a case. A video of the arbitration is freely available at http://software.west academic.com/lawyering-skills/. Peter Knapp and Ann Juergens, along with Roger Haydock, created and directed it so law students and lawyers could see a case brought to real life. P. Knapp, A. Juergens, and R. Haydock, Lawyering Video: Mediation and Arbitration (with Manual), West Academic. Another video of a trial is also available at the same website. P. Knapp, A. Juergens, and R. Haydock, Lawyering Video: Depositions and Trial (with Manual), West Academic. Future editions of this *Supplement* will add additional resources including demonstration lawyering skill videos.

This *Supplement* may be a mandatory or an optional book in your advocacy course. We believe the materials are an essential ingredient in the makings of an advocate, and we hope you will find the contents very useful, quite informative, and highly educational.

ROGER HAYDOCK
JOHN SONSTENG
William Mitchell College of Law
875 Summit Avenue
Saint Paul, MN 55105
roger.haydock@wmitchell.edu
john.sonsteng@wmitchell.edu

June 21, 2015

ACKNOWLEDGMENTS

We greatly acknowledge all those individuals listed in all the editions of our *Trial Advocacy* book.

We also owe a debt of special thanks to:

The Association of Trial Lawyers of America and William Cashman and John Skinkle who helped develop the trial transcript of *Riley v. Garfield House Apartments*.

Peter Knapp, Ann Juergens, and West for directing and producing the case and transcript of *Bingham v. Ecotronics*.

Steven Vincent Benet, Daniel Webster, and the Devil, for making *Scratch v. Stone* come to life, along with their Creator.

Finally, there are all those who have tirelessly drafted, edited, reviewed, debated, and enacted the federal rules of evidence and civil procedure that deserve all our thanks for developing rules to guide us and give us work.

INTRODUCTION

This *Supplement* has five sections and includes:

The Federal Rules of Evidence.

Selected Federal Rules of Civil Procedure.

A jury trial transcript, with commentary, *Riley v. Garfield House Apartments.*

An arbitration hearing transcript, with commentary, *Bingham v. Ecotronics.*

An administrative law hearing transcript, with commentary, *Scratch v. Stone.*

The federal rules readily permit readers of the companion *Trial Advocacy* text to refer to and rely on the provisions of the applicable rules.

The three transcripts provide complete and comprehensive examples of advocacy in the three primary forums: judicial, arbitral, and administrative. Each of these transcripts demonstrates successful advocacy strategies, tactics, and techniques.

This *Supplement*, the first of its kind, provides a very helpful and instructive guide to effective advocacy approaches. It is not enough to study separate and disparate elements of trial advocacy. It is essential to gain a full understanding of advocacy to review strategies, tactics, and techniques presented in complete cases.

Each transcript brings to life an entire presentation of a case. A personal injury case is tried before a jury; an employment dispute is tried before an arbitrator; a breach of contract case is tried before an administrative law judge. You can compare and contrast the similarities and the differences involved in the advocacy presentations before these three forums.

The transcripts also contain comments explaining the specific approaches used by the attorneys. These comments describe how the advocates implement various strategies, tactics, and techniques. You can analyze the effectiveness of the lawyers based on what you have studied in the companion *Trial Advocacy* book. References in this *Supplement* refer to the sections in the *Trial Advocacy Before Judges, Jurors, and Arbitrators* book.

TABLE OF CONTENTS

SUPPLEMENT TO

TRIAL

ADVOCACY BEFORE JUDGES, JURORS, AND ARBITRATORS

Fifth Edition

SECTION ONE

RULES OF EVIDENCE FOR UNITED STATES COURTS AND MAGISTRATES

Rules 101 Through 1103

RULES OF EVIDENCE FOR UNITED STATES COURTS AND MAGISTRATES

Including Amendments Effective December 1, 2014

Table of Rules

ARTICLE I. GENERAL PROVISIONS

Rule 101. Scope; Definitions

(a) **Scope.** These rules apply to proceedings in United States courts. The specific courts and proceedings to which the rules apply, along with exceptions, are set out in Rule 1101.

(b) **Definitions.** In these rules:

(1) "civil case" means a civil action or proceeding;

(2) "criminal case" includes a criminal proceeding;

(3) "public office" includes a public agency;

(4) "record" includes a memorandum, report, or data compilation;

(5) a "rule prescribed by the Supreme Court" means a rule adopted by the Supreme Court under statutory authority; and

(6) a reference to any kind of written material or any other medium includes electronically stored information.

Rule 102. Purpose

These rules should be construed so as to administer every proceeding fairly, eliminate unjustifiable expense and delay, and promote the development of evidence law, to the end of ascertaining the truth and securing a just determination.

Rule 103. Rulings on Evidence

(a) **Preserving a Claim of Error.** A party may claim error in a ruling to admit or exclude evidence only if the error affects a substantial right of the party and:

(1) if the ruling admits evidence, a party, on the record:

(A) timely objects or moves to strike; and

     (B) states the specific ground, unless it was apparent from the context; or

     (2) if the ruling excludes evidence, a party informs the court of its substance by an offer of proof, unless the substance was apparent from the context.

     (b) Not Needing to Renew an Objection or Offer of Proof. Once the court rules definitively on the record—either before or at trial—a party need not renew an objection or offer of proof to preserve a claim of error for appeal.

     (c) Court's Statement About the Ruling; Directing an Offer of Proof. The court may make any statement about the character or form of the evidence, the objection made, and the ruling. The court may direct that an offer of proof be made in question-and-answer form.

     (d) Preventing the Jury from Hearing Inadmissible Evidence. To the extent practicable, the court must conduct a jury trial so that inadmissible evidence is not suggested to the jury by any means.

     (e) Taking Notice of Plain Error. A court may take notice of a plain error affecting a substantial right, even if the claim of error was not properly preserved.

Rule 104.   Preliminary Questions

     (a) In General. The court must decide any preliminary question about whether a witness is qualified, a privilege exists, or evidence is admissible. In so deciding, the court is not bound by evidence rules, except those on privilege.

     (b) Relevance That Depends on a Fact. When the relevance of evidence depends on whether a fact exists, proof must be introduced sufficient to support a finding that the fact does exist. The court may admit the proposed evidence on the condition that the proof be introduced later.

     (c) Conducting a Hearing So That the Jury Cannot Hear It. The court must conduct any hearing on a preliminary question so that the jury cannot hear it if:

     (1) the hearing involves the admissibility of a confession;

     (2) a defendant in a criminal case is a witness and so requests; or

     (3) justice so requires.

     (d) Cross-Examining a Defendant in a Criminal Case. By testifying on a preliminary question, a defendant in a criminal case does not become subject to cross-examination on other issues in the case.

(e) Evidence Relevant to Weight and Credibility. This rule does not limit a party's right to introduce before the jury evidence that is relevant to the weight or credibility of other evidence.

Rule 105. Limiting Evidence That Is Not Admissible Against Other Parties or for Other Purposes

If the court admits evidence that is admissible against a party or for a purpose—but not against another party or for another purpose—the court, on timely request, must restrict the evidence to its proper scope and instruct the jury accordingly.

Rule 106. Remainder of or Related Writings or Recorded Statements

If a party introduces all or part of a writing or recorded statement, an adverse party may require the introduction, at that time, of any other part—or any other writing or recorded statement—that in fairness ought to be considered at the same time.

ARTICLE II. JUDICIAL NOTICE

Rule 201. Judicial Notice of Adjudicative Facts

(a) Scope. This rule governs judicial notice of an adjudicative fact only, not a legislative fact.

(b) Kinds of Facts That May Be Judicially Noticed. The court may judicially notice a fact that is not subject to reasonable dispute because it:

    (1) is generally known within the trial court's territorial jurisdiction; or

    (2) can be accurately and readily determined from sources whose accuracy cannot reasonably be questioned.

(c) Taking Notice. The court:

    (1) may take judicial notice on its own; or

    (2) must take judicial notice if a party requests it and the court is supplied with the necessary information.

(d) Timing. The court may take judicial notice at any stage of the proceeding.

(e) Opportunity to Be Heard. On timely request, a party is entitled to be heard on the propriety of taking judicial notice and the nature of the fact to be noticed. If the court takes judicial notice before notifying a party, the party, on request, is still entitled to be heard.

(f) Instructing the Jury. In a civil case, the court must instruct the jury to accept the noticed fact as conclusive. In a criminal case, the court must instruct the jury that it may or may not accept the noticed fact as conclusive.

ARTICLE III. PRESUMPTIONS IN CIVIL CASES

Rule 301. Presumptions in Civil Cases Generally

In a civil case, unless a federal statute or these rules provide otherwise, the party against whom a presumption is directed has the burden of producing evidence to rebut the presumption. But this rule does not shift the burden of persuasion, which remains on the party who had it originally.

Rule 302. Applying State Law to Presumptions in Civil Cases

In a civil case, state law governs the effect of a presumption regarding a claim or defense for which state law supplies the rule of decision.

ARTICLE IV. RELEVANCE AND ITS LIMITS

Rule 401. Test for Relevant Evidence

Evidence is relevant if:

(a) it has any tendency to make a fact more or less probable than it would be without the evidence; and

(b) the fact is of consequence in determining the action.

Rule 402. General Admissibility of Relevant Evidence

Relevant evidence is admissible unless any of the following provides otherwise:

- the United States Constitution;
- a federal statute;
- these rules; or
- other rules prescribed by the Supreme Court.

Irrelevant evidence is not admissible.

Rule 403. Excluding Relevant Evidence for Prejudice, Confusion, Waste of Time, or Other Reasons

The court may exclude relevant evidence if its probative value is substantially outweighed by a danger of one or more of the following: unfair prejudice, confusing the issues, misleading the jury, undue delay, wasting time, or needlessly presenting cumulative evidence.

Rule 404.   Character Evidence; Crimes or Other Acts

(a) Character Evidence.

(1) Prohibited Uses. Evidence of a person's character or character trait is not admissible to prove that on a particular occasion the person acted in accordance with the character or trait.

(2) Exceptions for a Defendant or Victim in a Criminal Case. The following exceptions apply in a criminal case:

(A) a defendant may offer evidence of the defendant's pertinent trait, and if the evidence is admitted, the prosecutor may offer evidence to rebut it;

(B) subject to the limitations in Rule 412, a defendant may offer evidence of an alleged victim's pertinent trait, and if the evidence is admitted, the prosecutor may:

(i) offer evidence to rebut it; and

(ii) offer evidence of the defendant's same trait; and

(C) in a homicide case, the prosecutor may offer evidence of the alleged victim's trait of peacefulness to rebut evidence that the victim was the first aggressor.

(3) Exceptions for a Witness. Evidence of a witness's character may be admitted under Rules 607, 608, and 609.

(b) Crimes, Wrongs, or Other Acts.

(1) Prohibited Uses. Evidence of a crime, wrong, or other act is not admissible to prove a person's character in order to show that on a particular occasion the person acted in accordance with the character.

(2) Permitted Uses; Notice in a Criminal Case. This evidence may be admissible for another purpose, such as proving motive, opportunity, intent, preparation, plan, knowledge, identity, absence of mistake, or lack of accident. On request by a defendant in a criminal case, the prosecutor must:

(A) provide reasonable notice of the general nature of any such evidence that the prosecutor intends to offer at trial; and

(B) do so before trial—or during trial if the court, for good cause, excuses lack of pretrial notice.

Rule 405.   Methods of Proving Character

(a) By Reputation or Opinion. When evidence of a person's character or character trait is admissible, it may be proved by testimony about the person's reputation or by testimony in the form of an opinion. On cross-examination of the character witness, the court may allow an inquiry into relevant specific instances of the person's conduct.

(b) By Specific Instances of Conduct. When a person's character or character trait is an essential element of a charge, claim, or defense, the character or trait may also be proved by relevant specific instances of the person's conduct.

Rule 406.   Habit; Routine Practice

Evidence of a person's habit or an organization's routine practice may be admitted to prove that on a particular occasion the person or organization acted in accordance with the habit or routine practice. The court may admit this evidence regardless of whether it is corroborated or whether there was an eyewitness.

Rule 407.   Subsequent Remedial Measures

When measures are taken that would have made an earlier injury or harm less likely to occur, evidence of the subsequent measures is not admissible to prove:

- negligence;
- culpable conduct;
- a defect in a product or its design; or
- a need for a warning or instruction.

But the court may admit this evidence for another purpose, such as impeachment or—if disputed—proving ownership, control, or the feasibility of precautionary measures.

Rule 408.   Compromise Offers and Negotiations

(a) Prohibited Uses. Evidence of the following is not admissible— on behalf of any party—either to prove or disprove the validity or amount of a disputed claim or to impeach by a prior inconsistent statement or a contradiction:

(1) furnishing, promising, or offering—or accepting, promising to accept, or offering to accept—a valuable consideration in compromising or attempting to compromise the claim; and

(2) conduct or a statement made during compromise negotiations about the claim—except when offered in a criminal case and when the negotiations related to a claim by a public office in the exercise of its regulatory, investigative, or enforcement authority.

(b) Exceptions. The court may admit this evidence for another purpose, such as proving a witness's bias or prejudice, negating a contention of undue delay, or proving an effort to obstruct a criminal investigation or prosecution.

Rule 409.   Offers to Pay Medical and Similar Expenses

Evidence of furnishing, promising to pay, or offering to pay medical, hospital, or similar expenses resulting from an injury is not admissible to prove liability for the injury.

Rule 410.   Pleas, Plea Discussions, and Related Statements

(a) Prohibited Uses. In a civil or criminal case, evidence of the following is not admissible against the defendant who made the plea or participated in the plea discussions:

   (1) a guilty plea that was later withdrawn;

   (2) a nolo contendere plea;

   (3) a statement made during a proceeding on either of those pleas under Federal Rule of Criminal Procedure 11 or a comparable state procedure; or

   (4) a statement made during plea discussions with an attorney for the prosecuting authority if the discussions did not result in a guilty plea or they resulted in a later-withdrawn guilty plea.

(b) Exceptions. The court may admit a statement described in Rule 410(a)(3) or (4):

   (1) in any proceeding in which another statement made during the same plea or plea discussions has been introduced, if in fairness the statements ought to be considered together; or

   (2) in a criminal proceeding for perjury or false statement, if the defendant made the statement under oath, on the record, and with counsel present.

Rule 411.   Liability Insurance

Evidence that a person was or was not insured against liability is not admissible to prove whether the person acted negligently or otherwise wrongfully. But the court may admit this evidence for another purpose, such as proving a witness's bias or prejudice or proving agency, ownership, or control.

Rule 412.   Sex-Offense Cases: The Victim's Sexual Behavior or Predisposition

(a) Prohibited Uses. The following evidence is not admissible in a civil or criminal proceeding involving alleged sexual misconduct:

(1) evidence offered to prove that a victim engaged in other sexual behavior; or

(2) evidence offered to prove a victim's sexual predisposition.

(b) Exceptions.

(1) Criminal Cases. The court may admit the following evidence in a criminal case:

    (A) evidence of specific instances of a victim's sexual behavior, if offered to prove that someone other than the defendant was the source of semen, injury, or other physical evidence;

    (B) evidence of specific instances of a victim's sexual behavior with respect to the person accused of the sexual misconduct, if offered by the defendant to prove consent or if offered by the prosecutor; and

    (C) evidence whose exclusion would violate the defendant's constitutional rights.

(2) Civil Cases. In a civil case, the court may admit evidence offered to prove a victim's sexual behavior or sexual predisposition if its probative value substantially outweighs the danger of harm to any victim and of unfair prejudice to any party. The court may admit evidence of a victim's reputation only if the victim has placed it in controversy.

(c) Procedure to Determine Admissibility.

(1) Motion. If a party intends to offer evidence under Rule 412(b), the party must:

    (A) file a motion that specifically describes the evidence and states the purpose for which it is to be offered;

    (B) do so at least 14 days before trial unless the court, for good cause, sets a different time;

    (C) serve the motion on all parties; and

    (D) notify the victim or, when appropriate, the victim's guardian or representative.

(2) Hearing. Before admitting evidence under this rule, the court must conduct an in camera hearing and give the victim and parties a right to attend and be heard. Unless the court orders otherwise, the motion, related materials, and the record of the hearing must be and remain sealed.

(d) Definition of "Victim." In this rule, "victim" includes an alleged victim.

Rule 413.   Similar Crimes in Sexual-Assault Cases

(a) Permitted Uses. In a criminal case in which a defendant is accused of a sexual assault, the court may admit evidence that the defendant committed any other sexual assault. The evidence may be considered on any matter to which it is relevant.

(b) Disclosure to the Defendant. If the prosecutor intends to offer this evidence, the prosecutor must disclose it to the defendant, including witnesses' statements or a summary of the expected testimony. The prosecutor must do so at least 15 days before trial or at a later time that the court allows for good cause.

(c) Effect on Other Rules. This rule does not limit the admission or consideration of evidence under any other rule.

(d) Definition of "Sexual Assault." In this rule and Rule 415, "sexual assault" means a crime under federal law or under state law (as "state" is defined in 18 U.S.C. § 513) involving:

    (1) any conduct prohibited by 18 U.S.C. chapter 109A;

    (2) contact, without consent, between any part of the defendant's body—or an object—and another person's genitals or anus;

    (3) contact, without consent, between the defendant's genitals or anus and any part of another person's body;

    (4) deriving sexual pleasure or gratification from inflicting death, bodily injury, or physical pain on another person; or

    (5) an attempt or conspiracy to engage in conduct described in subparagraphs (1)-(4).

Rule 414.   Similar Crimes in Child-Molestation Cases

(a) Permitted Uses. In a criminal case in which a defendant is accused of child molestation, the court may admit evidence that the defendant committed any other child molestation. The evidence may be considered on any matter to which it is relevant.

(b) Disclosure to the Defendant. If the prosecutor intends to offer this evidence, the prosecutor must disclose it to the defendant, including witnesses' statements or a summary of the expected testimony. The prosecutor must do so at least 15 days before trial or at a later time that the court allows for good cause.

(c) Effect on Other Rules. This rule does not limit the admission or consideration of evidence under any other rule.

(d) Definition of "Child" and "Child Molestation." In this rule and Rule 415:

(1) "child" means a person below the age of 14; and

(2) "child molestation" means a crime under federal law or under state law (as "state" is defined in 18 U.S.C. § 513) involving:

    (A) any conduct prohibited by 18 U.S.C. chapter 109A and committed with a child;

    (B) any conduct prohibited by 18 U.S.C. chapter 110;

    (C) contact between any part of the defendant's body—or an object—and a child's genitals or anus;

    (D) contact between the defendant's genitals or anus and any part of a child's body;

    (E) deriving sexual pleasure or gratification from inflicting death, bodily injury, or physical pain on a child; or

    (F) an attempt or conspiracy to engage in conduct described in subparagraphs (A)-(E).

Rule 415. Similar Acts in Civil Cases Involving Sexual Assault or Child Molestation

(a) Permitted Uses. In a civil case involving a claim for relief based on a party's alleged sexual assault or child molestation, the court may admit evidence that the party committed any other sexual assault or child molestation. The evidence may be considered as provided in Rules 413 and 414.

(b) Disclosure to the Opponent. If a party intends to offer this evidence, the party must disclose it to the party against whom it will be offered, including witnesses' statements or a summary of the expected testimony. The party must do so at least 15 days before trial or at a later time that the court allows for good cause.

(c) Effect on Other Rules. This rule does not limit the admission or consideration of evidence under any other rule.

ARTICLE V. PRIVILEGES

Rule 501. Privilege in General

The common law—as interpreted by United States courts in the light of reason and experience—governs a claim of privilege unless any of the following provides otherwise:

- the United States Constitution;
- a federal statute; or
- rules prescribed by the Supreme Court.

But in a civil case, state law governs privilege regarding a claim or defense for which state law supplies the rule of decision.

Rule 502. Attorney-Client Privilege and Work Product; Limitations on Waiver

The following provisions apply, in the circumstances set out, to disclosure of a communication or information covered by the attorney-client privilege or work-product protection.

(a) Disclosure Made in a Federal Proceeding or to a Federal Office or Agency; Scope of a Waiver. When the disclosure is made in a federal proceeding or to a federal office or agency and waives the attorney-client privilege or work-product protection, the waiver extends to an undisclosed communication or information in a federal or state proceeding only if:

(1) the waiver is intentional;

(2) the disclosed and undisclosed communications or information concern the same subject matter; and

(3) they ought in fairness to be considered together.

(b) Inadvertent Disclosure. When made in a federal proceeding or to a federal office or agency, the disclosure does not operate as a waiver in a federal or state proceeding if:

(1) the disclosure is inadvertent;

(2) the holder of the privilege or protection took reasonable steps to prevent disclosure; and

(3) the holder promptly took reasonable steps to rectify the error, including (if applicable) following Federal Rule of Civil Procedure 26(b)(5)(B).

(c) Disclosure Made in a State Proceeding. When the disclosure is made in a state proceeding and is not the subject of a state-court order concerning waiver, the disclosure does not operate as a waiver in a federal proceeding if the disclosure:

(1) would not be a waiver under this rule if it had been made in a federal proceeding; or

(2) is not a waiver under the law of the state where the disclosure occurred.

(d) Controlling Effect of a Court Order. A federal court may order that the privilege or protection is not waived by disclosure connected with the litigation pending before the court—in which event the disclosure is also not a waiver in any other federal or state proceeding.

(e) Controlling Effect of a Party Agreement. An agreement on the effect of disclosure in a federal proceeding is binding only on the parties to the agreement, unless it is incorporated into a court order.

(f) Controlling Effect of This Rule. Notwithstanding Rules 101 and 1101, this rule applies to state proceedings and to federal court-annexed and federal court-mandated arbitration proceedings, in the circumstances set out in the rule. And notwithstanding Rule 501, this rule applies even if state law provides the rule of decision.

(g) Definitions. In this rule:

(1) "attorney-client privilege" means the protection that applicable law provides for confidential attorney-client communications; and

(2) "work-product protection" means the protection that applicable law provides for tangible material (or its intangible equivalent) prepared in anticipation of litigation or for trial.

ARTICLE VI. WITNESSES

Rule 601.   Competency to Testify in General

Every person is competent to be a witness unless these rules provide otherwise. But in a civil case, state law governs the witness's competency regarding a claim or defense for which state law supplies the rule of decision.

Rule 602.   Need for Personal Knowledge

A witness may testify to a matter only if evidence is introduced sufficient to support a finding that the witness has personal knowledge of the matter. Evidence to prove personal knowledge may consist of the witness's own testimony. This rule does not apply to a witness's expert testimony under Rule 703.

Rule 603.   Oath or Affirmation to Testify Truthfully

Before testifying, a witness must give an oath or affirmation to testify truthfully. It must be in a form designed to impress that duty on the witness's conscience.

Rule 604.   Interpreter

An interpreter must be qualified and must give an oath or affirmation to make a true translation.

Rule 605.   Judge's Competency as a Witness

The presiding judge may not testify as a witness at the trial. A party need not object to preserve the issue.

Rule 606.   Juror's Competency as a Witness

(a) At the Trial. A juror may not testify as a witness before the other jurors at the trial. If a juror is called to testify, the court must give a party an opportunity to object outside the jury's presence.

(b) During an Inquiry Into the Validity of a Verdict or Indictment.

(1) Prohibited Testimony or Other Evidence. During an inquiry into the validity of a verdict or indictment, a juror may not testify about any statement made or incident that occurred during the jury's deliberations; the effect of anything on that juror's or another juror's vote; or any juror's mental processes concerning the verdict or indictment. The court may not receive a juror's affidavit or evidence of a juror's statement on these matters.

(2) Exceptions. A juror may testify about whether:

(A) extraneous prejudicial information was improperly brought to the jury's attention;

(B) an outside influence was improperly brought to bear on any juror; or

(C) a mistake was made in entering the verdict on the verdict form.

Rule 607.   Who May Impeach a Witness

Any party, including the party that called the witness, may attack the witness's credibility.

Rule 608.   A Witness's Character for Truthfulness or Untruthfulness

(a) Reputation or Opinion Evidence. A witness's credibility may be attacked or supported by testimony about the witness's reputation for having a character for truthfulness or untruthfulness, or by testimony in the form of an opinion about that character. But evidence of truthful character is admissible only after the witness's character for truthfulness has been attacked.

(b) Specific Instances of Conduct. Except for a criminal conviction under Rule 609, extrinsic evidence is not admissible to prove specific instances of a witness's conduct in order to attack or support the witness's character for truthfulness. But the court may, on cross-examination, allow them to be inquired into if they are probative of the character for truthfulness or untruthfulness of:

  (1) the witness; or

  (2) another witness whose character the witness being cross-examined has testified about.

By testifying on another matter, a witness does not waive any privilege against self-incrimination for testimony that relates only to the witness's character for truthfulness.

Rule 609. Impeachment by Evidence of a Criminal Conviction

(a) In General. The following rules apply to attacking a witness's character for truthfulness by evidence of a criminal conviction:

  (1) for a crime that, in the convicting jurisdiction, was punishable by death or by imprisonment for more than one year, the evidence:

    (A) must be admitted, subject to Rule 403, in a civil case or in a criminal case in which the witness is not a defendant; and

    (B) must be admitted in a criminal case in which the witness is a defendant, if the probative value of the evidence outweighs its prejudicial effect to that defendant; and

  (2) for any crime regardless of the punishment, the evidence must be admitted if the court can readily determine that establishing the elements of the crime required proving—or the witness's admitting—a dishonest act or false statement.

(b) Limit on Using the Evidence After 10 Years. This subdivision (b) applies if more than 10 years have passed since the witness's conviction or release from confinement for it, whichever is later. Evidence of the conviction is admissible only if:

  (1) its probative value, supported by specific facts and circumstances, substantially outweighs its prejudicial effect; and

  (2) the proponent gives an adverse party reasonable written notice of the intent to use it so that the party has a fair opportunity to contest its use.

(c) Effect of a Pardon, Annulment, or Certificate of Rehabilitation. Evidence of a conviction is not admissible if:

  (1) the conviction has been the subject of a pardon, annulment, certificate of rehabilitation, or other equivalent procedure based on a finding that the person has been rehabilitated, and the person has not been convicted of a later crime punishable by death or by imprisonment for more than one year; or

(2) the conviction has been the subject of a pardon, annulment, or other equivalent procedure based on a finding of innocence.

(d) Juvenile Adjudications. Evidence of a juvenile adjudication is admissible under this rule only if:

(1) it is offered in a criminal case;

(2) the adjudication was of a witness other than the defendant;

(3) an adult's conviction for that offense would be admissible to attack the adult's credibility; and

(4) admitting the evidence is necessary to fairly determine guilt or innocence.

(e) Pendency of an Appeal. A conviction that satisfies this rule is admissible even if an appeal is pending. Evidence of the pendency is also admissible.

Rule 610.   Religious Beliefs or Opinions

Evidence of a witness's religious beliefs or opinions is not admissible to attack or support the witness's credibility.

Rule 611.   Mode and Order of Examining Witnesses and Presenting Evidence

(a) Control by the Court; Purposes. The court should exercise reasonable control over the mode and order of examining witnesses and presenting evidence so as to:

(1) make those procedures effective for determining the truth;

(2) avoid wasting time; and

(3) protect witnesses from harassment or undue embarrassment.

(b) Scope of Cross-Examination. Cross-examination should not go beyond the subject matter of the direct examination and matters affecting the witness's credibility. The court may allow inquiry into additional matters as if on direct examination.

(c) Leading Questions. Leading questions should not be used on direct examination except as necessary to develop the witness's testimony. Ordinarily, the court should allow leading questions:

(1) on cross-examination; and

(2) when a party calls a hostile witness, an adverse party, or a witness identified with an adverse party.

Rule 612. Writing Used to Refresh a Witness's Memory

(a) Scope. This rule gives an adverse party certain options when a witness uses a writing to refresh memory:

(1) while testifying; or

(2) before testifying, if the court decides that justice requires the party to have those options.

(b) Adverse Party's Options; Deleting Unrelated Matter. Unless 18 U.S.C. § 3500 provides otherwise in a criminal case, an adverse party is entitled to have the writing produced at the hearing, to inspect it, to cross-examine the witness about it, and to introduce in evidence any portion that relates to the witness's testimony. If the producing party claims that the writing includes unrelated matter, the court must examine the writing in camera, delete any unrelated portion, and order that the rest be delivered to the adverse party. Any portion deleted over objection must be preserved for the record.

(c) Failure to Produce or Deliver the Writing. If a writing is not produced or is not delivered as ordered, the court may issue any appropriate order. But if the prosecution does not comply in a criminal case, the court must strike the witness's testimony or—if justice so requires—declare a mistrial.

Rule 613. Witness's Prior Statement

(a) Showing or Disclosing the Statement During Examination. When examining a witness about the witness's prior statement, a party need not show it or disclose its contents to the witness. But the party must, on request, show it or disclose its contents to an adverse party's attorney.

(b) Extrinsic Evidence of a Prior Inconsistent Statement. Extrinsic evidence of a witness's prior inconsistent statement is admissible only if the witness is given an opportunity to explain or deny the statement and an adverse party is given an opportunity to examine the witness about it, or if justice so requires. This subdivision (b) does not apply to an opposing party's statement under Rule 801(d)(2).

Rule 614. Court's Calling or Examining a Witness

(a) Calling. The court may call a witness on its own or at a party's request. Each party is entitled to cross-examine the witness.

(b) Examining. The court may examine a witness regardless of who calls the witness.

(c) Objections. A party may object to the court's calling or examining a witness either at that time or at the next opportunity when the jury is not present.

Rule 615.   Excluding Witnesses

At a party's request, the court must order witnesses excluded so that they cannot hear other witnesses' testimony. Or the court may do so on its own. But this rule does not authorize excluding:

(a) a party who is a natural person;

(b) an officer or employee of a party that is not a natural person, after being designated as the party's representative by its attorney;

(c) a person whose presence a party shows to be essential to presenting the party's claim or defense; or

(d) a person authorized by statute to be present.

ARTICLE VII. OPINIONS AND EXPERT TESTIMONY

Rule 701.   Opinion Testimony by Lay Witnesses

If a witness is not testifying as an expert, testimony in the form of an opinion is limited to one that is:

(a) rationally based on the witness's perception;

(b) helpful to clearly understanding the witness's testimony or to determining a fact in issue; and

(c) not based on scientific, technical, or other specialized knowledge within the scope of Rule 702.

Rule 702.   Testimony by Expert Witnesses

A witness who is qualified as an expert by knowledge, skill, experience, training, or education may testify in the form of an opinion or otherwise if:

(a) the expert's scientific, technical, or other specialized knowledge will help the trier of fact to understand the evidence or to determine a fact in issue;

(b) the testimony is based on sufficient facts or data;

(c) the testimony is the product of reliable principles and methods; and

(d) the expert has reliably applied the principles and methods to the facts of the case.

Rule 703.   Bases of an Expert's Opinion Testimony

An expert may base an opinion on facts or data in the case that the expert has been made aware of or personally observed. If experts in the particular field would reasonably rely on those kinds of facts or data in forming an opinion on the subject, they need not be admissible for the opinion to be admitted. But if the facts or data would otherwise be inadmissible, the proponent of the opinion may disclose them to the jury only if their probative value in helping the jury evaluate the opinion substantially outweighs their prejudicial effect.

Rule 704.   Opinion on an Ultimate Issue

(a) In General—Not Automatically Objectionable. An opinion is not objectionable just because it embraces an ultimate issue.

(b) Exception. In a criminal case, an expert witness must not state an opinion about whether the defendant did or did not have a mental state or condition that constitutes an element of the crime charged or of a defense. Those matters are for the trier of fact alone.

Rule 705.   Disclosing the Facts or Data Underlying an Expert's Opinion

Unless the court orders otherwise, an expert may state an opinion—and give the reasons for it—without first testifying to the underlying facts or data. But the expert may be required to disclose those facts or data on cross-examination.

Rule 706.   Court-Appointed Expert Witnesses

(a) Appointment Process. On a party's motion or on its own, the court may order the parties to show cause why expert witnesses should not be appointed and may ask the parties to submit nominations. The court may appoint any expert that the parties agree on and any of its own choosing. But the court may only appoint someone who consents to act.

(b) Expert's Role. The court must inform the expert of the expert's duties. The court may do so in writing and have a copy filed with the clerk or may do so orally at a conference in which the parties have an opportunity to participate. The expert:

(1) must advise the parties of any findings the expert makes;

(2) may be deposed by any party;

(3) may be called to testify by the court or any party; and

(4) may be cross-examined by any party, including the party that called the expert.

(c) Compensation. The expert is entitled to a reasonable compensation, as set by the court. The compensation is payable as follows:

(1) in a criminal case or in a civil case involving just compensation under the Fifth Amendment, from any funds that are provided by law; and

(2) in any other civil case, by the parties in the proportion and at the time that the court directs—and the compensation is then charged like other costs.

(d) Disclosing the Appointment to the Jury. The court may authorize disclosure to the jury that the court appointed the expert.

(e) Parties' Choice of Their Own Experts. This rule does not limit a party in calling its own experts.

ARTICLE VIII. HEARSAY

Rule 801.　Definitions That Apply to This Article; Exclusions From Hearsay

(a) Statement. "Statement" means a person's oral assertion, written assertion, or nonverbal conduct, if the person intended it as an assertion.

(b) Declarant. "Declarant" means the person who made the statement.

(c) Hearsay. "Hearsay" means a statement that:

(1) the declarant does not make while testifying at the current trial or hearing; and

(2) a party offers in evidence to prove the truth of the matter asserted in the statement.

(d) Statements That Are Not Hearsay. A statement that meets the following conditions is not hearsay:

(1) A Declarant-Witness's Prior Statement. The declarant testifies and is subject to cross-examination about a prior statement, and the statement:

(A) is inconsistent with the declarant's testimony and was given under penalty of perjury at a trial, hearing, or other proceeding or in a deposition;

(B) is consistent with the declarant's testimony and is offered:

(i) to rebut an express or implied charge that the declarant recently fabricated it or acted from a recent improper influence or motive in so testifying; or

(ii) to rehabilitate the declarant's credibility as a witness when attacked on another ground; or

(C) identifies a person as someone the declarant perceived earlier.

(2) An Opposing Party's Statement. The statement is offered against an opposing party and:

(A) was made by the party in an individual or representative capacity;

(B) is one the party manifested that it adopted or believed to be true;

(C) was made by a person whom the party authorized to make a statement on the subject;

(D) was made by the party's agent or employee on a matter within the scope of that relationship and while it existed; or

(E) was made by the party's coconspirator during and in furtherance of the conspiracy.

The statement must be considered but does not by itself establish the declarant's authority under (C); the existence or scope of the relationship under (D); or the existence of the conspiracy or participation in it under (E).

Rule 802.   The Rule Against Hearsay

Hearsay is not admissible unless any of the following provides otherwise:

- a federal statute;

- these rules; or

- other rules prescribed by the Supreme Court.

Rule 803.   Exceptions to the Rule Against Hearsay—Regardless of Whether the Declarant Is Available as a Witness

The following are not excluded by the rule against hearsay, regardless of whether the declarant is available as a witness:

(1) Present Sense Impression. A statement describing or explaining an event or condition, made while or immediately after the declarant perceived it.

(2) Excited Utterance. A statement relating to a startling event or condition, made while the declarant was under the stress of excitement that it caused.

(3) Then-Existing Mental, Emotional, or Physical Condition. A statement of the declarant's then-existing state of mind (such as motive, intent, or plan) or emotional, sensory, or physical condition (such as mental feeling, pain, or bodily health), but not including a statement of memory or belief to prove the fact remembered or believed unless it relates to the validity or terms of the declarant's will.

(4) Statement Made for Medical Diagnosis or Treatment. A statement that:

(A) is made for—and is reasonably pertinent to—medical diagnosis or treatment; and

(B) describes medical history; past or present symptoms or sensations; their inception; or their general cause.

(5) Recorded Recollection. A record that:

(A) is on a matter the witness once knew about but now cannot recall well enough to testify fully and accurately;

(B) was made or adopted by the witness when the matter was fresh in the witness's memory; and

(C) accurately reflects the witness's knowledge.

If admitted, the record may be read into evidence but may be received as an exhibit only if offered by an adverse party.

(6) Records of a Regularly Conducted Activity. A record of an act, event, condition, opinion, or diagnosis if:

(A) the record was made at or near the time by—or from information transmitted by—someone with knowledge;

(B) the record was kept in the course of a regularly conducted activity of a business, organization, occupation, or calling, whether or not for profit;

(C) making the record was a regular practice of that activity;

(D) all these conditions are shown by the testimony of the custodian or another qualified witness, or by a certification that complies with Rule 902(11) or (12) or with a statute permitting certification; and

(E) the opponent does not show that the source of information or the method or circumstances of preparation indicate a lack of trustworthiness.

(7) Absence of a Record of a Regularly Conducted Activity. Evidence that a matter is not included in a record described in paragraph (6) if:

(A) the evidence is admitted to prove that the matter did not occur or exist;

(B) a record was regularly kept for a matter of that kind; and

(C) the opponent does not show that the possible source of the information or other circumstances indicate a lack of trustworthiness.

(8) Public Records. A record or statement of a public office if:

    (A) it sets out:

        (i) the office's activities;

        (ii) a matter observed while under a legal duty to report, but not including, in a criminal case, a matter observed by law-enforcement personnel; or

        (iii) in a civil case or against the government in a criminal case, factual findings from a legally authorized investigation; and

    (B) the opponent does not show that the source of information or other circumstances indicate a lack of trustworthiness.

(9) Public Records of Vital Statistics. A record of a birth, death, or marriage, if reported to a public office in accordance with a legal duty.

(10) Absence of a Public Record. Testimony—or a certification under Rule 902—that a diligent search failed to disclose a public record or statement if:

    (A) the testimony or certification is admitted to prove that

        (i) the record or statement does not exist; or

        (ii) a matter did not occur or exist, if a public office regularly kept a record or statement for a matter of that kind; and

    (B) in a criminal case, a prosecutor who intends to offer a certification provides written notice of that intent at least 14 days before trial, and the defendant does not object in writing within 7 days of receiving the notice—unless the court sets a different time for the notice or the objection.

(11) Records of Religious Organizations Concerning Personal or Family History. A statement of birth, legitimacy, ancestry, marriage, divorce, death, relationship by blood or marriage, or similar facts of personal or family history, contained in a regularly kept record of a religious organization.

(12) Certificates of Marriage, Baptism, and Similar Ceremonies. A statement of fact contained in a certificate:

    (A) made by a person who is authorized by a religious organization or by law to perform the act certified;

    (B) attesting that the person performed a marriage or similar ceremony or administered a sacrament; and

(C) purporting to have been issued at the time of the act or within a reasonable time after it.

(13) Family Records. A statement of fact about personal or family history contained in a family record, such as a Bible, genealogy, chart, engraving on a ring, inscription on a portrait, or engraving on an urn or burial marker.

(14) Records of Documents That Affect an Interest in Property. The record of a document that purports to establish or affect an interest in property if:

(A) the record is admitted to prove the content of the original recorded document, along with its signing and its delivery by each person who purports to have signed it;

(B) the record is kept in a public office; and

(C) a statute authorizes recording documents of that kind in that office.

(15) Statements in Documents That Affect an Interest in Property. A statement contained in a document that purports to establish or affect an interest in property if the matter stated was relevant to the document's purpose—unless later dealings with the property are inconsistent with the truth of the statement or the purport of the document.

(16) Statements in Ancient Documents. A statement in a document that is at least 20 years old and whose authenticity is established.

(17) Market Reports and Similar Commercial Publications. Market quotations, lists, directories, or other compilations that are generally relied on by the public or by persons in particular occupations.

(18) Statements in Learned Treatises, Periodicals, or Pamphlets. A statement contained in a treatise, periodical, or pamphlet if:

(A) the statement is called to the attention of an expert witness on cross-examination or relied on by the expert on direct examination; and

(B) the publication is established as a reliable authority by the expert's admission or testimony, by another expert's testimony, or by judicial notice.

If admitted, the statement may be read into evidence but not received as an exhibit.

(19) Reputation Concerning Personal or Family History. A reputation among a person's family by blood, adoption, or marriage—or among a person's associates or in the community—concerning the person's birth, adoption, legitimacy, ancestry, marriage, divorce, death, relationship by blood, adoption, or marriage, or similar facts of personal or family history.

(20) Reputation Concerning Boundaries or General History. A reputation in a community—arising before the controversy—concerning boundaries of land in the community or customs that affect the land, or concerning general historical events important to that community, state, or nation.

(21) Reputation Concerning Character. A reputation among a person's associates or in the community concerning the person's character.

(22) Judgment of a Previous Conviction. Evidence of a final judgment of conviction if:

> **(A)** the judgment was entered after a trial or guilty plea, but not a nolo contendere plea;

> **(B)** the conviction was for a crime punishable by death or by imprisonment for more than a year;

> **(C)** the evidence is admitted to prove any fact essential to the judgment; and

> **(D)** when offered by the prosecutor in a criminal case for a purpose other than impeachment, the judgment was against the defendant.

The pendency of an appeal may be shown but does not affect admissibility.

(23) Judgments Involving Personal, Family, or General History, or a Boundary. A judgment that is admitted to prove a matter of personal, family, or general history, or boundaries, if the matter:

> **(A)** was essential to the judgment; and

> **(B)** could be proved by evidence of reputation.

(24) [Other Exceptions.] [Transferred to Rule 807.]

Rule 804. Exceptions to the Rule Against Hearsay—When the Declarant Is Unavailable as a Witness

(a) Criteria for Being Unavailable. A declarant is considered to be unavailable as a witness if the declarant:

(1) is exempted from testifying about the subject matter of the declarant's statement because the court rules that a privilege applies;

(2) refuses to testify about the subject matter despite a court order to do so;

(3) testifies to not remembering the subject matter;

(4) cannot be present or testify at the trial or hearing because of death or a then-existing infirmity, physical illness, or mental illness; or

(5) is absent from the trial or hearing and the statement's proponent has not been able, by process or other reasonable means, to procure:

    (A) the declarant's attendance, in the case of a hearsay exception under Rule 804(b)(1) or (6); or

    (B) the declarant's attendance or testimony, in the case of a hearsay exception under Rule 804(b)(2), (3), or (4).

But this subdivision (a) does not apply if the statement's proponent procured or wrongfully caused the declarant's unavailability as a witness in order to prevent the declarant from attending or testifying.

(b) The Exceptions. The following are not excluded by the rule against hearsay if the declarant is unavailable as a witness:

(1) Former Testimony. Testimony that:

    (A) was given as a witness at a trial, hearing, or lawful deposition, whether given during the current proceeding or a different one; and

    (B) is now offered against a party who had—or, in a civil case, whose predecessor in interest had—an opportunity and similar motive to develop it by direct, cross-, or redirect examination.

(2) Statement Under the Belief of Imminent Death. In a prosecution for homicide or in a civil case, a statement that the declarant, while believing the declarant's death to be imminent, made about its cause or circumstances.

(3) Statement Against Interest. A statement that:

    (A) a reasonable person in the declarant's position would have made only if the person believed it to be true because, when made, it was so contrary to the declarant's proprietary or pecuniary interest or had so great a tendency to invalidate the declarant's claim against someone else or to expose the declarant to civil or criminal liability; and

(B) is supported by corroborating circumstances that clearly indicate its trustworthiness, if it is offered in a criminal case as one that tends to expose the declarant to criminal liability.

(4) Statement of Personal or Family History. A statement about:

(A) the declarant's own birth, adoption, legitimacy, ancestry, marriage, divorce, relationship by blood, adoption, or marriage, or similar facts of personal or family history, even though the declarant had no way of acquiring personal knowledge about that fact; or

(B) another person concerning any of these facts, as well as death, if the declarant was related to the person by blood, adoption, or marriage or was so intimately associated with the person's family that the declarant's information is likely to be accurate.

(5) [Other Exceptions.] [Transferred to Rule 807.]

(6) Statement Offered Against a Party That Wrongfully Caused the Declarant's Unavailability. A statement offered against a party that wrongfully caused—or acquiesced in wrongfully causing—the declarant's unavailability as a witness, and did so intending that result.

Rule 805.   Hearsay Within Hearsay

Hearsay within hearsay is not excluded by the rule against hearsay if each part of the combined statements conforms with an exception to the rule.

Rule 806.   Attacking and Supporting the Declarant's Credibility

When a hearsay statement—or a statement described in Rule 801(d)(2)(C), (D), or (E)—has been admitted in evidence, the declarant's credibility may be attacked, and then supported, by any evidence that would be admissible for those purposes if the declarant had testified as a witness. The court may admit evidence of the declarant's inconsistent statement or conduct, regardless of when it occurred or whether the declarant had an opportunity to explain or deny it. If the party against whom the statement was admitted calls the declarant as a witness, the party may examine the declarant on the statement as if on cross-examination.

Rule 807.   Residual Exception

(a) In General. Under the following circumstances, a hearsay statement is not excluded by the rule against hearsay even if the statement is not specifically covered by a hearsay exception in Rule 803 or 804:

(1) the statement has equivalent circumstantial guarantees of trustworthiness;

(2) it is offered as evidence of a material fact;

(3) it is more probative on the point for which it is offered than any other evidence that the proponent can obtain through reasonable efforts; and

(4) admitting it will best serve the purposes of these rules and the interests of justice.

(b) Notice. The statement is admissible only if, before the trial or hearing, the proponent gives an adverse party reasonable notice of the intent to offer the statement and its particulars, including the declarant's name and address, so that the party has a fair opportunity to meet it.

ARTICLE IX. AUTHENTICATION AND IDENTIFICATION

Rule 901.   Authenticating or Identifying Evidence

(a) In General. To satisfy the requirement of authenticating or identifying an item of evidence, the proponent must produce evidence sufficient to support a finding that the item is what the proponent claims it is.

(b) Examples. The following are examples only—not a complete list—of evidence that satisfies the requirement:

(1) Testimony of a Witness with Knowledge. Testimony that an item is what it is claimed to be.

(2) Nonexpert Opinion About Handwriting. A nonexpert's opinion that handwriting is genuine, based on a familiarity with it that was not acquired for the current litigation.

(3) Comparison by an Expert Witness or the Trier of Fact. A comparison with an authenticated specimen by an expert witness or the trier of fact.

(4) Distinctive Characteristics and the Like. The appearance, contents, substance, internal patterns, or other distinctive characteristics of the item, taken together with all the circumstances.

(5) Opinion About a Voice. An opinion identifying a person's voice—whether heard firsthand or through mechanical or electronic transmission or recording—based on hearing the voice at any time under circumstances that connect it with the alleged speaker.

(6) Evidence About a Telephone Conversation. For a telephone conversation, evidence that a call was made to the number assigned at the time to:

(A) a particular person, if circumstances, including self-identification, show that the person answering was the one called; or

(B) a particular business, if the call was made to a business and the call related to business reasonably transacted over the telephone.

(7) Evidence About Public Records. Evidence that:

(A) a document was recorded or filed in a public office as authorized by law; or

(B) a purported public record or statement is from the office where items of this kind are kept.

(8) Evidence About Ancient Documents or Data Compilations. For a document or data compilation, evidence that it:

(A) is in a condition that creates no suspicion about its authenticity;

(B) was in a place where, if authentic, it would likely be; and

(C) is at least 20 years old when offered.

(9) Evidence About a Process or System. Evidence describing a process or system and showing that it produces an accurate result.

(10) Methods Provided by a Statute or Rule. Any method of authentication or identification allowed by a federal statute or a rule prescribed by the Supreme Court.

Rule 902.   Evidence That Is Self-Authenticating

The following items of evidence are self-authenticating; they require no extrinsic evidence of authenticity in order to be admitted:

(1) Domestic Public Documents That Are Sealed and Signed. A document that bears:

(A) a seal purporting to be that of the United States; any state, district, commonwealth, territory, or insular possession of the United States; the former Panama Canal Zone; the Trust Territory of the Pacific Islands; a political subdivision of any of these entities; or a department, agency, or officer of any entity named above; and

(B) a signature purporting to be an execution or attestation.

(2) Domestic Public Documents That Are Not Sealed but Are Signed and Certified. A document that bears no seal if:

(A) it bears the signature of an officer or employee of an entity named in Rule 902(1)(A); and

(B) another public officer who has a seal and official duties within that same entity certifies under seal—or its equivalent—that the signer has the official capacity and that the signature is genuine.

(3) Foreign Public Documents. A document that purports to be signed or attested by a person who is authorized by a foreign country's law to do so. The document must be accompanied by a final certification that certifies the genuineness of the signature and official position of the signer or attester—or of any foreign official whose certificate of genuineness relates to the signature or attestation or is in a chain of certificates of genuineness relating to the signature or attestation. The certification may be made by a secretary of a United States embassy or legation; by a consul general, vice consul, or consular agent of the United States; or by a diplomatic or consular official of the foreign country assigned or accredited to the United States. If all parties have been given a reasonable opportunity to investigate the document's authenticity and accuracy, the court may, for good cause, either:

(A) order that it be treated as presumptively authentic without final certification; or

(B) allow it to be evidenced by an attested summary with or without final certification.

(4) Certified Copies of Public Records. A copy of an official record—or a copy of a document that was recorded or filed in a public office as authorized by law—if the copy is certified as correct by:

(A) the custodian or another person authorized to make the certification; or

(B) a certificate that complies with Rule 902(1), (2), or (3), a federal statute, or a rule prescribed by the Supreme Court.

(5) Official Publications. A book, pamphlet, or other publication purporting to be issued by a public authority.

(6) Newspapers and Periodicals. Printed material purporting to be a newspaper or periodical.

(7) Trade Inscriptions and the Like. An inscription, sign, tag, or label purporting to have been affixed in the course of business and indicating origin, ownership, or control.

(8) Acknowledged Documents. A document accompanied by a certificate of acknowledgment that is lawfully executed by a notary public or another officer who is authorized to take acknowledgments.

(9) Commercial Paper and Related Documents. Commercial paper, a signature on it, and related documents, to the extent allowed by general commercial law.

(10) Presumptions Under a Federal Statute. A signature, document, or anything else that a federal statute declares to be presumptively or prima facie genuine or authentic.

(11) Certified Domestic Records of a Regularly Conducted Activity. The original or a copy of a domestic record that meets the requirements of Rule 803(6)(A)-(C), as shown by a certification of the custodian or another qualified person that complies with a federal statute or a rule prescribed by the Supreme Court. Before the trial or hearing, the proponent must give an adverse party reasonable written notice of the intent to offer the record—and must make the record and certification available for inspection—so that the party has a fair opportunity to challenge them.

(12) Certified Foreign Records of a Regularly Conducted Activity. In a civil case, the original or a copy of a foreign record that meets the requirements of Rule 902(11), modified as follows: the certification, rather than complying with a federal statute or Supreme Court rule, must be signed in a manner that, if falsely made, would subject the maker to a criminal penalty in the country where the certification is signed. The proponent must also meet the notice requirements of Rule 902(11).

Rule 903. Subscribing Witness's Testimony

A subscribing witness's testimony is necessary to authenticate a writing only if required by the law of the jurisdiction that governs its validity.

ARTICLE X. CONTENTS OF WRITINGS, RECORDINGS, AND PHOTOGRAPHS

Rule 1001. Definitions That Apply to This Article

In this article:

(a) A "writing" consists of letters, words, numbers, or their equivalent set down in any form.

(b) A "recording" consists of letters, words, numbers, or their equivalent recorded in any manner.

(c) A "photograph" means a photographic image or its equivalent stored in any form.

(d) An "original" of a writing or recording means the writing or recording itself or any counterpart intended to have the same effect by the person who executed or issued it. For electronically stored information, "original" means any printout—or other output readable by sight—if it accurately reflects the information. An "original" of a photograph includes the negative or a print from it.

(e) A "duplicate" means a counterpart produced by a mechanical, photographic, chemical, electronic, or other equivalent process or technique that accurately reproduces the original.

Rule 1002. Requirement of the Original

An original writing, recording, or photograph is required in order to prove its content unless these rules or a federal statute provides otherwise.

Rule 1003. Admissibility of Duplicates

A duplicate is admissible to the same extent as the original unless a genuine question is raised about the original's authenticity or the circumstances make it unfair to admit the duplicate.

Rule 1004. Admissibility of Other Evidence of Content

An original is not required and other evidence of the content of a writing, recording, or photograph is admissible if:

(a) all the originals are lost or destroyed, and not by the proponent acting in bad faith;

(b) an original cannot be obtained by any available judicial process;

(c) the party against whom the original would be offered had control of the original; was at that time put on notice, by pleadings or otherwise, that the original would be a subject of proof at the trial or hearing; and fails to produce it at the trial or hearing; or

(d) the writing, recording, or photograph is not closely related to a controlling issue.

Rule 1005. Copies of Public Records to Prove Content

The proponent may use a copy to prove the content of an official record—or of a document that was recorded or filed in a public office as authorized by law—if these conditions are met: the record or document is otherwise admissible; and the copy is certified as correct in accordance with

Rule 902(4) or is testified to be correct by a witness who has compared it with the original. If no such copy can be obtained by reasonable diligence, then the proponent may use other evidence to prove the content.

Rule 1006. Summaries to Prove Content

The proponent may use a summary, chart, or calculation to prove the content of voluminous writings, recordings, or photographs that cannot be conveniently examined in court. The proponent must make the originals or duplicates available for examination or copying, or both, by other parties at a reasonable time and place. And the court may order the proponent to produce them in court.

Rule 1007. Testimony or Statement of a Party to Prove Content

The proponent may prove the content of a writing, recording, or photograph by the testimony, deposition, or written statement of the party against whom the evidence is offered. The proponent need not account for the original.

Rule 1008. Functions of the Court and Jury

Ordinarily, the court determines whether the proponent has fulfilled the factual conditions for admitting other evidence of the content of a writing, recording, or photograph under Rule 1004 or 1005. But in a jury trial, the jury determines—in accordance with Rule 104(b)—any issue about whether:

(a) an asserted writing, recording, or photograph ever existed;

(b) another one produced at the trial or hearing is the original; or

(c) other evidence of content accurately reflects the content.

ARTICLE XI. MISCELLANEOUS RULES

Rule 1101. Applicability of the Rules

(a) To Courts and Judges. These rules apply to proceedings before:

- United States district courts;

- United States bankruptcy and magistrate judges;

- United States courts of appeals;

- the United States Court of Federal Claims; and

- the district courts of Guam, the Virgin Islands, and the Northern Mariana Islands.

(b) To Cases and Proceedings. These rules apply in:

- civil cases and proceedings, including bankruptcy, admiralty, and maritime cases;

- criminal cases and proceedings; and

- contempt proceedings, except those in which the court may act summarily.

(c) Rules on Privilege. The rules on privilege apply to all stages of a case or proceeding.

(d) Exceptions. These rules—except for those on privilege—do not apply to the following:

    (1) the court's determination, under Rule 104(a), on a preliminary question of fact governing admissibility;

    (2) grand-jury proceedings; and

    (3) miscellaneous proceedings such as:

- extradition or rendition;

- issuing an arrest warrant, criminal summons, or search warrant;

- a preliminary examination in a criminal case;

- sentencing;

- granting or revoking probation or supervised release; and

- considering whether to release on bail or otherwise.

(e) Other Statutes and Rules. A federal statute or a rule prescribed by the Supreme Court may provide for admitting or excluding evidence independently from these rules.

Rule 1102. Amendments

These rules may be amended as provided in 28 U.S.C. § 2072.

Rule 1103. Title

These rules may be cited as the Federal Rules of Evidence.

SECTION TWO

SELECTED FEDERAL RULES OF CIVIL PROCEDURE FOR THE UNITED STATES DISTRICT COURTS

SELECTED FEDERAL RULES OF CIVIL PROCEDURE FOR THE UNITED STATES DISTRICT COURTS

Effective September 16, 1938

Including Amendments Effective December 1, 2014

Table of Rules

TITLE VI. TRIALS

TITLE VII. JUDGMENT

TITLE VI. TRIALS

Rule 38.   Right to a Jury Trial; Demand

(a) Right Preserved. The right of trial by jury as declared by the Seventh Amendment to the Constitution—or as provided by a federal statute—is preserved to the parties inviolate.

(b) Demand. On any issue triable of right by a jury, a party may demand a jury trial by:

(1) serving the other parties with a written demand—which may be included in a pleading—no later than 14 days after the last pleading directed to the issue is served; and

(2) filing the demand in accordance with Rule 5(d).

(c) Specifying Issues. In its demand, a party may specify the issues that it wishes to have tried by a jury; otherwise, it is considered to have demanded a jury trial on all the issues so triable. If the party has demanded a jury trial on only some issues, any other party may—within 14 days after being served with the demand or within a shorter time ordered by the court—serve a demand for a jury trial on any other or all factual issues triable by jury.

(d) Waiver; Withdrawal. A party waives a jury trial unless its demand is properly served and filed. A proper demand may be withdrawn only if the parties consent.

(e) Admiralty and Maritime Claims. These rules do not create a right to a jury trial on issues in a claim that is an admiralty or maritime claim under Rule 9(h).

(As amended Feb. 28, 1966, eff. July 1, 1966; Mar. 2, 1987, eff. Aug. 1, 1987; Apr. 22, 1993, eff. Dec. 1, 1993; Apr. 30, 2007, eff. Dec. 1, 2007; Mar. 26, 2009, eff. Dec. 1, 2009.)

Rule 39.   Trial by Jury or by the Court

(a) When a Demand Is Made. When a jury trial has been demanded under Rule 38, the action must be designated on the docket as a jury action. The trial on all issues so demanded must be by jury unless:

(1) the parties or their attorneys file a stipulation to a nonjury trial or so stipulate on the record; or

(2) the court, on motion or on its own, finds that on some or all of those issues there is no federal right to a jury trial.

(b) When No Demand Is Made. Issues on which a jury trial is not properly demanded are to be tried by the court. But the court may, on motion, order a jury trial on any issue for which a jury might have been demanded.

(c) Advisory Jury; Jury Trial by Consent. In an action not triable of right by a jury, the court, on motion or on its own:

(1) may try any issue with an advisory jury; or

(2) may, with the parties' consent, try any issue by a jury whose verdict has the same effect as if a jury trial had been a matter of right, unless the action is against the United States and a federal statute provides for a nonjury trial.

(As amended Apr. 30, 2007, eff. Dec. 1, 2007.)

Rule 40.   Scheduling Cases for Trial

Each court must provide by rule for scheduling trials. The court must give priority to actions entitled to priority by a federal statute.

(As amended Apr. 30, 2007, eff. Dec. 1, 2007.)

Rule 41.   Dismissal of Actions

(a) Voluntary Dismissal.

(1) *By the Plaintiff.*

(A) *Without a Court Order.* Subject to Rules 23(e), 23.1(c), 23.2, and 66 and any applicable federal statute, the plaintiff may dismiss an action without a court order by filing:

(i) a notice of dismissal before the opposing party serves either an answer or a motion for summary judgment; or

(ii) a stipulation of dismissal signed by all parties who have appeared.

(B) *Effect.* Unless the notice or stipulation states otherwise, the dismissal is without prejudice. But if the plaintiff previously dismissed any federal- or state-court action based on or including the same claim, a notice of dismissal operates as an adjudication on the merits.

(2) *By Court Order; Effect.* Except as provided in Rule 41(a)(1), an action may be dismissed at the plaintiff's request only by court order, on terms that the court considers proper. If a defendant has pleaded a counterclaim before being served with the plaintiff's motion to dismiss, the action may be dismissed over the defendant's objection only if the counterclaim can remain pending for independent adjudication. Unless the order states otherwise, a dismissal under this paragraph (2) is without prejudice.

(b) Involuntary Dismissal; Effect. If the plaintiff fails to prosecute or to comply with these rules or a court order, a defendant may move to dismiss the action or any claim against it. Unless the dismissal order states otherwise, a dismissal under this subdivision (b) and any dismissal not under this rule—except one for lack of jurisdiction, improper venue, or failure to join a party under Rule 19—operates as an adjudication on the merits.

(c) Dismissing a Counterclaim, Crossclaim, or Third-Party Claim. This rule applies to a dismissal of any counterclaim, crossclaim, or third-party claim. A claimant's voluntary dismissal under Rule 41(a)(1)(A)(i) must be made:

(1) before a responsive pleading is served; or

(2) if there is no responsive pleading, before evidence is introduced at a hearing or trial.

(d) Costs of a Previously Dismissed Action. If a plaintiff who previously dismissed an action in any court files an action based on or including the same claim against the same defendant, the court:

(1) may order the plaintiff to pay all or part of the costs of that previous action; and

(2) may stay the proceedings until the plaintiff has complied.

(As amended Dec. 27, 1946, eff. Mar. 19, 1948; Jan. 21, 1963, eff. July 1, 1963; Feb. 28, 1966, eff. July 1, 1966; Dec. 4, 1967, eff. July 1, 1968; Mar. 2, 1987, eff. Aug. 1, 1987; Apr. 30, 1991, eff. Dec. 1, 1991; Apr. 30, 2007, eff. Dec. 1, 2007.)

Rule 42.   Consolidation; Separate Trials

(a) Consolidation. If actions before the court involve a common question of law or fact, the court may:

(1) join for hearing or trial any or all matters at issue in the actions;

(2) consolidate the actions; or

(3) issue any other orders to avoid unnecessary cost or delay.

(b) Separate Trials. For convenience, to avoid prejudice, or to expedite and economize, the court may order a separate trial of one or more separate issues, claims, crossclaims, counterclaims, or third-party claims. When ordering a separate trial, the court must preserve any federal right to a jury trial.

(As amended Feb. 28, 1966, eff. July 1, 1966; Apr. 30, 2007, eff. Dec. 1, 2007.)

Rule 43.   Taking Testimony

(a) In Open Court. At trial, the witnesses' testimony must be taken in open court unless a federal statute, the Federal Rules of Evidence, these rules, or other rules adopted by the Supreme Court provide otherwise. For good cause in compelling circumstances and with appropriate safeguards, the court may permit testimony in open court by contemporaneous transmission from a different location.

(b) Affirmation Instead of an Oath. When these rules require an oath, a solemn affirmation suffices.

(c) Evidence on a Motion. When a motion relies on facts outside the record, the court may hear the matter on affidavits or may hear it wholly or partly on oral testimony or on depositions.

(d) Interpreter. The court may appoint an interpreter of its choosing; fix reasonable compensation to be paid from funds provided by law or by one or more parties; and tax the compensation as costs.

(As amended Feb. 28, 1966, eff. July 1, 1966; Nov. 20, 1972, and Dec. 18, 1972, eff. July 1, 1975; Mar. 2, 1987, eff. Aug. 1, 1987; Apr. 23, 1996, eff. Dec. 1, 1996; Apr. 30, 2007, eff. Dec. 1, 2007.)

Rule 44.   Proving an Official Record

(a) Means of Proving.

    (1) *Domestic Record.* Each of the following evidences an official record—or an entry in it—that is otherwise admissible and is kept within the United States, any state, district, or commonwealth, or any territory subject to the administrative or judicial jurisdiction of the United States:

        (A) an official publication of the record; or

        (B) a copy attested by the officer with legal custody of the record—or by the officer's deputy—and accompanied by a certificate that the officer has custody. The certificate must be made under seal:

            (i) by a judge of a court of record in the district or political subdivision where the record is kept; or

            (ii) by any public officer with a seal of office and with official duties in the district or political subdivision where the record is kept.

    (2) *Foreign Record.*

        (A) *In General.* Each of the following evidences a foreign official record—or an entry in it—that is otherwise admissible:

            (i) an official publication of the record; or

    (ii) the record—or a copy—that is attested by an authorized person and is accompanied either by a final certification of genuineness or by a certification under a treaty or convention to which the United States and the country where the record is located are parties.

  (B) *Final Certification of Genuineness.* A final certification must certify the genuineness of the signature and official position of the attester or of any foreign official whose certificate of genuineness relates to the attestation or is in a chain of certificates of genuineness relating to the attestation. A final certification may be made by a secretary of a United States embassy or legation; by a consul general, vice consul, or consular agent of the United States; or by a diplomatic or consular official of the foreign country assigned or accredited to the United States.

  (C) *Other Means of Proof.* If all parties have had a reasonable opportunity to investigate a foreign record's authenticity and accuracy, the court may, for good cause, either:

    (i) admit an attested copy without final certification; or

    (ii) permit the record to be evidenced by an attested summary with or without a final certification.

(b) Lack of a Record. A written statement that a diligent search of designated records revealed no record or entry of a specified tenor is admissible as evidence that the records contain no such record or entry. For domestic records, the statement must be authenticated under Rule 44(a)(1). For foreign records, the statement must comply with (a)(2)(C)(ii).

(c) Other Proof. A party may prove an official record—or an entry or lack of an entry in it—by any other method authorized by law.

(As amended Feb. 28, 1966, eff. July 1, 1966; Mar. 2, 1987, eff. Aug. 1, 1987; Apr. 30, 1991, eff. Dec. 1, 1991; Apr. 30, 2007, eff. Dec. 1, 2007.)

Rule 44.1. Determining Foreign Law

A party who intends to raise an issue about a foreign country's law must give notice by a pleading or other writing. In determining foreign law, the court may consider any relevant material or source, including testimony, whether or not submitted by a party or admissible under the Federal Rules of Evidence. The court's determination must be treated as a ruling on a question of law.

(As added Feb. 28, 1966, eff. July 1, 1966; amended Nov. 20, 1972, eff. July 1, 1975; Mar. 2, 1987, eff. Aug. 1, 1987; Apr. 30, 2007, eff. Dec. 1, 2007.)

Rule 45.   Subpoena

(a) In General.

> **(1) *Form and Contents.***

>> **(A)** *Requirements—In General.* Every subpoena must:

>>> **(i)**   state the court from which it issued;

>>> **(ii)** state the title of the action and its civil-action number;

>>> **(iii)** command each person to whom it is directed to do the following at a specified time and place: attend and testify; produce designated documents, electronically stored information, or tangible things in that person's possession, custody, or control; or permit the inspection of premises; and

>>> **(iv)** set out the text of Rule 45(d)   and (e).

>> **(B)** *Command to Attend a Deposition—Notice of the Recording Method.* A subpoena commanding attendance at a deposition must state the method for recording the testimony.

>> **(C)** *Combining or Separating a Command to Produce or to Permit Inspection; Specifying the Form for Electronically Stored Information.* A command to produce documents, electronically stored information, or tangible things or to permit the inspection of premises may be included in a subpoena commanding attendance at a deposition, hearing, or trial, or may be set out in a separate subpoena. A subpoena may specify the form or forms in which electronically stored information is to be produced.

>> **(D)** *Command to Produce; Included Obligations.* A command in a subpoena to produce documents, electronically stored information, or tangible things requires the responding person to permit inspection, copying, testing, or sampling of the materials.

> **(2) *Issuing Court.*** A subpoena must issue from the court where the action is pending.

> **(3) *Issued by Whom.*** The clerk must issue a subpoena, signed but otherwise in blank, to a party who requests it. That party must complete it before service. An attorney also may issue and sign a subpoena if the attorney is authorized to practice in the issuing court.

> **(4) *Notice to Other Parties Before Service.*** If the subpoena commands the production of documents, electronically stored information, or tangible things or the inspection of premises

before trial, then before it is served on the person to whom it is directed, a notice and a copy of the subpoena must be served on each party.

(b) Service.

    (1) *By Whom and How; Tendering Fees.* Any person who is at least 18 years old and not a party may serve a subpoena. Serving a subpoena requires delivering a copy to the named person and, if the subpoena requires that person's attendance, tendering the fees for 1 day's attendance and the mileage allowed by law. Fees and mileage need not be tendered when the subpoena issues on behalf of the United States or any of its officers or agencies.

    (2) *Service in the United States.* A subpoena may be served at any place within the United States.

    (3) *Service in a Foreign Country.* 28 U.S.C. § 1783 governs issuing and serving a subpoena directed to a United States national or resident who is in a foreign country.

    (4) *Proof of Service.* Proving service, when necessary, requires filing with the issuing court a statement showing the date and manner of service and the names of the persons served. The statement must be certified by the server.

(c) Place of Compliance.

    (1) *For a Trial, Hearing, or Deposition.* A subpoena may command a person to attend a trial, hearing, or deposition only as follows:

        (A) within 100 miles of where the person resides, is employed, or regularly transacts business in person; or

        (B) within the state where the person resides, is employed, or regularly transacts business in person, if the person

            (i) is a party or a party's officer; or

            (ii) is commanded to attend a trial and would not incur substantial expense.

    (2) *For Other Discovery.* A subpoena may command:

        (A) production of documents, electronically stored information, or tangible things at a place within 100 miles of where the person resides, is employed, or regularly transacts business in person; and

        (B) inspection of premises at the premises to be inspected.

(d) **Protecting a Person Subject to a Subpoena; Enforcement.**

(1) *Avoiding Undue Burden or Expense; Sanctions.* A party or attorney responsible for issuing and serving a subpoena must take reasonable steps to avoid imposing undue burden or expense on a person subject to the subpoena. The court for the district where compliance is required must enforce this duty and impose an appropriate sanction—which may include lost earnings and reasonable attorney's fees—on a party or attorney who fails to comply.

(2) *Command to Produce Materials or Permit Inspection.*

(A) *Appearance Not Required.* A person commanded to produce documents, electronically stored information, or tangible things, or to permit the inspection of premises, need not appear in person at the place of production or inspection unless also commanded to appear for a deposition, hearing, or trial.

(B) *Objections.* A person commanded to produce documents or tangible things or to permit inspection may serve on the party or attorney designated in the subpoena a written objection to inspecting, copying, testing or sampling any or all of the materials or to inspecting the premises—or to producing electronically stored information in the form or forms requested. The objection must be served before the earlier of the time specified for compliance or 14 days after the subpoena is served. If an objection is made, the following rules apply:

(i) At any time, on notice to the commanded person, the serving party may move the court for the district where compliance is required for an order compelling production or inspection.

(ii) These acts may be required only as directed in the order, and the order must protect a person who is neither a party nor a party's officer from significant expense resulting from compliance.

(3) *Quashing or Modifying a Subpoena.*

(A) *When Required.* On timely motion, the court for the district where compliance is required must quash or modify a subpoena that:

(i) fails to allow a reasonable time to comply;

(ii) requires a person to comply beyond the geographical limits specified in Rule 45(c);

(iii) requires disclosure of privileged or other protected matter, if no exception or waiver applies; or

(iv) subjects a person to undue burden.

(B) *When Permitted.* To protect a person subject to or affected by a subpoena, the court for the district where compliance is required may, on motion, quash or modify the subpoena if it requires:

(i) disclosing a trade secret or other confidential research, development, or commercial information; or

(ii) disclosing an unretained expert's opinion or information that does not describe specific occurrences in dispute and results from the expert's study that was not requested by a party.

(C) *Specifying Conditions as an Alternative.* In the circumstances described in Rule 45(d)(3)(B), the court may, instead of quashing or modifying a subpoena, order appearance or production under specified conditions if the serving party:

(i) shows a substantial need for the testimony or material that cannot be otherwise met without undue hardship; and

(ii) ensures that the subpoenaed person will be reasonably compensated.

(e) Duties in Responding to a Subpoena.

(1) *Producing Documents or Electronically Stored Information.* These procedures apply to producing documents or electronically stored information:

(A) *Documents.* A person responding to a subpoena to produce documents must produce them as they are kept in the ordinary course of business or must organize and label them to correspond to the categories in the demand.

(B) *Form for Producing Electronically Stored Information Not Specified.* If a subpoena does not specify a form for producing electronically stored information, the person responding must produce it in a form or forms in which it is ordinarily maintained or in a reasonably usable form or forms.

(C) *Electronically Stored Information Produced in Only One Form.* The person responding need not produce the same electronically stored information in more than one form.

(D) *Inaccessible Electronically Stored Information.* The person responding need not provide discovery of electronically stored information from sources that the person identifies as not reasonably accessible because of undue burden or cost. On motion to compel discovery or for a protective order, the person responding must show that the information is not reasonably accessible because of undue burden or cost. If that showing is made, the court may nonetheless order discovery from such sources if the requesting party shows good cause, considering the limitations of Rule 26(b)(2)(C). The court may specify conditions for the discovery.

(2) *Claiming Privilege or Protection.*

(A) *Information Withheld.* A person withholding subpoenaed information under a claim that it is privileged or subject to protection as trial-preparation material must:

(i) expressly make the claim; and

(ii) describe the nature of the withheld documents, communications, or tangible things in a manner that, without revealing information itself privileged or protected, will enable the parties to assess the claim.

(B) *Information Produced.* If information produced in response to a subpoena is subject to a claim of privilege or of protection as trial-preparation material, the person making the claim may notify any party that received the information of the claim and the basis for it. After being notified, a party must promptly return, sequester, or destroy the specified information and any copies it has; must not use or disclose the information until the claim is resolved; must take reasonable steps to retrieve the information if the party disclosed it before being notified; and may promptly present the information under seal to the court for the district where compliance is required for a determination of the claim. The person who produced the information must preserve the information until the claim is resolved.

(f) **Transferring a Subpoena-Related Motion.** When the court where compliance is required did not issue the subpoena, it may transfer a motion under this rule to the issuing court if the person subject to the subpoena consents or if the court finds exceptional circumstances. Then, if the attorney for a person subject to a subpoena is authorized to practice in the court where the motion was made, the attorney may file papers and appear on the motion as an officer of the issuing court.

To enforce its order, the issuing court may transfer the order to the court where the motion was made.

(g) Contempt. The court for the district where compliance is required—and also, after a motion is transferred, the issuing court—may hold in contempt a person who, having been served, fails without adequate excuse to obey the subpoena or an order related to it.

(As amended Dec. 27, 1946, eff. Mar. 19, 1948; Dec. 29, 1948, eff. Oct. 20, 1949; Mar. 30, 1970, eff. July 1, 1970; Apr. 29, 1980, eff. Aug. 1, 1980; Apr. 29, 1985, eff. Aug. 1, 1985; Mar. 2, 1987, eff. Aug. 1, 1987; Apr. 30, 1991, eff. Dec. 1, 1991; Apr. 25, 2005, eff. Dec. 1, 2005; Apr. 12, 2006, eff. Dec. 1, 2006; Apr. 30, 2007, eff. Dec. 1, 2007; Apr. 16, 2013, eff. Dec. 1, 2013.)

Rule 46.   Objecting to a Ruling or Order

A formal exception to a ruling or order is unnecessary. When the ruling or order is requested or made, a party need only state the action that it wants the court to take or objects to, along with the grounds for the request or objection. Failing to object does not prejudice a party who had no opportunity to do so when the ruling or order was made.

(As amended Mar. 2, 1987, eff. Aug. 1, 1987; Apr. 30, 2007, eff. Dec. 1, 2007.)

Rule 47.   Selecting Jurors

(a) Examining Jurors. The court may permit the parties or their attorneys to examine prospective jurors or may itself do so. If the court examines the jurors, it must permit the parties or their attorneys to make any further inquiry it considers proper, or must itself ask any of their additional questions it considers proper.

(b) Peremptory Challenges. The court must allow the number of peremptory challenges provided by 28 U.S.C. § 1870.

(c) Excusing a Juror. During trial or deliberation, the court may excuse a juror for good cause.

(As amended Feb. 28, 1966, eff. July 1, 1966; Apr. 30, 1991, eff. Dec. 1, 1991; Apr. 30, 2007, eff. Dec. 1, 2007.)

Rule 48.   Number of Jurors; Verdict; Polling

(a) Number of Jurors. A jury must begin with at least 6 and no more than 12 members, and each juror must participate in the verdict unless excused under Rule 47(c).

(b) Verdict. Unless the parties stipulate otherwise, the verdict must be unanimous and must be returned by a jury of at least 6 members.

(c) **Polling.** After a verdict is returned but before the jury is discharged, the court must on a party's request, or may on its own, poll the jurors individually. If the poll reveals a lack of unanimity or lack of assent by the number of jurors that the parties stipulated to, the court may direct the jury to deliberate further or may order a new trial.

(As amended Apr. 30, 1991, eff. Dec. 1, 1991; Apr. 30, 2007, eff. Dec. 1, 2007; Mar. 26, 2009, eff. Dec. 1, 2009.)

Rule 49.   Special Verdict; General Verdict and Questions

(a) **Special Verdict.**

   (1) *In General.* The court may require a jury to return only a special verdict in the form of a special written finding on each issue of fact. The court may do so by:

   (A) submitting written questions susceptible of a categorical or other brief answer;

   (B) submitting written forms of the special findings that might properly be made under the pleadings and evidence; or

   (C) using any other method that the court considers appropriate.

   (2) *Instructions.* The court must give the instructions and explanations necessary to enable the jury to make its findings on each submitted issue.

   (3) *Issues Not Submitted.* A party waives the right to a jury trial on any issue of fact raised by the pleadings or evidence but not submitted to the jury unless, before the jury retires, the party demands its submission to the jury. If the party does not demand submission, the court may make a finding on the issue. If the court makes no finding, it is considered to have made a finding consistent with its judgment on the special verdict.

(b) **General Verdict with Answers to Written Questions.**

   (1) *In General.* The court may submit to the jury forms for a general verdict, together with written questions on one or more issues of fact that the jury must decide. The court must give the instructions and explanations necessary to enable the jury to render a general verdict and answer the questions in writing, and must direct the jury to do both.

   (2) *Verdict and Answers Consistent.* When the general verdict and the answers are consistent, the court must approve, for entry under Rule 58, an appropriate judgment on the verdict and answers.

(3) **Answers Inconsistent with the Verdict.** When the answers are consistent with each other but one or more is inconsistent with the general verdict, the court may:

(A) approve, for entry under Rule 58, an appropriate judgment according to the answers, notwithstanding the general verdict;

(B) direct the jury to further consider its answers and verdict; or

(C) order a new trial.

(4) **Answers Inconsistent with Each Other and the Verdict.** When the answers are inconsistent with each other and one or more is also inconsistent with the general verdict, judgment must not be entered; instead, the court must direct the jury to further consider its answers and verdict, or must order a new trial.

(As amended Jan. 21, 1963, eff. July 1, 1963; Mar. 2, 1987, eff. Aug. 1, 1987; Apr. 30, 2007, eff. Dec. 1, 2007.)

Rule 50.   Judgment as a Matter of Law in a Jury Trial; Related Motion for a New Trial; Conditional Ruling

(a) Judgment as a Matter of Law.

(1) *In General.* If a party has been fully heard on an issue during a jury trial and the court finds that a reasonable jury would not have a legally sufficient evidentiary basis to find for the party on that issue, the court may:

(A) resolve the issue against the party; and

(B) grant a motion for judgment as a matter of law against the party on a claim or defense that, under the controlling law, can be maintained or defeated only with a favorable finding on that issue.

(2) *Motion.* A motion for judgment as a matter of law may be made at any time before the case is submitted to the jury. The motion must specify the judgment sought and the law and facts that entitle the movant to the judgment.

(b) Renewing the Motion After Trial; Alternative Motion for a New Trial. If the court does not grant a motion for judgment as a matter of law made under Rule 50(a), the court is considered to have submitted the action to the jury subject to the court's later deciding the legal questions raised by the motion. No later than 28 days after the entry of judgment—or if the motion addresses a jury issue not decided by a verdict, no later than 28 days after the jury was discharged—the movant may file a renewed motion for judgment as a matter of law and may include an alternative or joint request for a new trial under Rule 59. In ruling on the renewed motion, the court may:

(1) allow judgment on the verdict, if the jury returned a verdict;

(2) order a new trial; or

(3) direct the entry of judgment as a matter of law.

(c) Granting the Renewed Motion; Conditional Ruling on a Motion for a New Trial.

(1) *In General.* If the court grants a renewed motion for judgment as a matter of law, it must also conditionally rule on any motion for a new trial by determining whether a new trial should be granted if the judgment is later vacated or reversed. The court must state the grounds for conditionally granting or denying the motion for a new trial.

(2) *Effect of a Conditional Ruling.* Conditionally granting the motion for a new trial does not affect the judgment's finality; if the judgment is reversed, the new trial must proceed unless the appellate court orders otherwise. If the motion for a new trial is conditionally denied, the appellee may assert error in that denial; if the judgment is reversed, the case must proceed as the appellate court orders.

(d) Time for a Losing Party's New-Trial Motion. Any motion for a new trial under Rule 59 by a party against whom judgment as a matter of law is rendered must be filed no later than 28 days after the entry of the judgment.

(e) Denying the Motion for Judgment as a Matter of Law; Reversal on Appeal. If the court denies the motion for judgment as a matter of law, the prevailing party may, as appellee, assert grounds entitling it to a new trial should the appellate court conclude that the trial court erred in denying the motion. If the appellate court reverses the judgment, it may order a new trial, direct the trial court to determine whether a new trial should be granted, or direct the entry of judgment.

(As amended Jan. 21, 1963, eff. July 1, 1963; Mar. 2, 1987, eff. Aug. 1, 1987; Apr. 30, 1991, eff. Dec. 1, 1991; Apr. 22, 1993, eff. Dec. 1, 1993; Apr. 27, 1995, eff. Dec. 1, 1995; Apr. 12, 2006, eff. Dec. 1, 2006; Apr. 30, 2007, eff. Dec. 1, 2007; Mar. 26, 2009, eff. Dec. 1, 2009.)

Rule 51.   Instructions to the Jury; Objections; Preserving a Claim of Error

(a) Requests.

(1) *Before or at the Close of the Evidence.* At the close of the evidence or at any earlier reasonable time that the court orders, a

party may file and furnish to every other party written requests for the jury instructions it wants the court to give.

(2) *After the Close of the Evidence.* After the close of the evidence, a party may:

    (A) file requests for instructions on issues that could not reasonably have been anticipated by an earlier time that the court set for requests; and

    (B) with the court's permission, file untimely requests for instructions on any issue.

(b) **Instructions.** The court:

    (1) must inform the parties of its proposed instructions and proposed action on the requests before instructing the jury and before final jury arguments;

    (2) must give the parties an opportunity to object on the record and out of the jury's hearing before the instructions and arguments are delivered; and

    (3) may instruct the jury at any time before the jury is discharged.

(c) **Objections.**

    (1) *How to Make.* A party who objects to an instruction or the failure to give an instruction must do so on the record, stating distinctly the matter objected to and the grounds for the objection.

    (2) *When to Make.* An objection is timely if:

        (A) a party objects at the opportunity provided under Rule 51(b)(2); or

        (B) a party was not informed of an instruction or action on a request before that opportunity to object, and the party objects promptly after learning that the instruction or request will be, or has been, given or refused.

(d) **Assigning Error; Plain Error.**

    (1) *Assigning Error.* A party may assign as error:

        (A) an error in an instruction actually given, if that party properly objected; or

        (B) a failure to give an instruction, if that party properly requested it and—unless the court rejected the request in a definitive ruling on the record—also properly objected.

    (2) *Plain Error.* A court may consider a plain error in the instructions that has not been preserved as required by Rule 51(d)(1) if the error affects substantial rights.

(As amended Mar. 2, 1987, eff. Aug. 1, 1987; Mar. 27, 2003, eff. Dec. 1, 2003; Apr. 30, 2007, eff. Dec. 1, 2007.)

Rule 52.   Findings and Conclusions by the Court; Judgment on Partial Findings

(a) Findings and Conclusions.

    (1) *In General.* In an action tried on the facts without a jury or with an advisory jury, the court must find the facts specially and state its conclusions of law separately. The findings and conclusions may be stated on the record after the close of the evidence or may appear in an opinion or a memorandum of decision filed by the court. Judgment must be entered under Rule 58.

    (2) *For an Interlocutory Injunction.* In granting or refusing an interlocutory injunction, the court must similarly state the findings and conclusions that support its action.

    (3) *For a Motion.* The court is not required to state findings or conclusions when ruling on a motion under Rule 12 or 56 or, unless these rules provide otherwise, on any other motion.

    (4) *Effect of a Master's Findings.* A master's findings, to the extent adopted by the court, must be considered the court's findings.

    (5) *Questioning the Evidentiary Support.* A party may later question the sufficiency of the evidence supporting the findings, whether or not the party requested findings, objected to them, moved to amend them, or moved for partial findings.

    (6) *Setting Aside the Findings.* Findings of fact, whether based on oral or other evidence, must not be set aside unless clearly erroneous, and the reviewing court must give due regard to the trial court's opportunity to judge the witnesses' credibility.

(b) Amended or Additional Findings. On a party's motion filed no later than 28 days after the entry of judgment, the court may amend its findings—or make additional findings—and may amend the judgment accordingly. The motion may accompany a motion for a new trial under Rule 59.

(c) Judgment on Partial Findings. If a party has been fully heard on an issue during a nonjury trial and the court finds against the party on that issue, the court may enter judgment against the party on a claim or defense that, under the controlling law, can be maintained or defeated only with a favorable finding on that issue. The court may, however, decline to render any judgment until the close of the evidence. A judgment on partial findings must be supported by findings of fact and conclusions of law as required by Rule 52(a).

(As amended Dec. 27, 1946, eff. Mar. 19, 1948; Jan. 21, 1963, eff. July 1, 1963; Apr. 28, 1983, eff. Aug. 1, 1983; Apr. 29, 1985, eff. Aug. 1, 1985; Apr. 30, 1991, eff. Dec. 1, 1991; Apr. 22, 1993, eff. Dec. 1, 1993; Apr. 27, 1995, eff. Dec. 1, 1995; Apr. 30, 2007, eff. Dec. 1, 2007; Mar. 26, 2009, eff. Dec. 1, 2009.)

Rule 53.   Masters

(a) Appointment.

(1) *Scope.* Unless a statute provides otherwise, a court may appoint a master only to:

  (A) perform duties consented to by the parties;

  (B) hold trial proceedings and make or recommend findings of fact on issues to be decided without a jury if appointment is warranted by:

   (i) some exceptional condition; or

   (ii) the need to perform an accounting or resolve a difficult computation of damages; or

  (C) address pretrial and posttrial matters that cannot be effectively and timely addressed by an available district judge or magistrate judge of the district.

(2) *Disqualification.* A master must not have a relationship to the parties, attorneys, action, or court that would require disqualification of a judge under 28 U.S.C. § 455, unless the parties, with the court's approval, consent to the appointment after the master discloses any potential grounds for disqualification.

(3) *Possible Expense or Delay.* In appointing a master, the court must consider the fairness of imposing the likely expenses on the parties and must protect against unreasonable expense or delay.

(b) Order Appointing a Master.

(1) *Notice.* Before appointing a master, the court must give the parties notice and an opportunity to be heard. Any party may suggest candidates for appointment.

(2) *Contents.* The appointing order must direct the master to proceed with all reasonable diligence and must state:

  (A) the master's duties, including any investigation or enforcement duties, and any limits on the master's authority under Rule 53(c);

  (B) the circumstances, if any, in which the master may communicate ex parte with the court or a party;

      (C) the nature of the materials to be preserved and filed as the record of the master's activities;

      (D) the time limits, method of filing the record, other procedures, and standards for reviewing the master's orders, findings, and recommendations; and

      (E) the basis, terms, and procedure for fixing the master's compensation under Rule 53(g).

   (3) *Issuing.* The court may issue the order only after:

      (A) the master files an affidavit disclosing whether there is any ground for disqualification under 28 U.S.C. § 455; and

      (B) if a ground is disclosed, the parties, with the court's approval, waive the disqualification.

   (4) *Amending.* The order may be amended at any time after notice to the parties and an opportunity to be heard.

(c) **Master's Authority.**

   (1) *In General.* Unless the appointing order directs otherwise, a master may:

      (A) regulate all proceedings;

      (B) take all appropriate measures to perform the assigned duties fairly and efficiently; and

      (C) if conducting an evidentiary hearing, exercise the appointing court's power to compel, take, and record evidence.

   (2) *Sanctions.* The master may by order impose on a party any noncontempt sanction provided by Rule 37 or 45, and may recommend a contempt sanction against a party and sanctions against a nonparty.

(d) **Master's Orders.** A master who issues an order must file it and promptly serve a copy on each party. The clerk must enter the order on the docket.

(e) **Master's Reports.** A master must report to the court as required by the appointing order. The master must file the report and promptly serve a copy on each party, unless the court orders otherwise.

(f) **Action on the Master's Order, Report, or Recommendations.**

   (1) *Opportunity for a Hearing; Action in General.* In acting on a master's order, report, or recommendations, the court must give the parties notice and an opportunity to be heard; may receive evidence; and may adopt or affirm, modify, wholly or partly reject or reverse, or resubmit to the master with instructions.

(2) *Time to Object or Move to Adopt or Modify.* A party may file objections to—or a motion to adopt or modify—the master's order, report, or recommendations no later than 21 days after a copy is served, unless the court sets a different time.

(3) *Reviewing Factual Findings.* The court must decide de novo all objections to findings of fact made or recommended by a master, unless the parties, with the court's approval, stipulate that:

(A) the findings will be reviewed for clear error; or

(B) the findings of a master appointed under Rule 53(a)(1)(A) or (C) will be final.

(4) *Reviewing Legal Conclusions.* The court must decide de novo all objections to conclusions of law made or recommended by a master.

(5) *Reviewing Procedural Matters.* Unless the appointing order establishes a different standard of review, the court may set aside a master's ruling on a procedural matter only for an abuse of discretion.

(g) **Compensation.**

(1) *Fixing Compensation.* Before or after judgment, the court must fix the master's compensation on the basis and terms stated in the appointing order, but the court may set a new basis and terms after giving notice and an opportunity to be heard.

(2) *Payment.* The compensation must be paid either:

(A) by a party or parties; or

(B) from a fund or subject matter of the action within the court's control.

(3) *Allocating Payment.* The court must allocate payment among the parties after considering the nature and amount of the controversy, the parties' means, and the extent to which any party is more responsible than other parties for the reference to a master. An interim allocation may be amended to reflect a decision on the merits.

(h) **Appointing a Magistrate Judge.** A magistrate judge is subject to this rule only when the order referring a matter to the magistrate judge states that the reference is made under this rule.

(As amended Feb. 28, 1966, eff. July 1, 1966; Apr. 28, 1983, eff. Aug. 1, 1983; Mar. 2, 1987, eff. Aug. 1, 1987; Apr. 30, 1991, eff. Dec. 1, 1991; Apr. 22, 1993, eff. Dec. 1, 1993; Mar. 27, 2003, eff. Dec. 1, 2003; Apr. 30, 2007, eff. Dec. 1, 2007; Mar. 26, 2009, eff. Dec. 1, 2009.)

TITLE VII. JUDGMENT

Rule 54.   Judgment; Costs

(a) Definition; Form. "Judgment" as used in these rules includes a decree and any order from which an appeal lies. A judgment should not include recitals of pleadings, a master's report, or a record of prior proceedings.

(b) Judgment on Multiple Claims or Involving Multiple Parties. When an action presents more than one claim for relief—whether as a claim, counterclaim, crossclaim, or third-party claim—or when multiple parties are involved, the court may direct entry of a final judgment as to one or more, but fewer than all, claims or parties only if the court expressly determines that there is no just reason for delay. Otherwise, any order or other decision, however designated, that adjudicates fewer than all the claims or the rights and liabilities of fewer than all the parties does not end the action as to any of the claims or parties and may be revised at any time before the entry of a judgment adjudicating all the claims and all the parties' rights and liabilities.

(c) Demand for Judgment; Relief to Be Granted. A default judgment must not differ in kind from, or exceed in amount, what is demanded in the pleadings. Every other final judgment should grant the relief to which each party is entitled, even if the party has not demanded that relief in its pleadings.

(d) Costs; Attorney's Fees.

   (1) *Costs Other Than Attorney's Fees.* Unless a federal statute, these rules, or a court order provides otherwise, costs—other than attorney's fees—should be allowed to the prevailing party. But costs against the United States, its officers, and its agencies may be imposed only to the extent allowed by law. The clerk may tax costs on 14 days' notice. On motion served within the next 7 days, the court may review the clerk's action.

   (2) *Attorney's Fees.*

      (A) *Claim to Be by Motion.* A claim for attorney's fees and related nontaxable expenses must be made by motion unless the substantive law requires those fees to be proved at trial as an element of damages.

      (B) *Timing and Contents of the Motion.* Unless a statute or a court order provides otherwise, the motion must:

         (i) be filed no later than 14 days after the entry of judgment;

  (ii) specify the judgment and the statute, rule, or other grounds entitling the movant to the award;

  (iii) state the amount sought or provide a fair estimate of it; and

  (iv) disclose, if the court so orders, the terms of any agreement about fees for the services for which the claim is made.

(C) *Proceedings.* Subject to Rule 23(h), the court must, on a party's request, give an opportunity for adversary submissions on the motion in accordance with Rule 43(c)or 78. The court may decide issues of liability for fees before receiving submissions on the value of services. The court must find the facts and state its conclusions of law as provided in Rule 52(a).

(D) *Special Procedures by Local Rule; Reference to a Master or a Magistrate Judge.* By local rule, the court may establish special procedures to resolve fee-related issues without extensive evidentiary hearings. Also, the court may refer issues concerning the value of services to a special master under Rule 53 without regard to the limitations of Rule 53(a)(1), and may refer a motion for attorney's fees to a magistrate judge under Rule 72(b) as if it were a dispositive pretrial matter.

(E) *Exceptions.* Subparagraphs (A)–(D) do not apply to claims for fees and expenses as sanctions for violating these rules or as sanctions under 28 U.S.C. § 1927.

(As amended Dec. 27, 1946, eff. Mar. 19, 1948; Apr. 17, 1961, eff. July 19, 1961; Mar. 2, 1987, eff. Aug. 1, 1987; Apr. 22, 1993, eff. Dec. 1, 1993; Apr. 29, 2002, eff. Dec. 1, 2002; Mar. 27, 2003, eff. Dec. 1, 2003; Apr. 30, 2007, eff. Dec. 1, 2007; Mar. 26, 2009, eff. Dec. 1, 2009.)

Rule 55. Default; Default Judgment

(a) **Entering a Default.** When a party against whom a judgment for affirmative relief is sought has failed to plead or otherwise defend, and that failure is shown by affidavit or otherwise, the clerk must enter the party's default.

(b) **Entering a Default Judgment.**

 (1) *By the Clerk.* If the plaintiff's claim is for a sum certain or a sum that can be made certain by computation, the clerk—on the plaintiff's request, with an affidavit showing the amount due—must enter judgment for that amount and costs against a defendant who has been defaulted for not appearing and who is neither a minor nor an incompetent person.

(2) **By the Court.** In all other cases, the party must apply to the court for a default judgment. A default judgment may be entered against a minor or incompetent person only if represented by a general guardian, conservator, or other like fiduciary who has appeared. If the party against whom a default judgment is sought has appeared personally or by a representative, that party or its representative must be served with written notice of the application at least 7 days before the hearing. The court may conduct hearings or make referrals—preserving any federal statutory right to a jury trial—when, to enter or effectuate judgment, it needs to:

   (A) conduct an accounting;

   (B) determine the amount of damages;

   (C) establish the truth of any allegation by evidence; or

   (D) investigate any other matter.

(c) **Setting Aside a Default or a Default Judgment.** The court may set aside an entry of default for good cause, and it may set aside a default judgment under Rule 60(b).

(d) **Judgment Against the United States.** A default judgment may be entered against the United States, its officers, or its agencies only if the claimant establishes a claim or right to relief by evidence that satisfies the court.

(As amended Mar. 2, 1987, eff. Aug. 1, 1987; Apr. 30, 2007, eff. Dec. 1, 2007; Mar. 26, 2009, eff. Dec. 1, 2009.)

Rule 56.   Summary Judgment

(a) **Motion for Summary Judgment or Partial Summary Judgment.** A party may move for summary judgment, identifying each claim or defense—or the part of each claim or defense—on which summary judgment is sought. The court shall grant summary judgment if the movant shows that there is no genuine dispute as to any material fact and the movant is entitled to judgment as a matter of law. The court should state on the record the reasons for granting or denying the motion.

(b) **Time to File a Motion.** Unless a different time is set by local rule or the court orders otherwise, a party may file a motion for summary judgment at any time until 30 days after the close of all discovery.

(c) Procedures.

    (1) *Supporting Factual Positions.* A party asserting that a fact cannot be or is genuinely disputed must support the assertion by:

        (A) citing to particular parts of materials in the record, including depositions, documents, electronically stored information, affidavits or declarations, stipulations (including those made for purposes of the motion only), admissions, interrogatory answers, or other materials; or

        (B) showing that the materials cited do not establish the absence or presence of a genuine dispute, or that an adverse party cannot produce admissible evidence to support the fact.

    (2) *Objection That a Fact Is Not Supported by Admissible Evidence.* A party may object that the material cited to support or dispute a fact cannot be presented in a form that would be admissible in evidence.

    (3) *Materials Not Cited.* The court need consider only the cited materials, but it may consider other materials in the record.

    (4) *Affidavits or Declarations.* An affidavit or declaration used to support or oppose a motion must be made on personal knowledge, set out facts that would be admissible in evidence, and show that the affiant or declarant is competent to testify on the matters stated.

(d) When Facts Are Unavailable to the Nonmovant. If a nonmovant shows by affidavit or declaration that, for specified reasons, it cannot present facts essential to justify its opposition, the court may:

    (1) defer considering the motion or deny it;

    (2) allow time to obtain affidavits or declarations or to take discovery; or

    (3) issue any other appropriate order.

(e) Failing to Properly Support or Address a Fact. If a party fails to properly support an assertion of fact or fails to properly address another party's assertion of fact as required by Rule 56(c), the court may:

    (1) give an opportunity to properly support or address the fact;

    (2) consider the fact undisputed for purposes of the motion;

    (3) grant summary judgment if the motion and supporting materials—including the facts considered undisputed—show that the movant is entitled to it; or

    (4) issue any other appropriate order.

(f) Judgment Independent of the Motion. After giving notice and a reasonable time to respond, the court may:

    (1) grant summary judgment for a nonmovant;

    (2) grant the motion on grounds not raised by a party; or

    (3) consider summary judgment on its own after identifying for the parties material facts that may not be genuinely in dispute.

(g) Failing to Grant All the Requested Relief. If the court does not grant all the relief requested by the motion, it may enter an order stating any material fact—including an item of damages or other relief—that is not genuinely in dispute and treating the fact as established in the case.

(h) Affidavit or Declaration Submitted in Bad Faith. If satisfied that an affidavit or declaration under this rule is submitted in bad faith or solely for delay, the court—after notice and a reasonable time to respond—may order the submitting party to pay the other party the reasonable expenses, including attorney's fees, it incurred as a result. An offending party or attorney may also be held in contempt or subjected to other appropriate sanctions.

(As amended Dec. 27, 1946, eff. Mar. 19, 1948; Jan. 21, 1963, eff. July 1, 1963; Mar. 2, 1987, eff. Aug. 1, 1987; Apr. 30, 2007, eff. Dec. 1, 2007; Mar. 26, 2009, eff. Dec. 1, 2009; Apr. 28, 2010, eff. Dec. 1, 2010.)

Rule 57.   Declaratory Judgment

These rules govern the procedure for obtaining a declaratory judgment under 28 U.S.C. § 2201. Rules 38 and 39 govern a demand for a jury trial. The existence of another adequate remedy does not preclude a declaratory judgment that is otherwise appropriate. The court may order a speedy hearing of a declaratory-judgment action.

(As amended Dec. 29, 1948, eff. Oct. 20, 1949; Apr. 30, 2007, eff. Dec. 1, 2007.)

Rule 58.   Entering Judgment

(a) Separate Document. Every judgment and amended judgment must be set out in a separate document, but a separate document is not required for an order disposing of a motion:

    (1) for judgment under Rule 50(b);

    (2) to amend or make additional findings under Rule 52(b);

    (3) for attorney's fees under Rule 54;

    (4) for a new trial, or to alter or amend the judgment, under Rule 59; or

(5) for relief under Rule 60.

(b) Entering Judgment.

(1) ***Without the Court's Direction.*** Subject to Rule 54(b) and unless the court orders otherwise, the clerk must, without awaiting the court's direction, promptly prepare, sign, and enter the judgment when:

(A) the jury returns a general verdict;

(B) the court awards only costs or a sum certain; or

(C) the court denies all relief.

(2) ***Court's Approval Required.*** Subject to Rule 54(b), the court must promptly approve the form of the judgment, which the clerk must promptly enter, when:

(A) the jury returns a special verdict or a general verdict with answers to written questions; or

(B) the court grants other relief not described in this subdivision (b).

(c) Time of Entry. For purposes of these rules, judgment is entered at the following times:

(1) if a separate document is not required, when the judgment is entered in the civil docket under Rule 79(a); or

(2) if a separate document is required, when the judgment is entered in the civil docket under Rule 79(a) and the earlier of these events occurs:

(A) it is set out in a separate document; or

(B) 150 days have run from the entry in the civil docket.

(d) Request for Entry. A party may request that judgment be set out in a separate document as required by Rule 58(a).

(e) Cost or Fee Awards. Ordinarily, the entry of judgment may not be delayed, nor the time for appeal extended, in order to tax costs or award fees. But if a timely motion for attorney's fees is made under Rule 54(d)(2), the court may act before a notice of appeal has been filed and become effective to order that the motion have the same effect under Federal Rule of Appellate Procedure 4 (a)(4) as a timely motion under Rule 59.

(As amended Dec. 27, 1946, eff. Mar. 19, 1948; Jan. 21, 1963, eff. July 1, 1963; Apr. 22, 1993, eff. Dec. 1, 1993; Apr. 29, 2002, eff. Dec. 1, 2002; Apr. 30, 2007, eff. Dec. 1, 2007.)

Rule 59.   New Trial; Altering or Amending a Judgment

(a) In General.

(1) *Grounds for New Trial.* The court may, on motion, grant a new trial on all or some of the issues—and to any party—as follows:

(A) after a jury trial, for any reason for which a new trial has heretofore been granted in an action at law in federal court; or

(B) after a nonjury trial, for any reason for which a rehearing has heretofore been granted in a suit in equity in federal court.

(2) *Further Action After a Nonjury Trial.* After a nonjury trial, the court may, on motion for a new trial, open the judgment if one has been entered, take additional testimony, amend findings of fact and conclusions of law or make new ones, and direct the entry of a new judgment.

(b) Time to File a Motion for a New Trial. A motion for a new trial must be filed no later than 28 days after the entry of judgment.

(c) Time to Serve Affidavits. When a motion for a new trial is based on affidavits, they must be filed with the motion. The opposing party has 14 days after being served to file opposing affidavits. The court may permit reply affidavits.

(d) New Trial on the Court's Initiative or for Reasons Not in the Motion. No later than 28 days after the entry of judgment, the court, on its own, may order a new trial for any reason that would justify granting one on a party's motion. After giving the parties notice and an opportunity to be heard, the court may grant a timely motion for a new trial for a reason not stated in the motion. In either event, the court must specify the reasons in its order.

(e) Motion to Alter or Amend a Judgment. A motion to alter or amend a judgment must be filed no later than 28 days after the entry of the judgment.

(As amended Dec. 27, 1946, eff. Mar. 19, 1948; Feb. 28, 1966, eff. July 1, 1966; Apr. 27, 1995, eff. Dec. 1, 1995; Apr. 30, 2007, eff. Dec. 1, 2007; Mar. 26, 2009, eff. Dec. 1, 2009.)

Rule 60.   Relief from a Judgment or Order

(a) Corrections Based on Clerical Mistakes; Oversights and Omissions. The court may correct a clerical mistake or a mistake arising from oversight or omission whenever one is found in a judgment, order, or other part of the record. The court may do so on motion or on its own, with or without notice. But after an appeal has been docketed in the appellate court and while it is pending, such a mistake may be corrected only with the appellate court's leave.

(b) Grounds for Relief from a Final Judgment, Order, or Proceeding. On motion and just terms, the court may relieve a party or its legal representative from a final judgment, order, or proceeding for the following reasons:

    (1) mistake, inadvertence, surprise, or excusable neglect;

    (2) newly discovered evidence that, with reasonable diligence, could not have been discovered in time to move for a new trial under Rule 59(b);

    (3) fraud (whether previously called intrinsic or extrinsic), misrepresentation, or misconduct by an opposing party;

    (4) the judgment is void;

    (5) the judgment has been satisfied, released, or discharged; it is based on an earlier judgment that has been reversed or vacated; or applying it prospectively is no longer equitable; or

    (6) any other reason that justifies relief.

(c) Timing and Effect of the Motion.

    (1) *Timing.* A motion under Rule 60(b) must be made within a reasonable time—and for reasons (1), (2), and (3) no more than a year after the entry of the judgment or order or the date of the proceeding.

    (2) *Effect on Finality.* The motion does not affect the judgment's finality or suspend its operation.

(d) Other Powers to Grant Relief. This rule does not limit a court's power to:

    (1) entertain an independent action to relieve a party from a judgment, order, or proceeding;

    (2) grant relief under 28 U.S.C. § 1655 to a defendant who was not personally notified of the action; or

    (3) set aside a judgment for fraud on the court.

(e) Bills and Writs Abolished. The following are abolished: bills of review, bills in the nature of bills of review, and writs of coram nobis, coram vobis, and audita querela.

(As amended Dec. 27, 1946, eff. Mar. 19, 1948; Dec. 29, 1948, eff. Oct. 20, 1949; Mar. 2, 1987, eff. Aug. 1, 1987; Apr. 30, 2007, eff. Dec. 1, 2007.)

Rule 61.   Harmless Error

Unless justice requires otherwise, no error in admitting or excluding evidence—or any other error by the court or a party—is ground for granting a new trial, for setting aside a verdict, or for vacating, modifying, or otherwise disturbing a judgment or order. At every stage of the proceeding, the court must disregard all errors and defects that do not affect any party's substantial rights.

(As amended Apr. 30, 2007, eff. Dec. 1, 2007.)

Rule 62.   Stay of Proceedings to Enforce a Judgment

(a) Automatic Stay; Exceptions for Injunctions, Receiverships, and Patent Accountings. Except as stated in this rule, no execution may issue on a judgment, nor may proceedings be taken to enforce it, until 14 days have passed after its entry. But unless the court orders otherwise, the following are not stayed after being entered, even if an appeal is taken:

    (1) an interlocutory or final judgment in an action for an injunction or a receivership; or

    (2) a judgment or order that directs an accounting in an action for patent infringement.

(b) Stay Pending the Disposition of a Motion. On appropriate terms for the opposing party's security, the court may stay the execution of a judgment—or any proceedings to enforce it—pending disposition of any of the following motions:

    (1) under Rule 50, for judgment as a matter of law;

    (2) under Rule 52(b), to amend the findings or for additional findings;

    (3) under Rule 59, for a new trial or to alter or amend a judgment; or

    (4) under Rule 60, for relief from a judgment or order.

(c) Injunction Pending an Appeal. While an appeal is pending from an interlocutory order or final judgment that grants, dissolves, or denies an injunction, the court may suspend, modify, restore, or grant an injunction on terms for bond or other terms that secure the opposing party's rights. If the judgment appealed from is rendered by a statutory three-judge district court, the order must be made either:

    (1) by that court sitting in open session; or

    (2) by the assent of all its judges, as evidenced by their signatures.

(d) Stay with Bond on Appeal. If an appeal is taken, the appellant may obtain a stay by supersedeas bond, except in an action described in Rule 62(a)(1) or (2). The bond may be given upon or after filing the notice of appeal or after obtaining the order allowing the appeal. The stay takes effect when the court approves the bond.

(e) Stay Without Bond on an Appeal by the United States, Its Officers, or Its Agencies. The court must not require a bond, obligation, or other security from the appellant when granting a stay on an appeal by the United States, its officers, or its agencies or on an appeal directed by a department of the federal government.

(f) Stay in Favor of a Judgment Debtor Under State Law. If a judgment is a lien on the judgment debtor's property under the law of the state where the court is located, the judgment debtor is entitled to the same stay of execution the state court would give.

(g) Appellate Court's Power Not Limited. This rule does not limit the power of the appellate court or one of its judges or justices:

(1) to stay proceedings—or suspend, modify, restore, or grant an injunction—while an appeal is pending; or

(2) to issue an order to preserve the status quo or the effectiveness of the judgment to be entered.

(h) Stay with Multiple Claims or Parties. A court may stay the enforcement of a final judgment entered under Rule 54(b) until   it enters a later judgment or judgments, and may prescribe terms necessary to secure the benefit of the stayed judgment for the party in whose favor it was entered.

(As amended Dec. 27, 1946, eff. Mar. 19, 1948; Dec. 29, 1948, eff. Oct. 20, 1949; Apr. 17, 1961, eff. July 19, 1961; Mar. 2, 1987, eff. Aug. 1, 1987; Apr. 30, 2007, eff. Dec. 1, 2007; Mar. 26, 2009, eff. Dec. 1, 2009.)

SECTION THREE

JURY TRIAL TRANSCRIPT

RITA RILEY v. GARFIELD HOUSE APARTMENTS

JURY TRIAL

Rita Riley v. Garfield House Apartments
TRANSCRIPT

The following transcript presents a jury trial, from jury selection to verdict. The trial demonstrates jury trial strategies, tactics, and techniques discussed in the companion *Trial Advocacy* text. Comments appear in the transcript explaining advocacy approaches. This case illustrates how lawyers try a jury trial, how the various stages of a case interrelate, how evidence is introduced, how case theories are presented, and how strategies and tactics affect the decision of a case.

The case involves a negligence action brought by Rita Riley, a young child, who was seriously scalded by hot water from a bathtub faucet in an apartment owned and operated by Garfield House Apartments. We have condensed the presentation of this trial in order to provide you with a transcript of reasonable and readable length. Not all theories, arguments, objections, tactics, approaches, and witnesses have been presented. Only two witnesses testify for each party, one lay witness and one expert. More witnesses would testify in an actual trial, including family members, treating physicians, medical personnel, adverse physicians, economists and other witnesses. The plaintiff proceeds first and calls Mary Riley, the mother of Rita Riley, and Dr. Pat Armstead, an expert witness. The defendant Garfield House Apartments calls Connie Austern, the manager at Garfield House Apartments, and Dr. Martin Thomas, an expert witness.

As you read through the transcript, consider the various strategies, tactics, and techniques presented and analyze the effectiveness of these trial lawyers and what you would have done similarly or differently to produce a favorable jury verdict. Section references in this supplement refer to sections in *Trial Advocacy Before Judges, Jurors, and Abritrators*.

Riley v. Garfield House Apartments

Judge's Preliminary Instructions and Jury Selection	Comments/Notes

Judge:

This is the case of Rita Riley versus Garfield House Apartments. Clerk, please call the jury panel.

Clerk:

1 As I call your name, please have a seat in the back of the jury box on the left-hand side.

Fran Piers. P-I-E-R-S. 629 University Avenue.

Maria Alvarez. A-L-V-A-R-E-Z. 4221 West 35th Street.

Marcus Bethume. B-E-T-H-U-M-E. 662 Pleasant.

Ann Beir. B-E-I-R. 75 Zinnia.

Jeff Scott. S-C-O-T-T. 608 Morgan Avenue North.

Clerk:

Mr. Scott will you please be seated in the front row, left-hand side.

Janice Strelson. S-T-R-E-L-S-O-N. 205 Garfield South.

Susan Flueg. F-L-U-E-G. 2140 Minnehaha Parkway.

Chris Gard. G-A-R-D. 948 Yosemite Avenue South.

1 This method of calling the jurors and placing them in the jury box is typical. The information provided by the jurors may be obtained by the court through questions answered by the jurors before being selected for a specific trial. If the information is made available to the attorneys in advance, much of the initial questioning can be eliminated. A six person jury is the typical number of jurors in civil cases. Additional jurors may serve as alternates who may also deliberate.

Trial Transcript 2

Riley v. Garfield House Apartments

Judge's Preliminary Instructions and Jury Selection	Comments/Notes
Judge: The clerk will swear the jury. Members of the jury panel please rise. **Clerk:** (The jury is sworn.) **Judge:** 2 Members of the jury panel, there are some things which are important for you to understand from the outset. At no time should you discuss this case with other members of the jury or with anyone else until after you have been instructed by this court at the conclusion of the trial when you begin your deliberations. The first thing we will do during this trial is to select six jurors to hear this case. I will begin by asking you some questions followed by the attorneys who will ask you questions. It is important you understand that the questions asked of you are not intended to embarrass you nor to pry into your personal affairs. That may be the result, but it is not the intent.	2 The initial instructions and comments by the judge are designed to describe the process of jury selection to the prospective jury members and to give them a brief description of the case. The description of the case should be as neutral as possible so that it does not influence the jury's opinion. See *Trial Advocacy* Section 5.1.

Riley v. Garfield House Apartments

**Judge's Preliminary
Instructions
and Jury Selection**

Comments/Notes

There are no right or wrong answers to the questions that will be put to you and you are not limited to answer questions with just a yes or a no. In fact, I encourage you to expand on any answers to the extent that you believe it is necessary to adequately answer the question.

There are eight of you on this panel and only six of you will hear the case, which means that two of you will be excused. The parties are allowed to excuse some of you and when they do, you will not be given a reason for it and you should not read into it that you are unfit to be a juror. That is not the case, it is simply to afford the parties the opportunity to have some choice in the jury that will hear their case.

I will now give you a brief description of what this case is about. On December 24, 3 years ago, plaintiff Rita Riley who was one year old, was in the

Riley v. Garfield House Apartments

Judge's Preliminary Instructions and Jury Selection	Comments/Notes
bathtub of her apartment when the water was turned on. The water was so hot that one-third of her body suffered burns. The defendant, Garfield House Apartments, owned the building Rita Riley lived in at the time of her injuries. The plaintiff has alleged that the defendant, the Garfield House Apartments, was negligent and caused the injuries. The defendant has denied this claim and has responded with a claim that the plaintiff's mother, Mary Riley, was negligent and the cause of the injuries. Some of the people who will be involved in this trial are in the courtroom. The attorney for the plaintiff and the parents of Rita Riley will please rise. Counsel for the defense, would you please stand too.	
3 Members of the Jury, do any of you know any of the lawyers or the parties, or Connie Austern who is an employee of Garfield House Apartments, or anyone involved with Garfield House Apartments?	3 The judge will generally introduce the attorneys and the parties and ask those present to stand and be identified. If a juror is acquainted with any attorney or party, or has a business relationship with any of these people, the judge may remove that juror from the panel. See *Trial Advocacy* Section 5.3 (I).

Riley v. Garfield House Apartments

Jury Selection	Comments/Notes
Does anyone know Dr. Martin Thomas or Dr. Pat Armstead, who we anticipate will be witnesses in this case? No one has indicated that they know any of the parties or witnesses and we will now proceed. Members of the jury panel, I have given you a list of questions which I would like you to answer beginning with juror number one, Fran Piers.	
4 Beginning with you, Mr. Piers, please respond to these questions. • Your employment? • Marital status? • Employment of spouse? • Family members employed and what they do? • Your education? • Any previous jury service and whether it was a criminal or civil trial? • Have you, or anyone in your family, ever sued or been sued? • Have you, or anyone in your family, ever been injured at your residence? By injury we	4 Some judges provide a questionnaire to the jury to speed up the process, others ask the questions themselves. Some judges require that the attorneys obtain this preliminary information by questioning each juror. See *Trial Advocacy* Section 5.4 (A).

Riley v. Garfield House Apartments

Jury Selection	Comments/Notes
mean something more than the normal cuts, scrapes, bumps or bruises.	
• Do you know anyone who is involved in the medical profession?	
5 Fran Piers:	5 The information provided by each of the jurors is very basic; however, it does give the attorneys preliminary background and provides them the opportunity to watch each of the jurors speak before the attorneys are given the opportunity to ask questions. The attorneys observe such things as independence, shyness, or sense of humor. See *Trial Advocacy* Section 5.7.
Auto repairman.	
Married, my spouse is a homemaker.	
I have three children under the age of 12, none of whom are employed.	
I have vocational training in auto repair.	
I do not have any previous jury service.	
I've never sued or been sued, nor has anyone in my family.	
I fell down the stairs about ten years ago and broke my arm.	
I have a neighbor who is a nurse in the hospital.	
Maria Alvarez:	
Manager for the telephone company.	
Single.	
Have no children.	

Riley v. Garfield House Apartments

Jury Selection	Comments/Notes
A bachelors degree from college.	

No previous jury service.

I sued a dry cleaner in small claims court for a dress that was ruined.

I have had no injuries.

I have a brother who is a physician and specializes in ear, nose and throat.

Marcus Bethume:

Mechanic.

Single, no children.

Have a GED degree.

No previous jury service.

Have been sued for work that I've done on cars in small claims court on two occasions, I won both times.

When I was younger, my dad cut off his thumb with a table saw.

Don't know anyone in the medical profession.

Ann Bier:

Supervisor in an insurance company.

Married.

Have two children, both of whom are employed. One is

Riley v. Garfield House Apartments

Jury Selection	Comments/Notes
22 years old, is a waitress, and is a student in college studying psychology, the other is 26 years old, is married, and is an insurance adjuster.	
I have some college courses but not a degree.	
I served on a jury 10 years ago in a criminal case.	
My daughter fell off her bike when she was a child and had some permanent teeth knocked out. My husband hurt his back real bad when he lifted a T.V. He had to have surgery.	
I've never sued or been sued.	
I have a friend who works in a doctors' office as a receptionist.	
Jeff Scott:	
Paint contractor.	
My wife died two years ago.	
Spouse was employed as an assembler in a factory.	
Family is two small children ages 3 and 5.	

Riley v. Garfield House Apartments

Jury Selection	Comments/Notes
Have some vocational education but not a degree.	

I have no previous jury service. Never been sued or sued anyone. No one has been seriously hurt.

Don't know anyone in the medical profession.

Janice Strelson:

Landscaper.

Single, no children.

Finished high school and served 3 years in the Army.

No previous jury service.

Have never sued or been sued.

Once I put my hand on an electric stove and burned my hand real bad.

Don't know anyone in the medical profession.

Susan Flueg:

Systems and programming supervisor at a local computer company.

Married, spouse is a hospital administrator.

Three children in grades 7 through 12. Have a BA degree from college. Previous jury service was about 10 years ago on a civil case.

Riley v. Garfield House Apartments	
Jury Selection	**Comments/Notes**

involving an automobile accident.

Have never sued or been sued.

No injuries.

Have a niece who is a medical technician in a doctor's office.

Chris Gard:

Welder.

Married, spouse does not work outside the home but works inside the home doing telephone solicitations.

Two small children, ages 6 and 9, who are in school.

I have completed some college courses during my four years in the Navy.

Have no previous jury service.

Have never been involved in a lawsuit.

My nine year old is always getting into things. He has had a broken leg and arm. He also fell on a metal fence post and got a big cut that needed thirty stitches to close up.

Riley v. Garfield House Apartments

| 1) Fran Piers | 2) Maria Alvarez | 3) Marcus Bethume | 4) Ann Bier |
| 5) Jeff Scott | 6) Janice Strelson | 7) Susan Flueg | 8) Chris Gard |

Jury Selection	Comments/Notes

Don't know anyone in the medical profession.

Judge:

6 Defense counsel, you may inquire.

Defendant's Counsel:

7 Q: Mr. Piers, what parts of your job as an auto repairman do you like best? And what parts do you like worst?

A: To tell you the truth, it's a lousy job. My boss is constantly harassing me to finish faster. There ain't much opportunity for advancement.

Q: Are there any things you can see that might improve with the job?

A: Only if the place gets sold to new owners.

Q: If you were the owner, how would you do things differently?

A: I'd get some decent working conditions, and I'd pay the workers a fair wage.

8 Q: Mr. Piers, we all really appreciate your candor. The beauty of the jury system is that it offers

6 The questions asked by the attorneys in this illustrative jury selection will not be complete. We include a reasonable number of representative questions and a variety of typical answers by the prospective jurors.

7 The defense attorney has chosen to ask the questions in the order that the jurors were seated. It is easy to remember the jurors' names if they are questioned in a specific order rather than in an unstructured fashion.

8 The attorney begins with an explanation of the jury system and then seeks a commitment from the juror. See *Trial Advocacy* Section 5.7 (E).

Riley v. Garfield House Apartments

1) Fran Piers	2) Maria Alvarez	3) Marcus Bethume	4) Ann Bier
5) Jeff Scott	6) Janice Strelson	7) Susan Flueg	8) Chris Gard

Jury Selection	Comments/Notes

an opportunity to people who aren't afraid to speak their mind to stand by their principles. If you believed that something was right would you stick to your guns as a juror?

A: Well, I reckon so.

9 Q: Ms. Alvarez, when you were in college did you also work?

A: Yes. I had a job working as a waitress 30 hours a week.

Q: That must have been tough. Did you sometimes wonder if it was worth it?

A: Yes, but I stuck it out because I figured a college education was worth it.

Q: Do you believe that hard work pays off in the end?

A: I certainly do.

Q: Did your brother work his way through undergraduate and medical school?

A: Yes.

Q: It sounds like in your family you were raised not to expect something for nothing?

9 The attorney continues by engaging the jurors in conversation. By showing interest in the jurors, the attorney begins to develop rapport with them. See *Trial Advocacy* Section 5.7 (C).

Trial Transcript 13

Riley v. Garfield House Apartments			
1) Fran Piers	2) Maria Alvarez	3) Marcus Bethume	4) Ann Bier
5) Jeff Scott	6) Janice Strelson	7) Susan Flueg	8) Chris Gard

Jury Selection	**Comments/Notes**

A: I like to think so.

Q: Can you tell us what people or what factors were the greatest influence on your life as you were growing up?

A: My parents and several of my teachers who were selfless and gave a lot to me.

Q: Thank you, Ms. Alvarez. Mr. Bethume, you told us that you are a mechanic. When you were sued over some car deals, how did you feel?

A: Well, I was ticked off at first.

10   Q: You probably know that our courts are wide open so that people can sue others? You wouldn't be biased or prejudiced against somebody just because you heard that they started a lawsuit would you?

A: No . . .

Q: On the other hand you recognize, in fairness, that just because a suit gets started doesn't mean the person who is suing has to win?

A: Right.

10   This question provides information about the judicial system not only to the individual juror but to the whole panel. The attorney obtains a commitment from the juror and also begins to work on any possible biases or prejudices that the jurors may have. See *Trial Advocacy* Section 5.7 (D).

Riley v. Garfield House Apartments

1) Fran Piers	2) Maria Alvarez	3) Marcus Bethume	4) Ann Bier
5) Jeff Scott	6) Janice Strelson	7) Susan Flueg	8) Chris Gard

Jury Selection	Comments/Notes

Q: Mr. Bethume, as a mechanic what's the most important part of your job?

A: I don't know what you . . .

Q: I mean what do you think good mechanics should be most careful about?

A: Oh, I think you should be sure you do a thorough job. No slipshod stuff, you know? Just put in an honest day's work.

Q: In what way do you think people can be of value when serving as a juror?

11   A: Well, I think it's important to give both sides a chance to tell their story. I mean I don't think you should make up your mind before you hear everything. And I think you should try to be fair to both sides.

11   This answer is consistent with the attorney's strategy and serves to educate the other jurors. If the answer had not been helpful, the attorney would have had to ask further questions to educate the juror. See *Trial Advocacy* Section 5.7 (B).

Q: Ms. Bier, please tell us how you rose to your position in the insurance company?

A: Hard work, mostly. After my first husband died, I got a job with Preferred Risk Insurance.

Riley v. Garfield House Apartments			
1) Fran Piers	2) Maria Alvarez	3) Marcus Bethume	4) Ann Bier
5) Jeff Scott	6) Janice Strelson	7) Susan Flueg	8) Chris Gard

Jury Selection	Comments/Notes

Company. My two children were by then in grade school so I was able to work a full 40 hours. I started out as an adjuster and rose to assistant supervisor and eventually became supervisor. I'm hoping to get the regional position, but I may have to move to take the job.

Q: What brings you the most satisfaction in your work?

A: Oh, I suppose knowing that I've tried to be fair with people . . . that's hard to say.

12   Q: Besides your work, what interests would you rank as similarly important to you?

12   This series of questions seeks specific information from a juror to help the attorneys exercise their challenges. See *Trial Advocacy* Section 5.8.

A: Well, my husband and family of course. And also I'm active in certain women's and political groups.

Q: Like?

A: Women Against Military Madness; NOW, and cochair of Representative Norton's re-election committee.

Q: Mr. Scott, you've told us you have two small

Riley v. Garfield House Apartments

1) Fran Piers	2) Maria Alvarez	3) Marcus Bethume	4) Ann Bier
5) Jeff Scott	6) Janice Strelson	7) Susan Flueg	8) Chris Gard

Jury Selection	Comments/Notes
children, ages three and five. If you could wish one thing for those children 20 years from now, what would it be?	

A: I'd hope they'd be honest, hardworking, abide by the law, respect other people's property, and be able to take care of themselves.

Q: When you're not working hard at your job as a painter, or taking care of your small children, how do you spend your time?

A: Well, my wife died two years ago. I really don't have much time. I do like to hunt. I have a nice rifle collection and some handguns. I also like to read.

Q: What do you like to read?

A: Mostly religious books and the Bible.

Q: In what way does your reading make life better for you?

A: I feel the Bible provides guidance for me and for my family. For every problem in life I feel there is a solution in the Bible.

Riley v. Garfield House Apartments			
1) Fran Piers	2) Maria Alvarez	3) Marcus Bethume	4) Ann Bier
5) Jeff Scott	6) Janice Strelson	7) Susan Flueg	8) Chris Gard

Jury Selection	**Comments/Notes**
Q: Thank you, Mr. Scott, Ms. Strelson, you've told the court that you are a landscaper. If I were a young person interested in being a landscaper, what recommendations would you have?	
13 A: I'd say go for it. It's like a beautiful life. You're free, you know? It's not easy, but what could be nicer . . . I mean working outside and all. Nature, and the clean air, and you're just free.	13 The attorney begins to get some answers from this juror that indicate that she may not have the same type of background or values as the rest of the jurors.
Q: Would you tell us when you started in this business?	
A: Sure. When I was 16, I was living with a group of people and we started this, like, concern for our environment. Eventually I started the landscaping business 10 years later.	
Q: Thanks for that information. I want to ask a question that isn't just for you, it's for everybody, but I forgot to ask it until now. Ms. Strelson, can you give us kind of a quick impression that you have of the legal system and the court system?	

Riley v. Garfield House Apartments

1) Fran Piers	2) Maria Alvarez	3) Marcus Bethume	4) Ann Bier
5) Jeff Scott	6) Janice Strelson	7) Susan Flueg	8) Chris Gard

Jury Selection	Comments/Notes

14   A: Well, I think it's not for the common people. I mean if you got enough money you can get away with just about anything. I think there is a lot of corruption and monkey business going on.

Q: Do you think it's possible to get a fair trial in our jury system?

A: Sure, if you've got the bucks.

14   The attorney chooses not to go further with this line of questioning. Further questioning of this juror may have a negative influence on the rest of the panel. If the defense wants a jury that may not be cohesive, this juror may serve that purpose and may make it more difficult for the plaintiff to get a verdict.

15   Q: Thanks Ms. Strelson. I know its not always easy to say exactly what's on your mind, but we appreciate your straight-forward manner.

A: Think nothing of it.

Q: Ms. Flueg, in your daily life what things demand most of your time?

A: Well I'd say mostly my job at Wong Computer Company and my two teenage boys. And I try to help my husband, too, you know, and I'd also say looking after my mother who is not in good health.

Q: Is your mother ill?

15   By thanking Ms. Strelson for her openness, the attorney gives a signal to the other jurors that they should also talk freely. See *Trial Advocacy* Section 5.7.

Riley v. Garfield House Apartments

1) Fran Piers	2) Maria Alvarez	3) Marcus Bethume	4) Ann Bier
5) Jeff Scott	6) Janice Strelson	7) Susan Flueg	8) Chris Gard

Jury Selection	Comments/Notes

A: She has had hip surgery and needs help keeping her house up.

Q: How much time does that take?

A: My boys and my husband and I try to spend a couple of hours a day with her. When we work together it's not so bad.

Q: It would help us to know what you had in mind when you said "helping my husband?"

A: Oh, I just meant with mowing the lawns, or sometimes doing little odd jobs and . . . Oh I don't know . . . just odds and ends . . . whatever needs to be done.

Q: Is your husband disabled in any way?

A: Oh no, it's just there's a lot of work.

Q: Can you fill me in a little bit more on what you mean?

A: Well we have four of them you know . . .

Q: I'm sorry?

Trial Transcript 20

Riley v. Garfield House Apartments

1) Fran Piers	2) Maria Alvarez	3) Marcus Bethume	4) Ann Bier
5) Jeff Scott	6) Janice Strelson	7) Susan Flueg	8) Chris Gard

---

Jury Selection	**Comments/Notes**

16   A: Four apartment buildings. So I need to collect rent, and make little repairs, that sort of thing.

Q: How long has your family been in the business of providing rental housing to people who need housing in this community?

A: Ten years now.

Q: Do you find being a property owner like that challenging?

A: Very much so. There's always some little problem that arises.

Q: How do you feel when you're able to solve a problem—big or small—that might arise with one of those dwelling units?

A: Pretty good. I like the feeling of being on top of things.

Q: Thank you, Ms. Flueg. Mr. Gard, what's the hardest part about being a welder?

A: I'd say working in cramped positions where it's awkward. And also it's kind of dirty.

16   By pursuing the questioning and asking straightforward questions, the attorney learns a great deal about this juror. There is an identification between this juror and the client. It is likely that the plaintiff will strike the juror using a peremptory challenge; however, the defense lawyer continues with the questioning to teach the other jurors about the case and the client. See *Trial Advocacy* Section 5.2.

Riley v. Garfield House Apartments

1) Fran Piers	2) Maria Alvarez	3) Marcus Bethume	4) Ann Bier
5) Jeff Scott	6) Janice Strelson	7) Susan Flueg	8) Chris Gard

Jury Selection	Comments/Notes

Q: When you come home after a tough day, what do you do?

A: Well, I like to rough-house with my two boys who are six and nine. Sometimes we go fishing in the summer. I also like to work on my car.

Q: When you think about what it might be like to be on a jury, what kinds of thoughts do you have?

A: I don't—I mean, what do you mean?

Q: Well, do you think it would be a tough job being on a jury where you might have to decide things in a way that one side won't like?

A: No. My uncle was on a jury and he says it was just a lot of people arguing but eventually they worked it out okay.

Q: Can you tell me a little more about what he meant when he said that they "worked it out okay?"

A: You know, it's like there'd be a little give here and a little take there and they worked it

Trial Transcript 22

Riley v. Garfield House Apartments

| 1) Fran Piers | 2) Maria Alvarez | 3) Marcus Bethume | 4) Ann Bier |
| 5) Jeff Scott | 6) Janice Strelson | 7) Susan Flueg | 8) Chris Gard |

Jury Selection	Comments/Notes

out so everybody was happy.

Q: Did your uncle seem to feel the jury system was a good thing?

17   A: Oh yeah.

Q: Is your uncle somebody you see a fair amount of and whom you admire?

A: Yeah. He's a big shot in a plumbing company.

18   **To the Court:**

I have no further questions.

Judge:

Plaintiff's counsel, you may inquire.

Plaintiff's Counsel:

19   Q: I represent Rita Riley. She is a small child and so really won't be able to speak on her own behalf, and I must speak for her. I would like to ask all of you this question: If Rita, through the adults who will be testifying for her—and I mean her mom and those people who cared for her— convinces you that she was terribly burned and her life has been changed

---

17   The attorney follows up on an answer and uses it to teach the other jurors that the system is a good system in contrast to the responses given by juror Strelson.

18   The judge does not require the defense attorney to make any peremptory or challenges for cause at this time and will permit the lawyers to do so at the end of all the questioning. The practice varies among jurisdictions. See *Trial Advocacy* Section 5.8.

19   Plaintiff's attorney and the plaintiff's case were briefly introduced to the jury at the beginning of the questioning. However, a great deal of information has already been obtained from the jurors and given to the jurors through the questions. The plaintiff's attorney has a brief opportunity to remind them about the case and the people involved. In this brief intro-

Riley v. Garfield House Apartments			
1) Fran Piers	2) Maria Alvarez	3) Marcus Bethume	4) Ann Bier
5) Jeff Scott	6) Janice Strelson	7) Susan Flueg	8) Chris Gard

Jury Selection	**Comments/Notes**

Jury Selection

forever, because of the defendant's negligence, is there anyone here who would refuse to award her substantial compensation for her past injuries and also to take care of her in the future?

Ms. Strelson:

20   Counsel, I was wondering . . .

Q: Yes, Ms. Strelson?

A: Does the federal government have a plan like, you know, social security, for people who are burned? I know my brother-in-law said . . .

21   Q: Ms. Strelson, that's a question that should be covered with the court later if the judge feels it's appropriate but neither I nor counsel for the defendant under our rules can get into a discussion on that. Thanks for responding to my question however. I do appreciate it. I take it by the absence of any raised hands there would be no problem in making a sufficient award of money even if it was necessary

Comments/Notes

duction the attorney uses words like "terribly burned" and "life changed forever" in order to begin the process of persuading the jury of the seriousness of the case and to begin developing a theory of the case. See *Trial Advocacy* Section 5.5.

20   Most jurors do not ask questions or speak without being asked questions although it does happen occasionally. This question from juror Strelson adds further information to indicate that she might be a disruptive influence on the jury.

21   The attorney properly suggests that the judge may respond to her question. See *Trial Advocacy* Section 5.4.

Riley v. Garfield House Apartments			
1) Fran Piers	2) Maria Alvarez	3) Marcus Bethume	4) Ann Bier
5) Jeff Scott	6) Janice Strelson	7) Susan Flueg	8) Chris Gard

Jury Selection	Comments/Notes

to make that award very substantial, as long as you were abiding by the law which the judge will give you at the end of the trial? Thank you.

22   Q: Now I want you to imagine something with me. We've all seen the interviewer on the street taking a poll about people's attitudes on things. If a young interviewer were to stop you on the street and ask you this question, I'd like to know how you'd answer it: "If you had to describe your point of view of life, would you describe yourself as a liberal, as a conservative or as something else?" Ms. Bier, how would you answer that question?

A: I'd have to say I'm sort of a liberal.

Q: And if that interviewer asked you to try to explain why you felt that way, what would you say?

A: I believe that I'd like to fight against the way big business sort of runs this country. I think we have some obligation towards people who can't make it on their own. Not everybody is rich and smart, you know.

22   The plaintiff's attorney uses a third person as a questioner to get very delicate information from the jurors. The attorney does not personally ask embarrassing questions, yet gives the jurors a chance to talk about something that they may find difficult if the attorney addressed the question directly. See *Trial Advocacy* Section 5.5 (A).

Riley v. Garfield House Apartments

1) Fran Piers	2) Maria Alvarez	3) Marcus Bethume	4) Ann Bier
5) Jeff Scott	6) Janice Strelson	7) Susan Flueg	8) Chris Gard

Jury Selection	Comments/Notes

23   Q: Now the nice thing about the jury system is that it is one of the great places in this country where people can openly and honestly disagree. Mr. Piers, how would you have answered that interviewer?

A: I go along with Ms. Bier. I'm not a radical, or anything like that, but I think big business is taking advantage of the little guy.

Q: Ms. Alvarez, nobody gets to escape this interviewer. What would you say?

A: I've never thought about it. Politics don't interest me.

Q: But if the interviewer said "I'm not just talking about politics. I mean in your neighborhood, your family, your work, everywhere . . . Do you think you're liberal or conservative?"

23   The attorney does not question the jurors in any order but moves around making sure that all of them get questioned. Some attorneys are able to remember all of the jurors' names without having to refer to notes. However, it is appropriate and necessary for many attorneys to use notes to make sure the name of each juror is pronounced correctly. See *Trial Advocacy* Section 5.7 (A).

Riley v. Garfield House Apartments

1) Fran Piers	2) Maria Alvarez	3) Marcus Bethume	4) Ann Bier
5) Jeff Scott	6) Janice Strelson	7) Susan Flueg	8) Chris Gard

Jury Selection	Comments/Notes

A: I'd say middle of the road.

Q: Mr. Bethume, this interviewer finds his way into your mechanic shop. What would you say?

A: I'd say I don't like labels. What's right is right. Then I'd probably say I was busy.

Q: Mr. Scott, say this interviewer finds you out in the field showing one of your young children how to hunt. How would you answer?

A: Definitely conservative. I think certain things the liberals wanted in this country got us in trouble. I mean like gun control and that kind of thing.

Q: Ms. Flueg, if you were interrupted in your busy life working at one of your apartment buildings and were asked those questions, what would you say?

A: Well, can I say "none of the above?" I mean I just feel that one should above all be responsible. If that means liberal or conservative, I don't know. I just think if we all did our duty and were responsible for our actions, it'd be a better world.

Riley v. Garfield House Apartments

1) Fran Piers	2) Maria Alvarez	3) Marcus Bethume	4) Ann Bier
5) Jeff Scott	6) Janice Strelson	7) Susan Flueg	8) Chris Gard

Jury Selection	Comments/Notes

Q: Mr. Gard, if you were walking along with your uncle and you were stopped by the interviewer, what would you say to answer those questions?

A: I think I'd say I'm a little bit of both.

24   Q: And finally Ms. Strelson, you've been sitting there patiently. What would you have said?

A: About what?

Q: About being liberal or conservative?

A: I'd say labels destroy the natural harmonies of the universe. I'd say that those words are just more evidence of the money-sickness of this planet. I'd refuse to buy into the materialism represented by modern political and social systems.

24   The final answers by Ms. Strelson are different than the answers provided by the other jurors. This juror may be a disruptive influence in deliberations and might make it more difficult for the plaintiff to get a verdict. See *Trial Advocacy* Section 5.2 (E).

Trial Transcript 28

Riley v. Garfield House Apartments

1) Fran Piers	2) Maria Alvarez	3) Marcus Bethume	4) Ann Bier
5) Jeff Scott	6) Janice Strelson	7) Susan Flueg	8) Chris Gard

Jury Selection	Comments/Notes

Plaintiff's Counsel to the Judge:

25 Your Honor, may we approach the bench for a moment?

Judge:

Yes, you may.

Colloquy at the Bench Plaintiff's Counsel:

Your Honor, I respectfully suggest that this latter juror, Ms. Strelson, be stricken for cause on grounds that she demonstrates a bias that would make it impossible for her to serve as a juror.

Defendant's Counsel:

26 I agree.

Judge:

Ms. Strelson, after hearing the questions of both lawyers and your answers, I believe that it may be difficult for you to sit as a member of this particular jury. Therefore I am going to excuse you at this time and ask you to return to the jury waiting room to be assigned to other duties. Thank you very much for your time. You may be excused now.

25 In making a request to strike a juror for cause, the attorney has chosen to enter into the discussion at the bench outside the hearing of the jury. If the attorney made the motion in the hearing of the jurors and the judge refused the motion, the discussion may influence the jurors negatively. See *Trial Advocacy* Section 5.8 (A).

26 The defense lawyer has chosen not to contest the motion to remove the juror for cause because she also appears to be an unfavorable defense juror. By joining in the motion, the defense attorney also indicates a willingness to be fair. See *Trial Advocacy* Section 5.8.

Trial Transcript 29

Riley v. Garfield House Apartments			
1) Fran Piers	2) Maria Alvarez	3) Marcus Bethume	4) Ann Bier
5) Jeff Scott	6) ~~Janice Strelson~~ Garrett Raymond	7) Susan Flueg	8) Chris Gard

Jury Selection	Comments/Notes

Judge:

27   Clerk, would you please draw the name of another juror.

Clerk:

As I call your name, please take the vacant seat in the jury box:

Garrett Raymond. R-A-Y-M-O-N-D. 4209 Columbus Avenue South.

Judge:

Mr. Raymond, would you please answer the following questions: (The judge repeats the preliminary questions asked of the other jurors).

Garrett Raymond:

A small business executive.

Single. Divorced, had been married for 10 years.

Have a 19 year old son who is studying engineering in college.

27   In this case the judge requested that the replacement jurors sit in the courtroom. When the clerk calls the name of juror Raymond, he replaces Ms. Strelson in seat number 6. A replacement is needed for Ms. Strelson so that each attorney will have the opportunity to exercise an equal number of peremptory challenges. Mr. Raymond will not have to be given the preliminary instructions because he has heard both the instructions and the previous questions. See *Trial Advocacy* Section 5.8 (D).

Riley v. Garfield House Apartments

1) Fran Piers	2) Maria Alvarez	3) Marcus Bethume	4) Ann Bier
5) Jeff Scott	6) Garrett Raymond	7) Susan Flueg	8) Chris Gard

Jury Selection	Comments/Notes

Have a Master's degree in business administration.

No previous jury service.

My company has been sued and I was involved in the lawsuit. It was settled before trial, however, for an undisclosed amount of money.

No injuries.

I know medical administrators because we provide small business services for them.

Judge:

Defense counsel may question Mr. Raymond.

28   **Defendant's Attorney:**

Q: Mr. Raymond, please tell us about this young son of yours who is studying engineering.

A: Well, he's a hardworking boy. Getting good grades. Behaves himself. Works part-time in my business.

Q: Have you been close to your son over the years?

A: Very.

28   The defense attorney has the right to proceed first. Both lawyers will address this juror in the same manner as the other jurors were questioned. See *Trial Advocacy* Section 5.4 (A).

Riley v. Garfield House Apartments

1) Fran Piers	2) Maria Alvarez	3) Marcus Bethume	4) Ann Bier
5) Jeff Scott	6) Garrett Raymond	7) Susan Flueg	8) Chris Gard

Jury Selection	Comments/Notes
Q: What kinds of values does he have that you most admire?	
A: He doesn't go along with the crowd. He is independent. He doesn't expect something for nothing. He takes responsibility. When he's wrong, he admits it. He doesn't blame somebody else.	
Q: If you could wish anything for your son in 20 years, what would it be?	
A: That he not be afraid to stand up for what's right. Sounds simple, I suppose, but that's what I feel.	
29 **Defendant's Attorney:**	29 Both attorneys would have asked more questions in a complete jury selection.
I have no other questions.	
Judge:	
Plaintiff's counsel, you may inquire.	
Plaintiff's Counsel:	
Q: Mr. Raymond, did you hear my question concerning the interviewer as you sat in the back of the courtroom?	
A: Yes, I did.	
Q: How would you answer the question?	

Riley v. Garfield House Apartments

1) Fran Piers	2) Maria Alvarez	3) Marcus Bethume	4) Ann Bier
5) Jeff Scott	6) Garrett Raymond	7) Susan Flueg	8) Chris Gard

Jury Selection	Comments/Notes

A: I'd say I'm conservative.

Q: Would you explain why you feel that way?

A: I'd say that I thought being conservative made you strong. Not looking for something for nothing.

Plaintiff's Counsel:

Thank you all very much. Your Honor, I have no further questions.

Judge:

30 Counsel, approach the bench. You may now each exercise your one peremptory challenge. Here is the list of jurors. Defense counsel, make your strike first.

Defendant's Attorney:

Your Honor, I strike juror number 1, Fran Piers.

Plaintiff's Counsel:

I strike number 7, Susan Flueg.

30 This procedure of striking jurors is one of several alternatives. The plaintiff must have an alternative juror to strike if the defense counsel strikes the juror that the plaintiff's counsel would have stricken. Most jurisdictions allow parties more than one peremptory challenge. See *Trial Advocacy* Section 5.8 (B).

Riley v. Garfield House Apartments			
1) ~~Fran Piers~~	2) Maria Alvarez	3) Marcus Bethume	4) Ann Bier
5) Jeff Scott	6) Garrett Raymond	7) ~~Susan Flueg~~	8) Chris Gard

Jury Selection	Comments/Notes

Judge:

31   The following two jurors please return to the jury assembly room. Juror number 1, Fran Piers, and juror number 7, Susan Fleug.

Thank you very much Mr. Piers and Ms. Flueg.

32   The six of you who remain are the jury in this case. Please rise so we may administer your oath.

(Oath administered.)

Judge:

33   Members of the Jury, now that you have been sworn I'll give you some preliminary instructions to guide you in your participation in the trial.

The evidence from which you will find the facts will consist of the testimony of witnesses, documents and other exhibits, and any facts the lawyers agree or stipulate to, or that the court may instruct you to find.

Certain things are not evidence and must not be con-

31   As you review the questions that the attorneys asked and determine if you would have removed the same jurors, consider the reasons why you may have made the same or different decisions.

32   The jurors were sworn earlier by the clerk and were required to answer questions truthfully. The second oath is to the panel that has been seated. At this time the jurors are required to swear that they will uphold their duty as jurors. See *Trial Advocacy* Section 2.2 (A).

33   These comments by the judge are typical. They provide general instructions for the jurors. However, the jurors have received a great deal of information in a very short period of time, and it will be difficult for them to recall the specific details of the instructions by the judge. The attorneys should not assume that the jurors understand the process or the case. See *Trial Advocacy* Section 2.9.

Riley v. Garfield House Apartments

1) Maria Alvarez	3) Marcus Bethume	4) Ann Bier
5) Jeff Scott	6) Garrett Raymond	7) Chris Gard

Jury Selection	Comments/Notes

sidered as such by you. I will list them for you now. Statements, arguments, and questions by lawyers are not evidence. Objections to questions are not evidence. Testimony that the court has excluded or told you to disregard is not evidence and must not be considered. Anything you may have seen or heard outside the courtroom is not evidence and must be disregarded. You are to decide the case solely on the evidence presented here in the courtroom.

In the course of the trial you're going to hear the testimony of witnesses, and you will have to make judgments about the credibility of the testimony. As you listen carefully to the witnesses, you should take note of such matters as their interest or lack of interest in the outcome of the case; their ability and their opportunity to know and remember and tell the facts; their manner; their

Riley v. Garfield House Apartments

1) Maria Alvarez	3) Marcus Bethume	4) Ann Bier
5) Jeff Scott	6) Garrett Raymond	7) Chris Gard

Jury Selection	Comments/Notes

experience; their frankness and sincerity or their lack of frankness or sincerity; the reasonableness or unreasonableness of the witnesses' testimony in light of all the other evidence in the case; and any other factors that bear on the question of believability and weight. You should in the last analysis rely on your own experience, your own judgment, and your own common sense.

It will be your duty to find from the evidence what the facts are. You and you alone are the judges of the facts. You will then have to apply those facts to the law as I will give it to you. You must follow that law whether you agree with it or not.

Nothing I may say or do during the course of the trial should be taken by you as indicating what your verdict should be.

Now, a few words about your conduct as jurors.

Riley v. Garfield House Apartments

1) Maria Alvarez	3) Marcus Bethume	4) Ann Bier
5) Jeff Scott	6) Garrett Raymond	7) Chris Gard

Jury Selection	Comments/Notes
First, you should not discuss the case among yourselves or with anyone else. At the end of the trial, you will have as much time as you need to discuss the case. That is at the end of the trial and not during the trial. Second, do not read or listen to anything regarding this case in any way. Third, do not research or investigate the case on your own or view websites or blogs. Finally, do not form any opinion until all the evidence is in. Keep an open mind until your deliberations at the end of the case.	

Riley v. Garfield House Apartments

Plaintiff's Opening Statement	Comments/Notes

Judge to Plaintiff's Counsel:

Counsel, you may now present your opening statement.

Plaintiff's Counsel:

1 On Christmas Eve, three years ago, one year old Rita Riley was scalded in her bath. She was burned, and she was scarred over more than one-third of her entire body. She was terribly hurt. As a result of

2 the injuries that Rita Riley received that night, she will never be the kind of person that she might have been.

She was hurt because the defendant corporation, who owned the building where she lived, had a water heater that did not work.

3 The evidence will show that the reason that the water heater did not work was because the defendant was negligent.

1 The jury's attention is immediately drawn to the tragedy. Counsel uses detailed impact words as transitions: "scalded," "burned," "scarred." Impact words such as "hurt" are repeated. Each sentence is logically linked to the preceding sentence so that the first paragraph traces the plaintiff's entire case. See *Trial Advocacy* Section 6.4 (B).

2 Right away, plaintiff's counsel tells the jury the story of what happened, why the jury should find for the plaintiff, and how to find for the plaintiff. The theory of this opening statement is consistent with and parallels the final argument. See *Trial Advocacy* Section 6.2 (C).

3 A legal conclusion is qualified with a prefatory clause—"the evidence will show"—because these comments approach argument. See *Trial Advocacy* Section 6.7 (B).

Riley v. Garfield House Apartments

Plaintiff's Opening Statement	Comments/Notes

4 The defendant was negligent, and therefore is responsible for what happened to that little girl, and must be held accountable for her injuries.

5 I'm here today on behalf of that little girl and her parents.

6 I will prove four things during the course of this trial. The first thing I will prove is that the defendant had a duty to Rita Riley. That duty was to provide a safe place for her to live. Secondly, I will prove that the defendant corporation breached that duty. The defendant failed to do something it was supposed to do: the defendant corporation failed to live up to its obligation to provide a safe place for that little girl. The third thing that I will prove is that the failure on the part of the defendant to fulfill its obligation was the direct cause of Rita Riley's injuries. Finally, I will prove that this little girl has been damaged. She has been scarred and disfigured. She has suffered pain, and she will continue to suffer pain, discomfort, and embarrassment for the rest of her life because of the burns she received that night.

4 Opening statement may include undisputed facts such as Rita's scalding and her disfigurement. It may also include disputed facts such as the elements of defendant's negligence. See *Trial Advocacy* Section 6.4 (C).

5 Counsel identifies with the plaintiff and her parents and begins to personalize them.

6 Only the elements of the case need to be defined; the judge will explain the law to the jury. Plaintiff's counsel must refer only to facts that will be presented through a witness, a document, or some other exhibit. At the outset, plaintiff's counsel establishes the scene of the accident, introduces the plaintiff by personalizing her as a tragically disfigured child, and de-personalizes the defendant, a corporation. This presentation of the facts gets the attention and empathy of the jury. Counsel explains the purpose of the evidence which will prove the elements of defendant's negligence. See *Trial Advocacy* Section 6.1 (B).

Riley v. Garfield House Apartments

Plaintiff's Opening Statement	Comments/Notes
7 On that Christmas Eve three years ago, Rita Riley and her mom and dad lived at the Garfield House Apartments here in our city. They had lived there since Rita was born. The defendant corporation owned those apartments. That Christmas Eve, Rita's mother, Mary, was giving Rita a bath. She had given her daughter baths frequently, almost every day of Rita's first year of life. She always ran the water the same way. The water control had a single lever. When it was up and pointed to the right the water was supposed to run cold; to the middle, comfortably warm; pointed to the left, hot. When the lever was down the water was off. She first turned the water all the way to "hot" and let it run. She did this because the water in this apartment often took a long,	7 The attorney begins a chronological description of the accident, first the event, then the injuries, and finally the future damages. See *Trial Advocacy* Section 6.3 (A).

Riley v. Garfield House Apartments

Plaintiff's Opening Statement	Comments/Notes
long time to heat up. She ran the water until it was hot, and when it became hot, she put the plug in the bathtub. After some hot water was run, she turned the water to "cold" and ran cold water until the temperature was appropriate for a little child and until there was about an inch and a half of water in the tub. She then shut the water off, placed her baby in the tub and watched her splash and play around. Rita liked to take baths.	
8 Mary stayed with her daughter for about five minutes, and then she went into the next room to take care of some laundry. She was approximately ten feet away, but she wasn't concerned because she had done this before and there had never	8 Defendant's strongest theory of non-liability is parental negligence because Mary Riley left the infant alone in the bathtub. To mitigate the effect, plaintiff's counsel candidly brings out the weakness first. Counsel takes the jury through the scene of the bath preparation, the bath itself, and the accident in a clear, straightforward way. See *Trial Advocacy* Section 6.4 (F).
9 been any problem. She was also able to hear Rita laughing and splashing in the bathtub. She was gone for less than a minute. And then she heard two distinct sounds at the exact same time. She heard the sound of position. Rita must have pushed the handle up. Mary pulled the lever straight down to shut it off. The water that was coming out was steaming hot and was running	9 The use of impact words like "laughing and splashing," creates a picture of a happy baby and a confident mother. These terms contrast sharply with the "screams."

Riley v. Garfield House Apartments

Plaintiff's Opening Statement	Comments/Notes
directly on to her daughter. She pulled Rita out of the tub. She tried to run cold water over the burns, but even the cold water stayed warm. Mary called an ambulance. She knew how badly her daughter was burned, because everywhere she touched Rita, her skin would come off in her hands. Rita was taken immediately to the hospital emergency room and stayed in the hospital for months. She has had skin grafts and continues to require serious medical care. She is not healed even today.	

Riley v. Garfield House Apartments

Plaintiff's Opening Statement	Comments/Notes
10 The medical bills for Rita total over one hundred, fifty-seven thousand dollars. Over the next ten to fifteen years, Rita will have to have more operations and the doctor bills will be much more.	10 The financial damages, present and future, are included as a part of the chronological presentation. Counsel has decided not to provide the jurors with a specific amount of damages for pain and suffering, but to defer a specific request until summation. See *Trial Advocacy* Section 6.4 (O).
11 At the time of this accident, Connie Austern was the manager for the defendant, Garfield House Apartments. You will learn that Ms. Austern had no training and no experience in operating or maintaining a water heater. Ms. Austern did not know how to operate the thermostat, which is the device that controls the temperature of the water for the entire apartment complex. She had never once read the owner's manual. She didn't even know where the owner's manual was.	11 The testimony of each witness is outlined. In this section, counsel refers to the defense witness Connie Austern. The jury is told what to look for. The evidence will show that Connie Austern had no reasonable experience or training in inspecting and maintaining the water heater. This reinforces the plaintiff's theory that the defendant Garfield House Apartments was negligent and highlights what will be brought out on cross-examination. See *Trial Advocacy* Section 6.4 (D).
12 At the time of this accident, a vandalism problem existed in the basement of the Garfield House Apartments, where the water heater was located. In response to that problem, Ms. Austern put up a fence of	12 The description of the security for the water heater is specific and described in terms favoring the plaintiff. This adds to the persuasive weight of the defendant's breach of duty.

Trial Transcript 43

Riley v. Garfield House Apartments

Plaintiff's Opening Statement	Comments/Notes
two-by-fours and a little chicken wire screen. When the vandals knocked that fence down, she put the same fence back up, even though that fence was not doing what it was supposed to do. That fence was not keeping the vandals away from that water heater.	
13 You will hear the testimony of Dr. Pat Armstead, who has a Ph.D. in the field of mechanical engineering. Dr. Armstead will tell you what should be the proper security and mainte-	13 The credentials of plaintiff's expert are mentioned in the opening statement.
14 nance of a water heater in an apartment building. You will learn that the water heater in the basement of the Garfield Apartment was not properly maintained and was not properly secured.	14 The theme—improper maintenance and improper security—is repeated and summarizes this section of the opening. See *Trial Advocacy* Section 6.3 (B).
15 Rita and her parents moved out of the Garfield House Apartments a few weeks after the accident. The building was completely remodeled and changed the following summer. We have never been able to get that faucet or the water heater examined and analyzed because they were destroyed during the remodeling.	15 The faucet and heater are not available to plaintiff or the jury. This weakness in the evidence is represented in the best light. See *Trial Advocacy* Section 6.5 (H).

Riley v. Garfield House Apartments

Plaintiff's Opening Statement	Comments/Notes
16 The defendant corporation was negligent because it had a duty to provide a safe place to live, and it didn't do what it was supposed to do. The defendant led the Rileys to believe that they could be safe, but they were not, and that's what the law calls negligence. The defendant was negligent because the person that it put in charge of that water heater was not properly trained, had no experience in maintaining a water heater, and didn't know how to operate the thermostat. The defendant was also negligent because it did not secure the water heater properly.	16 Plaintiff's counsel is drawing a legal conclusion that the defendant was negligent. No qualifying remarks such as, "the evidence will show," were used. The extent to which this type of presentation may be used depends upon the judge, court rules and practice, and the opposing attorney. Qualifying remarks such as "the evidence will show" or "I will prove" may prevent an objection. See *Trial Advocacy* Section 6.5 (J).
17 At the end of the trial, I will ask you to return a verdict for Rita Riley and to award her an adequate amount of money to compensate her not only for the injuries that she has suffered but for the injuries that she continues to suffer today, and	17 Plaintiff's counsel offers a concise summary of the vital facts, a compelling statement justifying a verdict for Rita Riley, and a dramatic summary of the major theme and damages. Counsel has presented the opening statement in an understandable

Riley v. Garfield House Apartments

Plaintiff's Opening Statement	Comments/Notes
for the injuries, and the pain, and the humiliation that she will suffer for the rest of her life. I will ask you to return that verdict not on the basis of sympathy. I will ask you to return that verdict on the basis of the facts and the evidence you are about to see and hear. Thank you.	and simple format. Each element of negligence will be consistent with plaintiff's closing argument because counsel has already composed the closing argument and has directed everything to that summation. See *Trial Advocacy* Section 6.1 (A).

Riley v. Garfield House Apartments

Defendant's Opening Statement	Comments/Notes
Judge to Defendant's Attorney:	
Are you ready to give your opening statement?	
Defendant's Attorney:	
Yes I am, your Honor.	
1 Members of the Jury, sometimes when a child is hurt in an accident, it's nobody's fault. Sometimes when a child is hurt, it's somebody's fault, but it can't be determined with legal certainty whose fault it was. Today the evidence will show that tragically sometimes the	1 Defense counsel acknowledges the tragedy, but puts the tragedy into a context consistent with the defense's theory of the case. See *Trial Advocacy* Section 6.1 (A).
2 person who loves that child the most is the person responsible for that child's injuries.	2 The focus of the theory of the case is quickly and clearly established: Plaintiff's mother, not defendant, is responsible. See *Trial Advocacy* Section 6.5 (A).
3 Before any plaintiff can place the blame, the burden, the responsibility for an accident on anyone, they must prove the case. The plaintiff may only prove a case on the basis of the facts and on the evidence, not on speculation or sympathy.	3 Defense counsel avoids over-personalizing Rita Riley by calling her "the plaintiff." In addition, counsel refers to the plaintiff with the plural pronoun "they." While not proper grammatically, this linguistic device works subliminally on the jurors, reminding them that Rita's mother's responsibility is attributable to Rita. See *Trial Advocacy* Section 6.4 (D).
4 On the basis of the facts and the evidence of this case, the plaintiff will not be able	4 Defense counsel attempts to personalize his clients by referring to them as "owners" and not as a corporation.

Trial Transcript 47

Riley v. Garfield House Apartments

Defendant's Opening Statement	Comments/Notes
to show the owners of the Garfield House Apartments are responsible for what happened to Rita Riley on that night.	The phrase "on the basis of the facts and evidence" averts opposing counsel's objection to improper argument and allows defense counsel to qualify a legal conclusion. See *Trial Advocacy* Section 6.7 (B).
5 In order for the plaintiff to win today, the plaintiff does have to prove four things. The plaintiff must prove that the owners of the Garfield House Apartments had a duty to the plaintiff, which of course they did. They had a duty to every tenant in that building to provide a reasonably safe place to live, a reasonably safe place. They did provide that reasonably safe place. However, they did not have a duty to protect people from themselves, or their own carelessness.	5 Defense counsel demonstrates how the facts cannot support the plaintiff's case. Enumerating each element of negligence, defense counsel tells the jury how the evidence will not support plaintiff's case. Defense counsel clearly and candidly acknowledges the one element of negligence that defendant admits which is the duty to plaintiff. Counsel turns this admission into a strength by defining the scope of that duty—to maintain a reasonably safe habitation, not to protect people from their own carelessness. See *Trial Advocacy* Section 6.4 (F).
6 Secondly, the plaintiff must prove the defendants breached that duty, that they failed to do something that they were supposed to do. The evidence will not permit the plaintiff to prove the owners of the Garfield House Apartments breached their duty. The defendants did what they were supposed to do. They maintained a reasonably safe place for their tenants	6 Counsel effectively enumerates each element of negligence with transitions: first, second, third, fourth. Counsel uses this step-by-step format to show the jury how defendant's reasonableness contrasts with plaintiff's parents' carelessness. See *Trial Advocacy* Section 6.3 (B).

Riley v. Garfield House Apartments

Defendant's Opening Statement	Comments/Notes
Thirdly, the plaintiff must prove, somehow, that the owners of the Garfield House Apartments were directly responsible for what happened that night. However, it was not the owners of the Garfield House Apartments or Connie Austern who left that child alone in that bathtub on December 24.	
Finally, the plaintiff must prove damages. They must prove the actual money costs of injuries. The medical bills are real, but any other damages may not be proved using conjecture or speculation, and may not be based upon sympathy alone. The plaintiff must prove those money costs on the basis of real facts and real evidence.	
7 On December 24, Rita Riley's mother did leave her alone in a bathtub, and while that child was left alone, without any supervision, that active, smart, one-year-old girl turned on the water and got tragically burned. At the time of this incident, the	7 Defense counsel uses a chronological format. This clear and effective presentation follows plaintiff's format, and it allows defense counsel to contrast plaintiff's story so that the jury will find it more difficult to give credence to plaintiff's case. See *Trial Advocacy* Section 6.3 (A).

Riley v. Garfield House Apartments

Defendant's Opening Statement	Comments/Notes
8 mother, Mary Riley, was aware of how hot the water was in the apartment. Rita's mother knew the hot water was so hot that while doing the dishes in the kitchen sink she had to use a towel to touch the hot water faucet because she couldn't touch it with her bare hands. It was too hot. She also realized how hot the water was because she'd burned herself in the shower about a week before the plaintiff was burned. She will tell you a sudden rush of hot water came through the pipes and burned her leg.	8 Defense counsel acknowledges plaintiff's mother's trouble with scalding water. This fact is turned to the defense's advantage by showing that plaintiff's mother was aware, yet despite her knowledge, she left the child alone. See *Trial Advocacy* Section 6.5 (H).
9 But you will learn that Rita's mother never told Connie Austern or anyone else at the Garfield House Apartments about the water in that apartment. In fact, the plaintiff will be unable to prove that any of the tenants had ever complained to the management of the Garfield House Apartments about the water being too hot.	9 Seeming admissions of dangerous conditions—faucets too hot to touch, sudden rushes of hot water—are minimized by the fact that Mary Riley failed to act reasonably given her knowledge. Impact words that ordinarily would bolster plaintiff's case are used to strengthen defendant's case. See *Trial Advocacy* Section 6.4 (J).

Riley v. Garfield House Apartments

Defendant's Opening Statement	Comments/Notes
Connie Austern is the maintenance manager of the Garfield House Apartments. On December 24, 3 years ago,	
10　Connie Austern had been with the Garfield House Apartments for six years and still works there today. She enjoys the work, and she does a good job. At the time of the accident, Ms. Austern routinely inspected the water heater in the basement of the Garfield House Apartments—regularly! Even though there were no complaints.	10　Rather than stating conclusions that Connie Austern was conscientious about maintaining the water heater, counsel establishes credibility by using words such as "routine" inspection and "immediate" response to vandalism. See *Trial Advocacy* Section 6.4 (I).
When there was a vandalism problem in the basement where the water heater and the washer and dryer were located, Ms. Austern put a fence up to keep the vandals away from the water heater. And on the few occasions when the vandals tampered with the fence itself, Ms. Austern fixed the fence immediately and inspected the thermostat to make sure that the water temperature gauge was where it was supposed to be. She made sure that the vandals hadn't tampered with the thermostat.	

Trial Transcript 51

Riley v. Garfield House Apartments

Defendant's Opening Statement	Comments/Notes
You will learn that the owners of the Garfield House Apartments had gone to the trouble and the expense of having a service contract placed on that water heater. They had a service contract with Metro Appliance, a group of professionals who repair water heaters. The terms of the service contract were that the owners of the Garfield House Apartments paid an annual fee to Metro Appliance. In return for that fee, all Connie Austern had to do, if there was a problem of any kind with that water heater, was to call Metro Appliance, and they would come out and repair the water heater for no charge because the fee had already been	
11 paid. But Connie Austern never had the opportunity to call Metro Appliance because Rita's parents never told the owners or management or Connie Austern about any problem.	11 Presenting defendant's theory of the facts, counsel avoids the inference that defendant failed to act by continuing the theme of parental responsibility. Had plaintiff's parents reasonably acted on their knowledge, defendant would have had the "opportunity" to utilize the service contract. See *Trial Advocacy* Section 6.4 (H).

Riley v. Garfield House Apartments

Defendant's Opening Statement	Comments/Notes
You will hear the testimony of Dr. Martin Thomas, a Ph.D. in the field of mechanical engineering. Dr. Thomas is a specialist in building and apartment safety. You will learn that before the building was remodeled and the water heater removed, Dr. Thomas went to the Garfield House Apartments, ran tests of the water temperature, inspected that water heater and did not recommend any changes concerning how that water heater was secured or maintained. None!	
12 The evidence will show that the owners of the Garfield House Apartments were not negligent. They were not negligent because they had absolutely no warning about the problems with the temperature of the water in that building.	12 Using the qualifying clause, "the evidence will show," defense counsel traces the facts and shows how defendant reasonably met its duty. The jury knows what the defendant did in response to vandalism and in response to maintaining a dangerous machine by hiring an expert. The jury knows how not to find for plaintiff. See *Trial Advocacy* Section 6.5 (G).
13 They were not negligent because Connie Austern did what she was supposed to do. She inspected that water heater on a regular basis, and she installed a fence around that water heater when there	13 While the jury may want to find for the infant plaintiff, counsel shows why the jury must not assign blame to Garfield House Apartments. In clear, simple language, defense counsel lays out the

---

Riley v. Garfield House Apartments

Defendant's Opening Statement	Comments/Notes
was a vandalism problem. The owners had a service contract. They had gone to the trouble and expense of putting a service contract on that water heater, but they never had the opportunity to use it. The summer after this accident the city historical society provided funds to restore the building which housed the Garfield House Apartments to its original appearance and to change the Garfield House Apartments from apartments to condominiums. The entire	theory of the case, rebutting plaintiff. The themes of the reasonable defendant and the careless parent are developed and will be used during the final argument. See *Trial Advocacy* Section 6.1 (A).
14 building was remodeled and changed. Because condominiums have to have individual water heaters, new plumbing and water heaters were added throughout the building. Unfortunately, the old water heating system is gone, and no one can presently test it or show you how it worked or if there was any problem with the system. The owners of the Garfield House Apartments are not responsible for what happened that night because it was not	14 The loss of the faucet and water heater is explained in a straightforward way so that the defense does not appear to have acted improperly by destroying evidence.

Trial Transcript 54

Riley v. Garfield House Apartments

Defendant's Opening Statement	Comments/Notes
15 the owner of the Garfield Apartments, it was not Connie Austern, it was not the people who designed or the people who installed the water heater that left that child alone, unattended, and unsupervised in that tub on the night of the accident. It was Mary Riley who left that child alone and she knew that the water got too hot.	15 This conclusion supports a verdict for the defendant. See *Trial Advocacy* Section 6.3 (C).
16 At the end of this trial, members of the Jury, I will ask you to return a verdict for the defendant because that will be the correct and fair verdict in this case. Thank you.	16 The Defense ends with a clear statement about the result requested.

Riley v. Garfield House Apartments	
Plaintiff's Direct Examination of Mary Riley	**Comments/Notes**

Judge to Plaintiff's Counsel:

Counsel, are you ready to proceed with the presentation of your case?

Plaintiff's Counsel:

Yes I am, your Honor.

Judge:

Call your first witness.

Plaintiff's Counsel:

I call Mary Riley to testify.

Clerk:

Ms. Riley, will you please step forward and take your place in the witness box. Do you swear that your testimony will be the whole truth and nothing but the truth, so help you God?

Ms. Riley:

I do.

Clerk:

Please state your name, spelling your last name.

Ms. Riley:

Mary Louise Riley. R-i-l-e-y.

Riley v. Garfield House Apartments	
Plaintiff's Direct Examination of Mary Riley	**Comments/Notes**

Plaintiff's Counsel:

1 Q: Ms. Riley, where do you live?

A: I live in Waterville.

Q: How old are you?

A: I'm twenty-nine.

Q: Are you married?

A: Yes, I am.

Q: How long have you been married?

A: Seven years.

Q: Where did you live on December 24, 3 years ago?

A: The Garfield House Apartments.

Q: Where are the Garfield House Apartments located?

A: 721 Pine Street.

Q: How long did you live at the Garfield House Apartments?

A: Four years.

Q: When did you move out?

A: A few weeks after Rita was burned. It was the middle of January.

Q: Have you ever been back to those apartments?

A: No.

Q: What's your husband's name?

A: John Riley.

1 Simple questions about the witness' family life and personal history help the witness' own level of self-confidence. The similarity in Mary Riley's background with that of the jurors' background helps humanize the witness. See *Trial Advocacy* Section 7.8 (A).

Riley v. Garfield House Apartments

Plaintiff's Direct Examination of Mary Riley	Comments/Notes
Q: How old is he?	
A: He's twenty-nine also.	
Q: Besides working in the home, do you work outside the home?	
A: Yes, I do.	
Q: What do you do?	
2 A: I'm a substitute English teacher.	2 Note how the preliminary questions reinforce the credibility of the plaintiff's parents as a stable, educated young couple. Early highlighting of Mary Riley's college background and her responsibility to children in her capacity as a substitute English teacher helps the plaintiff meet the obvious weakness in the case against Garfield Apartments: it was irresponsible of Mary Riley to leave a one-year-old baby alone in a bathtub. See *Trial Advocacy* Section 7.6 (A).
Q: Where did you go to college?	
A: I went to the University of Minnesota.	
Q: What kind of work does your husband do?	
A: He's a computer programmer.	
Q: Did he go to college?	
A: Yes, he did.	
Q: Where did he go?	
A: He also went to the University of Minnesota.	
Q: Does he travel on his job?	
A: Yes, quite a bit.	
Q: On December 24, 3 years ago, was he home?	
A: No.	
A: He was stuck in a snowstorm in Denver.	
Q: When did you expect him?	
A: In the early morning on Christmas Day.	

Riley v. Garfield House Apartments

Plaintiff's Direct Examination of Mary Riley	Comments/Notes
3 Q: You and your husband have children? A: Yes, we do. Q: How many?	3 Delaying the introduction of the injured child to the end of the preliminary questions helps the jury focus on the parents' background.
4 A: One. A little girl. Rita. Q: How old was she on December 24? A: She was one year old.	4 This series of very simple incremental questions proceeds logically from the background facts established in the earlier preliminary questions. The progression of questions serves not only to introduce the young plaintiff but also to prepare a sympathetic reception of the plaintiff due to her tender age and the magnitude of her pain and suffering. The precise magnitude of her pain and suffering will be developed throughout the case as plaintiff's counsel establishes the element of damages. See *Trial Advocacy* Section 7.8 (B).
5 Q: Ms. Riley, on Christmas Eve at 7:30 in the evening, what happened to your little daughter? A: She was terribly burned with hot, scalding water. Q: Where did that occur?	5 The plaintiff's opening statement has established the theory of this case. Mary Riley now sets the scene.
6 A: In our bathtub in the Garfield House Apartments. Q: How was your baby scalded?	6 The location of the accident is set at the apartment building, owned by the defendant.

Riley v. Garfield House Apartments

Plaintiff's Direct Examination of Mary Riley	Comments/Notes
7 A: Well, I prepared her bath, and I put her in. And I had to leave the room for a short period of time to hang up some clothes.	7 The plaintiff's mother is asked to describe how the tragedy occurred. First, there is a broad chronological description, then counsel asks the plaintiff's mother to repeat the critical point of the event: the action of the water on the baby's body. See *Trial Advocacy* Section 7.8 (C).
8 Q: What happened then?	
A: I remember standing in the closet, hanging up the clothes and hearing Rita splashing around and laughing in the bathtub. And, then all of a sudden, I heard the water come on, and at the exact same time, Rita screamed.	8 Counsel must be careful not to ask questions calling for broad and unfocused responses allowing opposing counsel to break the flow of the direct examination with objections. The first question may be too broad, calling for a narrative; the next series of questions is more effective. The testimony is focused and the event is described as the lawyer wants it described. There is little possibility that the witness will add inadmissible testimony and there should be no objections. See *Trial Advocacy* Section 7.7 (C).
Q: How long did she scream?	
A: Just a few seconds.	
Q: What did you do?	
A: I dropped everything and ran back to the bathroom. And there was Rita under the faucet.	

Riley v. Garfield House Apartments

Plaintiff's Direct Examination of Mary Riley	Comments/Notes
9 Q: Ms. Riley, when you ran back into the bathroom, tell us exactly what you saw. A: Well, there was Rita on her hands and knees under the water faucet. And there was hot water streaming all over her body. Q: Could you see where the faucet lever was? A: Yes. Q: Where? A: Straight up on medium. Q: How did you know the water was hot? A: It was steaming. Q: By steaming, what do you mean? A: Like a kettle boiling, steam was coming off the water and off Rita. Q: And when you saw the steaming water, what did you do? A: Well, I pulled her away and turned on the cold water. I was going to put Rita underneath it. Q: Did it get cold? A: No, only medium warm. Q: And then?	9 Counsel controls a distressed witness and directs the testimony by asking short, simple questions. Counsel uses a previous answer as a part of the next question. This technique helps emphasize to the jury the mother's immediate response to her baby: she "dropped everything" and ran to the child's aid. Counsel's attention to the testimony of the witness also serves to channel the witness back to the appropriate narration of her own efforts to save the baby from further injury. See *Trial Advocacy* Section 7.8 (D).

Riley v. Garfield House Apartments

Plaintiff's Direct Examination of Mary Riley	Comments/Notes
10 A: Well, she struggled against me, and I noticed that every time she moved where I touched her, her skin came off in my hands. Q: What did you do? A: Well, I ran into the kitchen where I finally got cold water after it ran a long time, I threw a towel into the water, and I wrapped her up in it. Q: And then what? A: I took her into the bedroom, and put her down on the bed. Q: What did you do then? A: I called the ambulance. Q: And then what happened? A: They came, and I rode with Rita to the hospital.	10 The empathy of the jury is elicited by Mary Riley's ability to use simple language to describe essential facts: the water is so hot it is "steaming"; the skin of the "struggling" baby comes off in her mother's hands. Note how counsel emphasizes impact words by repeating them in follow-up questions. These questions, in turn, also elicit answers with impact such as the image of a boiling kettle. See *Trial Advocacy* Section 7.8 (F).
11 Q: Let's go back in time before the hot water scalded Rita. Tell us exactly how you prepared the bath for Rita. A: I always prepared Rita's bath the same way. I gave her lots of baths, usually every day. I turned the water lever to hot and waited until the water got hot.	11 The attorney uses an introductory statement to provide a transition between two events.

Riley v. Garfield House Apartments

Plaintiff's Direct Examination of Mary Riley	Comments/Notes
Q: Why did you do that?	
A: Sometimes it would take a long time to get hot, other times it was hot right away. It never ran the same way.	
Q: Then what did you do?	
A: When the water got hot, I put in the plug and ran some hot water. Then I turned the faucet to cold and mixed the hot and cold so I would have about an inch and one half of medium warm water in the tub.	
Q: Then what?	
A: I turned off the faucet by pulling the lever straight down.	12 To establish the correct foundation for this piece of illustrative evidence, counsel must show:
Plaintiff's Counsel to the Court:	• The faucet is relevant to the case.
12 Your Honor, may I approach the witness with an exhibit?	• The witness recognizes and can identify the exhibit.
Judge:	• The witness recalls what the faucet looked like at the relevant time, the time of the accident.
Yes, you may.	• The faucet is substantially similar to the faucet that was involved in the accident.
Plaintiff's Counsel:	
Q: I'm handing you what I have had marked for identification as Plaintiff's Exhibit One for identification. Please look this over carefully. Do you recognize it?	• The illustrative exhibit would assist the witness in testifying. See *Trial Advocacy* Section 8.6 (A).

Riley v. Garfield House Apartments	
Plaintiff's Direct Examination of Mary Riley	**Comments/Notes**
A: Yes, I do.	
Q: What is it?	
A: It's a faucet.	
Q: How do you recognize it?	
A: Well, it's the kind of faucet we had in the bathtub in the Garfield House Apartments.	
Q: Do you know if this is the same faucet?	
A: I have no idea.	
Q: Why?	
A: Because I've never been back to Garfield House Apartments and have not seen the faucet since we moved out.	
Q: Is Exhibit One a fair and accurate representation of how the handle of the faucet operated in your apartment? That is, does this one look exactly like the one in your apartment looked?	
A: Yes, it does.	
Q: Would Exhibit One help you explain to us what happened the night Rita was burned?	
A: Yes, it would.	
Plaintiff's Counsel to the Judge:	
Your Honor, we offer Plaintiff's Exhibit One. Counsel? (Shows exhibit to opposing counsel.)	

Riley v. Garfield House Apartments

Plaintiff's Direct Examination of Mary Riley	Comments/Notes
Defendant's Attorney: Objection, your Honor. This exhibit is not the faucet that was involved in the accident. It has no probative value. **Judge:** You may respond. **Plaintiff's Counsel:** We offer Plaintiff's Exhibit One as demonstrative evidence to show the handle positions of the faucet. **Judge:** Very well. Objection overruled. Exhibit One is received. **Plaintiff's Counsel:** 13 May the witness step down, your Honor, to show the exhibit to the jury and to demonstrate exactly what she did? **Judge:** Yes. **Plaintiff's Counsel:** Q: Ms. Riley, will you walk up close to the jury and use Plaintiff's Exhibit One to demonstrate exactly what you did with that faucet when you prepared Rita's bath on Christmas Eve three years ago?	13 The witness is directed to use the exhibit to demonstrate the event. The exhibit helps the witness communicate and gives the witness a chance to work closely with the attorney and the jury to explain complex facts. See *Trial Advocacy* Section 8.7 (A).

Riley v. Garfield House Apartments

Plaintiff's Direct Examination of Mary Riley	Comments/Notes
A: Well, I pushed this lever up to turn it on. And then I pushed the lever all the way left to hot on the faucet. Q: And now you are turning the faucet all the way to the left. A: Yes. Q: How do you know it's on hot? A: Well because there's a big "H" on this side. Q: Then what did you do? A: I put the plug in and let some hot water run. I then turned it all the way to the right to cold to the big "C". Q: And now you have pushed the lever all the way to the right, and then what? A: I mixed the cold with the hot until the tub was filled with about an inch and a half of warm water. Q: Then what, Ms. Riley? A: I tested the water with my hand and felt that it was warm and not hot. I moved the lever to the middle position and down to the off position until the water stopped flowing.	

Riley v. Garfield House Apartments

Plaintiff's Direct Examination of Mary Riley	Comments/Notes
Q: Thank you. Will you return to the witness stand? . . . Now, Ms. Riley, when you turned the water off, where was the lever?	
A: Straight down at off.	
Q: Had you ever known hot water to come out of it when the arrow was on medium?	
A: No, never.	
Q: How did you know the water was off?	
A: Because it wasn't dripping and it was on off.	
Q: Ms. Riley, returning to the accident, what part of your daughter's body was scalded?	
14 A: Rita's face was scalded, her shoulders, most of the sides of her body: her arms, her back, her legs.	14 Counsel takes the witness back to a significant point in her testimony: the description of the plaintiff's injuries. Rita, the infant plaintiff, cannot testify herself; so it is imperative that her attorney have the witness who can best speak for Rita—her mother. See *Trial Advocacy* Section 7.8 (B).
Q: Why did you leave your daughter alone in the bathroom?	

Riley v. Garfield House Apartments

Plaintiff's Direct Examination of Mary Riley	Comments/Notes
15 A: Well, I was comfortable with leaving her there because I'd done it before. I was only going to the other room for a minute to hang up clothes, and I could hear her back in the bathroom, so I didn't think there'd be any problem. I could always run back and help her if I heard anything.	15 The way this major weakness in the case is handled is critical. It is important the jury understand the normal nature of Rita's bath preparation and how Mary Riley regulated the temperature of the water. The credibility of Mary Riley must be enhanced. She shows a quick and responsible reaction to her baby's screams. See *Trial Advocacy* Section 7.7 (C).
Q: Where was she in the bathtub when you left her?	Because this is a weakness in the case, the explanation should be carefully structured. An alternative approach would be to ask Ms. Riley specific questions instead of a broad question:
A: She was in the middle of the tub.	**Example:**
Q: And how was she positioned?	Q: Why did you leave Rita alone in the bathtub?
A: She was sitting facing the front of the tub.	A: Well, I was comfortable with leaving her there . . .
Q: Had Rita ever touched the faucet before?	Q: Why were you comfortable?
A: No, never. She never seemed interested, and I had told her not to touch it.	A: Because I had left her alone before for a very short time when I was in the next room.
	Q: Were you worried?
	A: No.
	Q: Why not?

Riley v. Garfield House Apartments

Plaintiff's Direct Examination of Mary Riley	Comments/Notes

16   Q: Ms. Riley, have you had any other experiences with scalding hot water in that apartment?

A: Yes, I have.

Q: When?

17   A: Well, when we first moved into the apartment, we learned how hot the hot water was, and once I was in the kitchen doing dishes, and I had to turn off the faucet with a towel because it got so hot.

Q: Were both faucets on at the time, . . . the hot and the cold?

A: No, just the hot water tap was on.

Q: Have you had any other problems?

A: About a week before Rita was burned, I was in the shower, and I had turned the dial toward the hot setting to warm it up, and all of a sudden, scalding water came surging out and burned my leg.

Q: Have you had other problems with the hot water?

A: Well, when we had the hot water tap on, we had problems daily.

A: Because I could hear her and could run to her in a second or two.

Q: Did you ever leave her and go to another part of the apartment beyond the very next room?

A: Never.

Q: What room were you in on Christmas Eve?

A: In the next room.

Q: What were you doing in the next room?

A: Hanging some clothes in the closet.

Q: While you were hanging clothes, how far from Rita were you?

A: I was less than ten feet.

16   Since the negligence of the plaintiff's mother is exposed at about mid-point in Mary Riley's direct examination, the impact of this negligence is minimized. It also serves to enhance the credibility of the witness because plaintiff's counsel is presenting the weakness, not hiding it. See *Trial Advocacy* Section 7.8 (D).

17   Counsel explores an issue in the minds of the jurors: if Mary Riley experienced two burns herself because of the

Riley v. Garfield House Apartments

Plaintiff's Direct Examination of Mary Riley	Comments/Notes
Q: Please give us an example of those problems. A: Well, anytime someone flushed the toilet in another apartment, our hot water turned scalding. Q: Ms. Riley, have you ever reported those problems to the people at Garfield House Apartments? A: No. Q: Why not? A: Well, we knew from other tenants that they had reported it. Nothing had ever been done, so we didn't think it would help. **Defendant's Attorney:** Objection, your Honor. Hearsay. **Judge to Plaintiff's Counsel:** Counsel, you wish to be heard on this objection? **Plaintiff's Counsel:** Yes I do, your Honor. **Judge:** Would both attorneys please approach the bench.	excessively hot water, she should have alerted Garfield Apartments. Again, counsel candidly raises the issue, and the witness offers a reasonable explanation.

Riley v. Garfield House Apartments

Plaintiff's Direct Examination of Mary Riley	Comments/Notes
18 **At the Bench Out of the Hearing of the Jury:**	**18** Plaintiff's lawyer has to decide whether to argue the point and interrupt the flow of the direct or get on with the examination. See *Trial Advocacy* Section 7.6 (B).

18   **At the Bench Out of the Hearing of the Jury:**

Plaintiff's Counsel:

Your Honor, this is an exception to the rule against hearsay. I do not intend to prove the truth of what was told to Ms. Riley. However, what she was told goes to Mary Riley's state of mind, and her reason for not reporting. She understood reporting problems did no good.

Judge to Plaintiff's Counsel:

You have not proved sufficient foundation.   The   defense objection is sustained.

Defendant's Attorney:

Your Honor, we request a curative instruction.

Judge:

Members of the Jury, you are to disregard the last answer and not to consider any of it as evidence in this case. Continue, counsel.

Riley v. Garfield House Apartments

Plaintiff's Direct Examination of Mary Riley	Comments/Notes
Plaintiff's Counsel: 19 Q: On January 8, just before you moved out of the Garfield House Apartments, did you go to the basement area of the building? A: Yes, I did. **Defendant's Attorney:** Objection, irrelevant. **Judge:** Overruled. Q: Why? A: I wanted to look at the water heater.	19 Rather than try to rephrase the question so that it calls for a response explaining the witness' state-of-mind, counsel decides to move on because the answer has already been heard by the jury. The question was asked in good faith as there is a reasonable argument for the admission of the testimony. The jury has heard the testimony as the objection came after the answer. The opposing attorney could only have anticipated this hearsay response through discovery. A relevancy objection in response to the question "why didn't you report the problems" would have been appropriate and may have been sustained. Had there been a timely objection, plaintiff's attorney would have had to make an offer of proof at the bench and the hearsay answer may have been prevented. Once the response is in front of the jury, an instruction to disregard is an available remedy. See *Trial Advocacy* Section 4.6 (A).

Riley v. Garfield House Apartments

Plaintiff's Direct Examination of Mary Riley	Comments/Notes
Plaintiff's Counsel:	

20   Q: Why did you want to do that?

A: I had seen the chicken wire around it when I had been in the basement before, and I wanted to see if someone could tamper with the heater.

Q: What did you do?

A: I took a broom that was by the door to the water heater room, and I tore a little hole in the wire and pushed the broom handle through to see if I could reach the heater.

Q: Could you?

A: Yes, it was easy.

Q: Why did you do that with the broom?

A: I thought maybe somebody had fooled around with the heater or something like that.

Q: Did you touch the heater with the broom handle or change any setting on it?

A: No.

Q: Did you tell anybody what you had done?

A: No.

Q: Why?

---

20   There are three major factual weaknesses in the plaintiff's case: Mary Riley left her daughter alone in the bathtub, she never reported problems with hot water, and she tampered with the wire enclosure after the accident. While the last incident does not directly relate to the accident, it still may seem to be a foolish thing to do and relates to Mary Riley's judgment and common sense. If plaintiff's counsel does not bring this event out on direct examination and offer an explanation, the witness may appear to be vulnerable on cross. Weaknesses in a case cannot be avoided by pretending they do not exist. The direct examiner has chosen to deal with all the problems on direct examination rather than try to rehabilitate the witness on re-direct examination. See *Trial Advocacy* Section 7.9 (A).

Trial Transcript 73

Riley v. Garfield House Apartments

Plaintiff's Direct Examination of Mary Riley	Comments/Notes
A: I don't know, I just didn't, and we moved shortly afterward.	
21 Q: Ms. Riley, was Rita in the hospital when you moved? A: Yes. Q: How long was your daughter in the hospital? A: Six days followed by periodic visits and stays. Q: When your daughter came out of the hospital, was she different? A: Yes. Q: How was she different?	21 This preliminary question is a transition to a new area of questions. It is not an improper leading question because the witness has testified that the child was taken to the hospital. See *Trial Advocacy* Section 7.7 (B).
22 A: Well, she changed physically and emotionally. Q: How is she changed physically? A: She is scarred. She has lost movement in her right hand. She can't stand to be held because of the painful grafts. Q: How is she changed emotionally? A: She can never sleep through the night. She's very clingy. I can never leave her alone. She's afraid of water. She struggles against taking baths.	22 By framing a question around an earlier response of the witness about the physical disfigurement of the plaintiff child, counsel reinforces damages.

Trial Transcript 74

Riley v. Garfield House Apartments

Plaintiff's Direct Examination of Mary Riley	Comments/Notes
23 Q: Ms. Riley, I'm showing you what has been marked for identification as Plaintiff's Exhibit Two. Do you recognize it?	23 To establish the foundation for this photograph exhibit, counsel must show:

A: Yes, I do.

Q: What is it?

A: It's a picture of Rita.

Q: When was that picture taken?

A: Two weeks before the accident.

Q: Who took it?

A: Her dad.

Q: Does that picture fairly and accurately represent or show what your daughter looked like before she was burned on Christmas Eve?

A: Yes, it does.

Plaintiff's Counsel to the Judge:

Your Honor, we offer Plaintiff's Exhibit Two. Counsel, would you like to examine Plaintiff's Exhibit Two? (Showing photograph to opposing counsel.)

Defendant's Attorney:

No, thank you. No objections.

Comments/Notes column:

- The exhibit is relevant to the case.
- The witness is familiar with the image depicted on the photograph at the relevant time of the event.
- The photograph fairly and accurately represents something that is relevant to the case. See *Trial Advocacy* Section 8.6 (J).

Riley v. Garfield House Apartments

Plaintiff's Direct Examination of Mary Riley	**Comments/Notes**

Judge:

Exhibit Two is received.

Plaintiff's Counsel:

Q: Ms. Riley, I'm handing you what's been marked for identification as Plaintiffs Exhibit Three. What is it?

A: It's a photograph of Rita that I took just two weeks ago.

Q: Does this photo accurately represent what Rita looks like now?

A: Yes, it does.

Plaintiff's Counsel to the Judge:

24Your Honor, we offer Plaintiffs Exhibit Three. Counsel? (Showing photograph to opposing counsel.)

Defendant's Attorney:

No objections.

Judge:

Exhibit Three is received.

Plaintiff's Counsel:

Q: Ms. Riley, have you had any bills, medical bills, for the injuries to your daughter?

A: Yes, we have.

Q: Have you had many of them?

24Counsel must make a decision at this point: whether the jury should see a photograph of the scarred child now or later. In deciding, counsel must consider whether the photograph will evoke a negative response or sympathy, whether it will distract the jury too much and whether a later introduction would be too late for effect. In this case, defense counsel probably would prefer that Rita Riley's disfigurement be handled through photographic exhibit than by her actually appearing in court. Rita Riley will appear in court, at a later time in the trial. See *Trial Advocacy* Section 7.4 (F).

Riley v. Garfield House Apartments	
Plaintiff's Direct Examination of Mary Riley	**Comments/Notes**
A: Yes, we've had a lot of bills.	
Q: Did you keep them?	
A: Yes, we did.	
Q: Did you make a record of those bills?	
A: Yes, I did.	
Q: When did you do that?	
A: I made it a couple of weeks ago when you asked me to make a list.	
Q: Is that list accurate and complete?	
A: Yes, it is.	
Q: Would this list assist you in describing the bills to us?	
A: Yes, it would.	
Q: Ms. Riley, I'm showing you what's been marked for identification as Plaintiff's Exhibit Four. Do you recognize it?	
A: Yes, I do.	
Q: What is it?	
A: It's the list of bills that I made.	
Q: Is that list the same as when you made it?	
A: Yes, it is.	
Q: Have there been any changes to that list?	
A: No.	

Trial Transcript 77

Riley v. Garfield House Apartments

Plaintiff's Direct Examination of Mary Riley	Comments/Notes
Plaintiff's Counsel to the Judge: Your Honor, opposing counsel and I have agreed the list of bills prepared by Ms. Riley is an accurate list of the bills paid by the Rileys for Rita's medical treatment. We offer Plaintiff's Exhibit Four. **Defendant's Attorney:** That is correct your Honor. I have no objection. **Judge:** Exhibit Four is received. **Plaintiff's Counsel:** Q: Ms. Riley, would you tell us what the total expenses were for your daughter's medical treatment? 25 A: One Hundred, Fifty-seven thousand, eight hundred and seventy-five dollars. ($157,875.00) Q: Do you know exactly what the future medical costs for her injuries will be? A: Only what the doctor told us.	25 Exhibits are frequently admitted in evidence through stipulation. Opposing counsel does not contest the accuracy of the bills, and the summary exhibit is an efficient way of providing information to the jury. See *Trial Advocacy* Section 8.6 (K).

Riley v. Garfield House Apartments

Plaintiff's Direct Examination of Mary Riley	Comments/Notes
26Q: How has all this affected your lives? A: Well, we can't take Rita out in the sun. Q: Why? A: Because everywhere she was burned is terribly sensitive to the sun. Q: What else? A: We have to work with Rita to teach her not to go outside in the sun or use anything but lukewarm water to bathe in because her burns will always be sensitive. Q: Please continue. A: We have to work with Rita so she can deal with the future skin operations and her pain and discomfort. Q: Are you having to make financial plans because of this accident? A: Yes. Q: What?	26 Mary Riley has been a responsible witness in her narrative responses throughout direct examination. She has not added improper testimony. Appropriately, counsel allows her to describe the family members' individual reaction to the baby's injuries. These questions are especially effective at the close of her examination. See *Trial Advocacy* Section 7.6 (B).
27 A We are planning to save to help pay for the huge medical and counseling bills we expect to have for Rita. Q: Ms. Riley, how else have these injuries to your little daughter affected you?	27 This series of questions demonstrates how potential costs and future damages may be presented through a lay witness. Medical experts, financial planners and life expectancy tables are used to provide specific testimony to establish this evidence.

Trial Transcript 79

Riley v. Garfield House Apartments

Plaintiff's Direct Examination of Mary Riley	Comments/Notes
A: I used to love to hold and cuddle my baby. Then after she was burned, I was afraid to touch her. Q: Have these injuries to your daughter affected your husband in any other way? 28 A: My husband is so depressed about Rita he can't even talk about it. Q: And how have the injuries affected your little daughter? A: Rita's not the same little girl she used to be. She doesn't laugh and play like she used to. She doesn't react to other people like she used to. She doesn't hold and hug me the way she used to. **Plaintiff's Counsel to the Judge:** No further questions, your Honor.	28 Lay witnesses can testify about health. It is not improper for Mary Riley to describe her husband's state of depression. This is a common disability that lay people confront in their daily interactions with others. See *Trial Advocacy* Section 4.8 (C).

Riley v. Garfield House Apartments	
Defendant's Cross-Examination of Mary Riley	**Comments/Notes**

Judge to Defendant's Attorney:

You may cross-examine.

Defendant's Attorney:

Thank you, your Honor.

1 Q: At the time your daughter was injured on Christmas Eve, she was one year old, correct, Ms. Riley?

A: That's right.

Q: And she could sit up?

A: Yes.

Q: And she could walk and crawl?

A: Yes.

Q: She could scoot around pretty well, couldn't she?

A: Yes, she could.

1 Counsel must make a tactical decision about this witness. A compassionate discrediting cross-examination will reduce Ms. Riley's credibility and emphasize her failure to act as a responsible mother. An aggressive attack on the plaintiff's mother may cause resentment on the part of the jury toward the corporate defendant and sympathy toward the plaintiff's family. A supportive cross-examination can re-emphasize the points established in the direct examination that indicate Mary Riley knew the dangerous condition and knew her baby was vulnerable. Mary Riley's direct examination testimony focused on the excessively hot water, and the lack of corrective measures by Garfield House Apartments. The cross-examination must be structured to prevent the possibility of Mary Riley repeating damaging evidence. See *Trial Advocacy* Section 9.1.

Riley v. Garfield House Apartments

Defendant's Cross-Examination of Mary Riley	Comments/Notes
2 Q: And she could pull herself up, isn't that right? A: Yes. Q: And when you held her, she could grab onto your hand? A: Yeah. Q: She could hold your hand pretty hard, couldn't she? A: Yes, she could. Q: And she could play with her blocks? A: Yeah. Q: She could pick them up? A: Yes. Q: She could pick up her other toys? A: Yes. Q: She could move her toys around? A: Yes. Q: She could throw them? A: Oh, Yeah. Q: Now, Ms. Riley, at the time your daughter was injured on Christmas Eve, you were into the holiday season, isn't that right?	2 Counsel's questioning builds upon Rita's motor development first brought out on direct. Rita's ability to crawl, scoot around, grab objects, haul herself up—all these abilities in a one-year-old baby serve to reemphasize the contributory negligence of her mother, Mary Riley, who left her baby alone in water, in a slippery tub, near a hot water faucet that had earlier burned the mother herself. Counsel's cross-examination should build upon the doubt in the minds of the jurors: Why did Mary Riley leave a one-year-old baby alone in a bathroom, especially when she knew of a special hazard? Counsel addresses this doubt and begins the examination with a series of short questions that lead the jury to infer Mary Riley's contributory negligence. See *Trial Advocacy* Section 9.1 (A).

Riley v. Garfield House Apartments

Defendant's Cross-Examination of Mary Riley	Comments/Notes
3 A: Yes, it was Christmas. Q: This was your daughter's first Christmas? A: Yes. Q: And it was a busy time for you, wasn't it? A: Yes. Q: You were expecting your husband home the next morning? A: Yes.	3 The short simple questions control the witness. When an area of examination is complete, the attorney has a transition question to direct the attention to a new area. The transition question is followed by another series of short questions. See *Trial Advocacy* Section 9.3 (A).
4 Q: You were looking forward to spending the time, the holidays, with your parents? A: Yes. Q: Taking care of last minute gift wrapping? A: Yes. Q: Last minute food preparation? A: That's right. Q: You cleaned up the house. A: Yes, it was already clean. Q: You finished the laundry? A: Yes. Q: You were doing many of the things that were necessary to get prepared for the holidays, weren't you? A: Yes.	4 Counsel connects the general suggestion of negligence on the part of Rita's mother with the specific conditions on Christmas Eve: Mary Riley was too distracted to exercise proper care in the supervision of her baby.

Riley v. Garfield House Apartments

Defendant's Cross-Examination of Mary Riley	**Comments/Notes**

Q: Ms. Riley, when you left your daughter in the bathroom, you were comfortable leaving her there?

A: Yes, I was.

Q: You weren't concerned she might roll over in that water and possibly drown, were you?

A: I don't think . . . No, I wasn't.

Q: And you weren't concerned she might slip from the side of that tub into the water, were you?

A: Well, I could have heard her if that happened, and I could have helped her.

5 Q: Ms. Riley, when your daughter was injured, you assumed she reached up and turned on that water, isn't that correct?

A: That's right.

Q: And you'd never known her to do that before, had you?'

A: No.

Q: But you did know she was capable of pulling herself up, right?

A: Yes.

Q: When you were in that closet, and you heard the water come on and your baby scream, it shocked you, didn't it?

5 Counsel has had Mary Riley agree that the child was mobile, active, and that Mary was busy. Counsel seeks to demonstrate Mary should not have been comfortable leaving a one-year-old baby in a bathtub and should not have assumed the child would be all right. The answers are consistent with the defense theory the assumptions are not valid and Mary's "comfort" is not consistent with common sense. See *Trial Advocacy* Section 9.3 (B).

Riley v. Garfield House Apartments

Defendant's Cross-Examination of Mary Riley	Comments/Notes
A: Yes, it did.	
Q: You were very concerned about her, weren't you?	
A: Yes, I was.	
Q: And you ran back to the bathroom?	
A: Yes.	
Q: And as you came in through the door of that bathroom, you saw what you testified was hot water coming out on her body, right?	
A: Steaming hot water.	
Q: That's right, and you were upset?	
A: Yes.	
Q: You were frightened?	
A: Yes.	
Q: You were terrified of what was happening to her?	
6 A: Yes, I was.	6 While Mary Riley's "shock" is a normal reaction, that state of mind is inconsistent with her exact perception, her opportunity to observe, her memory, and her ability to reconstruct and testify about the precise events.
Q: And you ran over, and you pulled her out of the tub?	
A: Yes, I did.	
Q: As fast as you could?	
A: Yes.	
Q: And you turned off the hot water?	
A: Yes, I did. It was steaming hot.	

Trial Transcript 85

Riley v. Garfield House Apartments	
Defendant's Cross-Examination of Mary Riley	**Comments/Notes**
Q: Ms. Riley, you had problems with hot water in your apartment before the accident, didn't you?	
A: Yes, we did.	
Q: In fact, you had to use a towel to touch the faucet at times?	
A: Yes.	
Q: You were burned at the kitchen sink?	
A: Yes.	
Q: And you were burned in the bathroom shower?	
A: That's right.	
7 Q: And it really didn't matter what time of day it was, did it?	7 These questions and answers repeat some of the direct examination testimony and support a key defense theory. See *Trial Advocacy* Section 9.2 (F).
A: No.	
Q: And you assumed that Garfield House Apartments would not do anything about the hot water if you reported it to them, didn't you?	
A: Yes, I did.	
8 Q: And you assumed that your baby would not be injured in that tub when you left her alone, didn't you?	8 The attorney has worked the word "assume" into the cross-examination on a number of occasions. This theme word may be used as the basis of the final argument: that the mother's actions and the plaintiff's case are built on assumptions not facts.
A: Yes, I did.	
Q: You never reported your problems with hot water to Garfield House Apartments, did you?	

Trial Transcript 86

Riley v. Garfield House Apartments

Defendant's Cross-Examination of Mary Riley	Comments/Notes
A: No. Because nothing would be done.	
Q: You assumed nothing would be done?	
A: Yes.	
Q: You never reported it to Connie Austern?	
A: No.	
Q: You never reported it to the owners of the complex?	
A: No.	
9 Q: You didn't report it to anyone working for Connie Austern, did you?	9 Counsel builds a series of negatives: Mary Riley failed to take action based on her assumption Garfield House would not correct the problem. The inference counsel instills in the jury is Mary Riley's assumptions are wrong and the failure is hers, not the defendant's. The cross-examination ends on a strong line of questioning to reinforce the jury's perception of Mary Riley's failure to take responsibility: why did Mary Riley fail to report a hazard that had already harmed her and that endangered other tenants, her guests, and her baby? See *Trial Advocacy* Section 9.3 (E).
A: No.	
Q: You didn't report it to anyone, did you?	
A: Just my husband.	
Q: After the accident and before you moved you went in the basement?	
A: Yes.	
Q: You poked a hole in the wire and poked at the water thermostat with a broomstick, didn't you?	
A: Yes, I did.	
Q: You didn't get the thermostat to move, did you?	

Riley v. Garfield House Apartments

Defendant's Cross-Examination of Mary Riley	Comments/Notes
10 A: No, I couldn't.	10 Even if there had been some vandalism, Mary Riley could not get that thermostat to move. This series of questions is consistent with the theme that Mary Riley uses bad judgment and was negligent when she failed to report possible problems.
Q: You didn't report that to anybody either, did you?	
A: No, I didn't.	
Defendant's Attorney:	11 Defense counsel decided not to cross-examine Ms. Riley with regard to damages. Neutral witnesses such as doctors and psychiatrists can be examined concerning the speculative nature of healing, pain, and the necessity of future medical treatment. The risk of alienating the jury by questioning the mother about delicate issues is too great, particularly when other witnesses will be available. Even without other witnesses, the speculative nature of the damages may be effectively raised in final argument without having to cross-examine the mother. See *Trial Advocacy* Section 9.2 (C).
11 I have no further questions.	

Riley v. Garfield House Apartments

Defendant's Cross-Examination of Mary Riley	Comments/Notes
Plaintiff's Counsel:	
12 I have no redirect questions, Your Honor. Thank you, Ms. Riley.	12 Plaintiff's counsel decides no redirect is necessary. See *Trial Advocacy* Section 7.9 (B).

Riley v. Garfield House Apartments

Plaintiff's Direct Examination of Dr. Armstead	Comments/Notes

Judge:

Counsel, call your next witness.

Plaintiff's Counsel:

I call Dr. Pat Armstead.

(Witness is sworn in by the Clerk)

Q: Doctor, where did you receive your doctoral degree?

1 A: I received my Ph.D. in engineering at UCLA 9 years ago.

Q: Did you specialize in a specific area of engineering?

A: Within the engineering field, I specialized in safety engineering and engineering statistics.

2 Q: Doctor, please tell us what other degrees you have and where you obtained them?

A: I received my master's degree from Massachusetts Institute of Technology. My major field of study was safety engineering. I received my bachelor of science degree in mechanical engineering from Texas Tech 20 years ago.

1 Dr. Armstead is testifying as an expert safety analyst. Counsel must provide the proper foundation showing the witness has appropriate engineering education, experience, professional accomplishments, publications, teaching, and other credentials. See *Trial Advocacy* Section 10.1 (B).

2 Open-ended questions are frequently used to establish expert qualifications as an efficient way to provide a great deal of information. Counsel must control the witness and not let the narrative go on too long or become unfocused or boring. See *Trial Advocacy* Section 10.4 (B).

Riley v. Garfield House Apartments

Plaintiff's Direct Examination of Dr. Armstead	Comments/Notes
Q: Are you professionally registered in any fields?	
A: I'm professionally registered in the state of California in mechanical engineering and safety engineering.	
Q: How did you become professionally registered?	
A: By successfully passing a series of licensing examinations and tests in mechanical and safety engineering.	
Q: Where do you currently work, Doctor?	
A: For the past 4 years, I have been the Associate Director of the Association for Safety Analysis.	
Q: Where did you work before taking the position at the Association for Safety Analysis?	
3 A: For 3 years before that, I was a consultant in private practice with Pat Armstead Associates. We consulted with attorneys on matters of mechanical engineering and safety engineering. I was in the United States Air Force Corps of Engineers for 2 years. And before that I was employed as a	3 If the expert's answers appear too rehearsed, the credibility of the expert may be reduced. The expert here goes beyond the scope of the question and adds the duration and type of employment to the expected answer, the name of the employer. While the answers provide admissible information, the witness has demonstrated a

Riley v. Garfield House Apartments	
Plaintiff's Direct Examination of Dr. Armstead	**Comments/Notes**
plant mechanic and safety engineer at the American Can Company.	willingness to take control of the testimony away from the attorney. See *Trial Advocacy* Section 10.5 (A).
Q: Do you have any teaching experience?	
A: Yes. Currently I have a position as a research professor at the University of California, Los Angeles. I teach courses at the graduate and undergraduate levels in safety engineering, thermodynamics, and engineering statistics. I also do research at UCLA in risk analysis and human factors in	
4 safety design of multi-unit dwellings, including apartment buildings.	4 The expert, perhaps appearing too well coached, again responds to the question by reciting the remainder of the expert's resume. These questions are important for both legal and persuasive foundation. The information from the witness must be provided in an interesting way, and the witness must be prepared to testify with enthusiasm and sincerity.
Q: Doctor, in your position as Associate Director of the Association of Safety Analysis, what do you do?	Background information helps humanize the witness as well as set forth expert qualifications. Teaching experience reinforces expertise in the witness' field and also makes the expert appear less clinical and more human. See *Trial Advocacy* Section 10.4 (C).

Riley v. Garfield House Apartments

Plaintiff's Direct Examination of Dr. Armstead	Comments/Notes
5 A: Well, I provide a consulting service for attorneys, providing risk analysis, rendering opinions on industrial accidents and their causes, and rendering opinions on consumer product failures. I also consult with industrial commercial clients to make sure that their products comply with federal, state, and local regulations. Q: Doctor, do you belong to any professional associations? A: Yes. I am currently a member of the National Academy of Sciences. Q: Do you do any writing?	5 The attorney must determine if the examination should be controlled and the testimony presented in a structure determined by the lawyer and not the witness. Control could have been established by breaking the questions into shorter segments. See *Trial Advocacy* Section 10.5 (B). **Example:** Q: Doctor, in addition to your research at UCLA on risk analysis and safety design, have you made any other contributions to your field? A: Yes, I serve as Associate Director of the Association of Safety Analysis and contribute to the ASA blog. Q: What do you do as Associate Director of the Association of Safety Analysis? A: I provide consulting services for attorneys, prepare risk analysis, provide opinions on the causes of industrial accidents, and render opinions on consumer product failures.

Riley v. Garfield House Apartments

Plaintiff's Direct Examination of Dr. Armstead	Comments/Notes
6 A: Yes. I've written scores of articles in the field of safety engineering published in various scholastic and scientific journals.	6 "Scores of articles" is not plausible, particularly if not all are published in respected scholastic journals. Counsel should ask the witness clarifying questions that establish that these articles include safety tip columns for newspapers and magazines. Otherwise, opposing counsel may embarrass the expert by challenging the content of articles this witness has passed off as scholarly. See *Trial Advocacy* Section 10.5 (C).
Q: Doctor, do you have any experience with scald victims, people who are burned by hot water?	
A: Yes, in my position with the Association for Safety Analysis, I've consulted on numerous cases where individuals have been burned by hot water.	
Q: Doctor, I'm going to ask you a yes-or-no question. Based on your training, your years of experience of working with scald victims, and your education in the field of safety engineering, are you able to determine the temperature of water that causes burns? Yes or no, please.	7 Counsel establishes the sources of the safety analyst's opinions as foundation for the opinion to follow. The "Yes" or "No" instruction indicates to the witness that this is a preliminary foundation question. It informs the witness not to blurt out an answer until the foundation has been established. The court is also informed that the direct examiner understands the rules.
7 A: Yes, I am.	

Trial Transcript 94

Riley v. Garfield House Apartments

Plaintiff's Direct Examination of Dr. Armstead	Comments/Notes
8 Q: How are you able to do that?	8 This unusual foundation is necessary because a nonmedical witness claims to be able to determine the temperature of hot water that causes injury.
9 A: Well, there is a direct correlation between the degree of burns and the temperature of the water. First degree burns are usually caused by water between 130 and 150 degrees Fahrenheit. Second degree burns are caused by water with a temperature range of 150 to 180 degrees. Third degree burns are caused by water with a temperature over 180 degrees Fahrenheit. Based on that direct correlation and either by examining the scald victim or pictures of the victim along with a review of the medical records, the temperature of the water that caused the burns can be determined quite accurately.	9 Note the length of the expert's narrative compared to the brief question. Experts are permitted to give narrative responses in regard to substantive as well as to qualification testimony as a way to speed up an examination. Here, the expert gives the three ranges of water temperatures correlated to first, second, and third degree burns. Control of the witness and the structure of the testimony is even more important when critical evidence is addressed by the witness. See *Trial Advocacy* Section 10.5 (E).
Q: Doctor, do you have an opinion in this case regarding the temperature of the water that scalded Rita Riley?	
A: Yes, I do.	
Q: What information did you rely upon to come to that opinion?	

Riley v. Garfield House Apartments

Plaintiff's Direct Examination of Dr. Armstead	Comments/Notes
A: Well, I examined the medical reports of Rita Riley, which stated that she has third degree burns over 36 percent of her body. I also have examined pictures of the little girl after the accident.	
10 Q: Are these types of things—the medical reports and pictures of scald victims—an expert in the field of safety engineering would normally use in rendering an opinion?	10 Counsel emphasizes the particular sources on which Dr. Armstead bases the opinion on Rita Riley's burns. Counsel reemphasizes that these sources—medical records and photographs—are established means experts use to determine temperature. See *Trial Advocacy* Section 10.5 (C).
A: Yes, they are.	
Q: Doctor, what is your opinion as to the temperature of the water that burned Rita Riley?	
A: Based on the medical reports and the pictures that I examined of Rita Riley, I would state that the water that caused her burns was approximately 205 degrees Fahrenheit.	
11 Q: Doctor, we have been informed by the defendant that the water heater in the basement of the Garfield House Apartments at the time of this accident was a Rood water heater—a Rood water heater model	11 The lengthy factual inventory risks an objection from opposing counsel that plaintiff's counsel is testifying. Plaintiff's counsel should introduce the defendant's admission about the AST75–300 model. See Fed.R.Evid. 801(d)(2). See *Trial Advocacy* Section 4.8 (F).

Riley v. Garfield House Apartments

Plaintiff's Direct Examination of Dr. Armstead	Comments/Notes
number AST75–300. Are you familiar with Rood water heaters?	

A: Yes, I am.

Q: Are you familiar with this particular model of water heater?

A: Yes.

Q: How are you familiar with this particular Rood water heater?

A: While I was doing my undergraduate work at Texas Tech I was employed by Rood Manufacturing in their safety design department. The Rood model number AST75–300 was one of the first water heaters I actually worked on. I helped design that unit and was involved in discussions concerning the safety of that particular water heater.

Q: Doctor, based on your teaching, your years of education, and your experience with water heaters in general, do you have an opinion as to the proper way to secure a water heater in an apartment? Yes or no, please.

A: Yes.

Riley v. Garfield House Apartments

Plaintiff's Direct Examination of Dr. Armstead

Comments/Notes

12   Q: Does that opinion include the water heater in the basement of the Garfield House Apartments?

A: Yes, it does.

Q: What is that opinion, Doctor?

A: A water heater should be secured so vandals or any unauthorized people do not have access to the water heater, so they cannot tamper with the controls of the water heater or cause damage to the heater itself.

Q: Why is that?

A: Well, if vandals are allowed access to the water heater, they can adjust various control dials, including the thermostat which controls the temperature for the water throughout the entire building. If a vandal were to turn the thermostat up, it would be possible that people within the apartment could be scalded.

Q: Doctor, once again, based on your training, your years of experience, and your education in the field of safety engineering and mechanical

12   Counsel continues to establish one of the plaintiff's case theories: Defendant improperly inspected and maintained the water heater. See *Trial Advocacy* Section 10.5.

Riley v. Garfield House Apartments

Plaintiff's Direct Examination of Dr. Armstead	Comments/Notes

engineering, do you have an opinion concerning the proper maintenance of a water heater in the basement of an apartment building?

A: Yes, I do.

Q: And does that opinion also include the water heater in the basement of the Garfield Apartments?

A: Yes, it does.

Q: What is that opinion, Doctor?

A: The water heater must be properly maintained to ensure that it's functioning properly. It must be inspected regularly, and tests must be done to make sure the water being produced by that water heater is not excessively hot. If the water heater is not properly maintained, it's very possible the water heater will malfunction and excessively hot water will be produced and cause burns to the tenants in the apartment.

Riley v. Garfield House Apartments

Plaintiff's Direct Examination of Dr. Armstead	Comments/Notes
13 Q: Now, Doctor, I want to direct your attention specifically to the water heater in the basement of the Garfield Apartment where the Rileys lived. Do you have an opinion whether that water heater was properly secured? A: Yes, I do. Q: What information did you use to come to that opinion? A: Well, I've read the deposition transcripts of Dr. Martin Thomas, of Connie Austern, and of John Riley and Mary Riley. I've also examined photographs of the water heater, and recommendations made by Rood Manufacturing in the owner's manual for this model. Q: Doctor, are these types of things the kind of information that an expert in your field of safety engineering and mechanical engineering would normally use when rendering opinions? A: Yes, they are.	13 The opinion of the expert continues to be focused on the particular water heater, photographs of it, and deposition testimony about it. See *Trial Advocacy* Section 10.5 (A).

Riley v. Garfield House Apartments

Plaintiff's Direct Examination of Dr. Armstead	Comments/Notes
14 Q: Doctor, what is your opinion concerning the security of the water heater in the basement of the Garfield Apartment where the Rileys resided? A: The security of that particular water heater was inadequate because the chicken wire fence around that water heater did not keep vandals or other unauthorized persons away from the water heater or the controls of the water heater. The two-by-fours and chicken wire that were used to make that fence were not sturdy, so the fence could be easily knocked down. Also, even if the fence was not knocked down, the holes within the screen were so large that the thermostat and other controls on the water heater could be adjusted by the use of a long thin stick through the holes. Q: Do you also have an opinion whether that water heater in the basement of the Garfield Apartment was properly maintained at the time of this accident?	14 By dividing the overall opinion into two parts—security and maintenance—the standards on which safety analysts base their findings are re-emphasized. This bolsters Dr. Armstead's credibility and assists the jury's participation in those findings. The breakdown of "security" allows the witness to elaborate on the skimpy enclosure, chicken wire mesh, and two-by-fours. See *Trial Advocacy* Section 10.5 (B).

Trial Transcript 101

Riley v. Garfield House Apartments

Plaintiff's Direct Examination of Dr. Armstead	Comments/Notes
A: Yes, I do.	
Q: What information did you rely on to come to that opinion?	
A: Well, the same information I used to come to the opinion concerning the security of the water heater.	
Q: And are those the types of things an expert in your field would use when consulting and rendering opinions?	
A: Yes, they are.	
Q: Doctor, what is your opinion concerning the maintenance of the water heater in the basement of the Garfield House Apartment where the Rileys lived?	
15 A: Well, the water heater in the basement of the Garfield Apartments was improperly maintained for numerous reasons.	15 Similarly, the breakdown of "maintenance" allows the witness to run through the litany of the defendant's failures already established by prior testimony.
Q: Why?	
A: First off, the person that was put in charge of that water heater, Ms. Austern, had no training or experience in water heater maintenance inspection. She did not know how to adjust the thermostat, how to activate	

Riley v. Garfield House Apartments

Plaintiff's Direct Examination of Dr. Armstead	Comments/Notes
the pressure relief valve, or how to test the thermostat to make sure that it was accurate. In fact, she had not even read the owner's manual so that she could refer to it in case other problems would arise. Because of her	
16 lack of knowledge it is obvious the water heater was not properly maintained. Q: Go on, please? A: It was also improperly maintained because the people with whom the apartment complex had a service contract were never called over to inspect it. The service contract is a great idea, but unless the people with whom you have the service contract regularly inspect the water heater at least once a year, whether there are problems or not, the service contract does you absolutely no good. For the service contract to have any effect on	16 The litany includes all Connie Austern's deficiencies beginning with her lack of knowledge and builds to a conclusion the jury cannot escape: the heater was not properly cared for. See *Trial Advocacy* Section 10.5 (F).
17 the proper maintenance of this water heater at all, those people had to come out and look at that water heater and they did not.	17 The expert debunks the service contract as a viable defense. The contract contained no terms requiring periodic inspection.

Trial Transcript 103

Riley v. Garfield House Apartments	
Plaintiff's Direct Examination of Dr. Armstead	**Comments/Notes**
Plaintiff's Counsel to the Judge:	
18 Thank you, Doctor. No further questions.	18 Counsel need not ask another question. The expert's last words, "they did not," restates the negative inference counsel wants the jury to apply to the case: the defendant failed to comply with the duty to tenants and the defendant's negligence directly caused Rita Riley's injuries. See *Trial Advocacy* Section 10.2.

Riley v. Garfield House Apartments

Defendant's Cross-Examination of Dr. Armstead	Comments/Notes
Judge to Defendant's Attorney: Counsel, you may cross-examine. **Defendant's Attorney:** 1 Q: Doctor, your Ph.D. is in the field of mechanical engineering, isn't that correct? A: Yes, that's right. Q: And in the field of mechanical engineering you work with machines, don't you? A: Yes, I do. Q: You are not a medical doctor, are you? A: No. Q: You're not a burn specialist? A: No. 2 Q: And you're not a pediatrician— a doctor that treats children—are you? A: No, I'm not. Q: Now Doctor, you are familiar with the Rood model AST75–300 water heater? A: Yes. Q: That model is the one at issue in this case? A: Yes.	1 On direct, Dr. Armstead has asserted that the water which burned Rita Riley was about 205 degrees F. and that she had particular knowledge of the safety design of the Rood water heater AST75–300 period. She also testified that the defendant failed to adequately secure the water heater because the chicken wire was easily penetrated by a long stick that could reach the controls. She further testified the defendant failed to properly inspect the water heater because without an owner's manual, Connie Austern could not make necessary adjustments to the thermostat. Defense counsel will cross-examine Dr. Armstead on these issues and her credibility. See *Trial Advocacy* Section 10.6 2 Counsel establishes that mechanical training, not medical training, is the basis of Dr. Armstead's expertise. Once Dr. Armstead admits she is not a medical doctor, the questions about her not being a burn specialist and not being a pediatrician make sense, and while to the same point they are not repetitious. However, any more than this limited number of questions may become improper and boring.

Riley v. Garfield House Apartments

Defendant's Cross-Examination of Dr. Armstead	Comments/Notes
Q: That was the first water heater you ever worked on?	
A: That's true.	
Q: And when you were working on it, you were a junior in college at Texas Tech?	
A: That's also true.	
Q: You were taking general education courses during those first two years of college, weren't you?	
A: Yes.	
Q: Those were required courses?	
A: Yes, they were.	
Q: They were the same courses that everyone takes during their first two years of college?	
A: Basically.	
Q: And these courses are required before anyone gets into their major field of study?	
A: That's correct.	
Q: You took English?	
A: Yes.	
Q: Some history?	
A: Yes.	
Q: Philosophy?	
A: Yes.	

Riley v. Garfield House Apartments	
Defendant's Cross-Examination of Dr. Armstead	**Comments/Notes**
Q: During this time you didn't take any engineering courses?	
A: That's right.	
Q: The two science courses you took were psychology and biology, isn't that true?	
A: That's true.	
Q: You spent the nine years between your sophomore year at Texas Tech and your Ph.D. at UCLA studying science and engineering?	
A: That's true.	
Q: And during those nine years you did not work for the Rood Manufacturing Company, did you?	
A: No, I didn't.	
Q: And during that time you never worked with water heaters?	
A: No, I didn't.	
Q: Doctor, most of your work is consulting with attorneys, is it not?	
A: Yes, it is.	
Q: And when you are hired by an attorney, you do the studies that you think are necessary to render an opinion, isn't that true?	

Trial Transcript 107

Riley v. Garfield House Apartments	
Defendant's Cross-Examination of Dr. Armstead	**Comments/Notes**
A: Yes, it is.	
Q: And the attorney pays you to do the studies, correct?	
A: That's correct.	
Q: And the attorney pays your traveling expenses—whatever's necessary to do those studies—isn't that true?	
A: Yes, that's true.	
3 Q: And after you have done the studies you consider necessary, you issue a report, right?	3 Dr. Armstead is subject to impeachment based on lack of knowledge, bias, prejudice, and interest. See *Trial Advocacy* Section 10.6 (B).
A: That's usually how it's done.	
Q: That's how you do it?	
A: Yes.	
Q: And, if necessary, you testify at trial, don't you?	
A: Yes, I do.	
Q: When you're consulting with an attorney, that attorney pays you to do the study?	
A: Or the client.	
Q: And the attorney pays you to write the report?	
A: Yes.	
Q: You get paid when you testify at trial, don't you?	
A: I receive compensation for my time spent in court.	

Trial Transcript 108

Riley v. Garfield House Apartments

Defendant's Cross-Examination of Dr. Armstead	Comments/Notes
Q: In this case, the plaintiff has paid your fee and expenses relating to your report and trial testimony? A: Yes. Q: Doctor, you usually testify for plaintiffs in cases such as these, don't you? A: No, that's not true. I testify for plaintiffs and defendants. Q: So, Doctor, you'll testify for whoever pays your fee, is that correct? A: I'll testify for both sides. That's correct. 4 Q: Whoever pays your fee? A: Yes. Q: Doctor, when you render an opinion, you base that opinion on many different facts and assumptions, don't you? A: Yes, I do. Q: And the more facts you base that opinion on, the more likely that opinion will be accurate, isn't that true? A: Yes. Q: And it's possible if some of the facts were to change, the opinion itself would change, isn't it?	4 Dr. Armstead's business requires that she frequently testifies. The fact Dr. Armstead works for both defense and plaintiffs may be interpreted two ways, either that she is indiscriminate or that she is impartial in conducting her analysis. Counsel could also have established that when the Doctor is hired, she knows a party has hired her to arrive at an opinion which supports that party's case. See *Trial Advocacy* Section 10.6 (C).

Riley v. Garfield House Apartments

Defendant's Cross-Examination of Dr. Armstead	Comments/Notes
5 A: Yes, it's possible. 6 Q: Now, Doctor, isn't it true that all the information you received concerning this specific Rood water heater in the basement of the Garfield House Apartments came from the plaintiff's attorney? A: Yes, that's true. Q: In this particular case, you never tested the water temperature in plaintiff's apartment, did you? A: No, I did not. Q: You never tested the temperature of the water in the sink of the plaintiff's apartment? A: No, I did not. Q: You never tested the temperature of the water in the basement of the Garfield House Apartments? A: No, I didn't. Q: In fact, you did not run any tests of the water temperature in the Garfield House Apartments, did you?	5 Dr. Armstead's report reflects what the interested party wants to hear. If the facts were from an unbiased source or if the facts were established by on-site testing, Dr. Armstead's opinion might be different. 6 The opinions of the witness are based on data supplied by plaintiff's attorney, a biased source. Dr. Armstead has not verified the facts before making her report. See *Trial Advocacy* Section 10.4 (C).

Riley v. Garfield House Apartments

Defendant's Cross-Examination of Dr. Armstead	Comments/Notes
7 A: No, I did not. Q: You never inspected the pressure relief valve on the water heater in the basement of the Garfield Apartments, did you? A: No, I didn't. Q: You never inspected the water pipes going to and from that water heater, isn't that true? A: That's true. Q: You never inspected the heating source of that water? A: No. Q: You didn't inspect the thermostat on that water heater either, did you, Doctor? A: No. Q: In fact, you never inspected that water heater at all? A: No, I did not. Q: You didn't inspect the fence around that water heater in the basement of the Garfield House Apartments? A: No. Q: You never had an opportunity to shake that fence to determine how sturdy it was?	7 Counsel discredits the damaging testimony of Dr. Armstead by a series of short, specific leading questions emphasizing Dr. Armstead's failure to test and inspect. See *Trial Advocacy* Section 9.3 (A).

Trial Transcript 111

Riley v. Garfield House Apartments

Defendant's Cross-Examination of Dr. Armstead	Comments/Notes
A: No, I didn't.	
Q: And, of course, you never had the opportunity to take a long stick and try to stick it through the holes in the screen and adjust the thermostat?	
A: No, I didn't.	
Q: In fact, Doctor, you've never been to the Garfield House Apartments, have you?	
A: No, I have not.	
Defendant's Attorney to the Judge:	
8 No further questions, your Honor.	8 Counsel repeats negatives like "never" and "didn't" several times. This series of negative questions requires Dr. Armstead to admit the sources for the report were biased and she had never been on site. The psychological effect on the jury is an incremental loss of respect for the integrity of Dr. Armstead's opinion. See *Trial Advocacy* Section 9.3 (F).

Riley v. Garfield House Apartments

Defendant's Direct Examination of Connie Austern	Comments/Notes
Judge to Plaintiff's Counsel: Counsel, do you have other witnesses?	
Plaintiff's Counsel: 9 I do not, your Honor. The plaintiff rests at this time.	9 Defense counsel decides not to make a directed verdict motion, and need not in this jurisdiction, to preserve post-trial motions. See *Trial Advocacy* Section 12.5 (A).
Judge to Defendant's Attorney: Counsel, are you prepared to call your first witness?	
Defendant's Attorney: I am, your Honor. The defense calls Connie Austern. (Witness is sworn by the Clerk). Q: Ms. Austern, how old are you?	
1 A: I'm forty.	1 This series of questions humanizes the witness and puts her at ease. See *Trial Advocacy* Section 7.7 (A).
Q: Where do you live? A: At 212 Main Street. Q: And where do you work? A: I manage the Garfield House Condominiums. Q: Where is the building located? A: 721 Pine Street. Q: Are you married? A: Yes, I am. Q: What is your husband's name? A: John.	

Riley v. Garfield House Apartments

Defendant's Direct Examination of Connie Austern	Comments/Notes
Q: And how old is he?	
A: He's forty-five.	
Q: Where does he work?	
A: He works as a physical therapist at the Medical Center.	
2 Q: Ms. Austern, you and your husband have children?	2 Leading questions can be occasionally used to establish the undisputed background of a witness. See *Trial Advocacy* Section 7.7 (B).
A: Yes, we do.	
Q: How many?	
A: Two. A boy and a girl, eight and eleven.	
Q: And what are their names?	
A: Blake and Megan.	
Q: Did you go to college, Ms. Austern?	
A: Yes, I did.	
Q: Where did you go?	
A: I went to the University of North Carolina.	
Q: What did you major in?	
A: I was an English major.	
Q: Ms. Austern, why did you become a maintenance manager of an apartment building?	

Riley v. Garfield House Apartments

Defendant's Direct Examination of Connie Austern	Comments/Notes
3 A: Well, I had four brothers, and I was the only female in the family, and the whole time we were growing up, I was competing with the guys. They were always fixing cars and doing painting and mowing and things like that, and it looked like fun. So I tried to keep up. I learned a lot of those things right along with them, and I decided when I was looking for a part-time job in college it would be a fun thing to do. So I did it, and still enjoy doing it now.	3 This common sense explanation makes the witness believable. The background provides many common points of identification with the jury. The witness' answer is narrative and appropriate.
Q: How long have you worked at the Garfield House?	
A: For almost 9 years.	
4 Q: How large is that building?	4 This background information establishes Ms. Austern as a stable employee and a responsible person. Her record of good management helps to establish her consistency, an element necessary to the defense of this case. See *Trial Advocacy* Section 7.8 (A).
A: It is a single building with forty-eight condominium units.	
Q: Has your job substantially changed since you started?	
A: Yes.	
Q: How so?	
A: About 2 years ago, the Garfield Apartments were converted into condominiums.	

Trial Transcript 115

Riley v. Garfield House Apartments	
Defendant's Direct Examination of Connie Austern	**Comments/Notes**
This meant that a lot of the utility type services became self-contained.	
Q: How did this change your job?	
A: For now there is no central water heater or single electric meter. All the units have their own. Since the residents own their units outright, they are responsible for monitoring their own utility services. This means I no longer have a water heater to check on.	
Q: Before the change, what kind of general duties were you responsible for as maintenance manager?	
A: I managed all the physical operations of the building.	
Q: Did you do rental work?	
A: No.	
Q: Who did?	
A: The owners of the building hired a real estate company to handle that work.	
Q: Did you supervise any employees?	

Riley v. Garfield House Apartments

Defendant's Direct Examination of Connie Austern	Comments/Notes
5 A: Yes. I had two part-time maintenance men. They each worked twenty hours a week for me. Q: What were your specific duties? A: We kept the grounds. I made sure the building was maintained, and I also took care of any equipment we needed to do those jobs. Q: As far as the grounds were concerned, what kind of specific types of activities did you get involved in? A: We did mowing, fertilizing, shoveling, trimming, things like that. Q: What kind of things did you do as far as the building was concerned? A: Well, there's a wide array of things. I checked leaky faucets. I plastered walls. I caulked windows. I changed light bulbs. I vacuumed hallways. I had painting done. Just a variety of things. Q: And what kind of activities did you get involved in with respect to equipment around the place?	5 Short, specific questions allow counsel to control the witness' testimony establishing her credibility as an employee, responsible for her own tasks, and those of her helpers. See *Trial Advocacy* Section 7.7 (C).

Riley v. Garfield House Apartments

Defendant's Direct Examination of Connie Austern	Comments/Notes
6 A: We had a furnace, a water heater, and there were the things like the lawn mowers and the snowblowers and things like that which needed to be kept up. Q: Did you have tools and equipment to take care of those maintenance activities? A: Yes. I had a shop downstairs. Q: Where was your tool room located in the building? A: In the basement. Q: Did it take up the entire basement? A: No. There were separate rooms. It was only in one corner of a room. Q: And what else was in the basement? A: There was a water heater room and furnace room. There were some storage cabinets for the tenants, and that's about it. Q: Did you keep all of your equipment materials there? A: No. We had a separate storage garage for all the flammable things and	6 Counsel can take advantage of this witness' ability to narrate essential information. Here, the witness can explain her control over equipment, specifically the water heater. See *Trial Advocacy* Section 7.8 (B).

Riley v. Garfield House Apartments

Defendant's Direct Examination of Connie Austern	Comments/Notes
lawn mowers and snowblowers. Q: Now, Ms. Austern, you mentioned that you had worked with the water heater. What did that involve?	
7 A: We had a standard review. It was a maintenance check. Q: What did that maintenance check include? A: Every six to eight weeks I would check the temperature control, the temperature setting, to make sure it was on medium, and I also inspected the outside of the heater to make sure it looked okay.	7 The attorney has used part of an earlier answer as a transition taking the testimony from the general to the specific, focusing on the key facts. See *Trial Advocacy* Section 7.8 (C).
8 Q: What do you mean by "looked okay"? A: That nothing had been moved and the gauges were at the same settings. Q: Was there any other kind of inspection done on it? A: No. Q: Did you do any kind of repair work on the particular water heater in the Garfield House Apartments?	8 Counsel is listening to the testimony and has the witness explain an unclear response.

Riley v. Garfield House Apartments

Defendant's Direct Examination of Connie Austern	Comments/Notes

A: No.

Q: Why not?

A: Well, that was a sophisticated machine, and I'm not trained or qualified to touch those things. We had a service contract for that.

Q: Who had the service contract?

A: Metro Appliances.

Q: And what did that service contract involve?

A: They were to come in and inspect the water heater periodically, and we could call them too. They were on call if we had any problems. The contract was renewed each year.

Q: Had there been any changes made on that water heater by Metro Appliances?

A: Yes, there had.

Q: What were they?

A: Well, they put a new temperature dial on. They put a safety relief valve on, and they put a temperature relief valve on.

Q: When were these changes made?

Riley v. Garfield House Apartments

Defendant's Direct Examination of Connie Austern	Comments/Notes

A: I believe it was about 9 years ago.

9 Q: Why were they made?

A: Well, new valves were required because of a new law. All landlords had to put them on. As for the temperature dial, I'm not sure why they changed that.

Q: When you say "they made these changes," whom do you mean?

10 A: The service contract people, Metro Appliances.

11 Q: Now, Ms. Austern, had you ever had any problems with vandalism three years ago?

A: Yes, we had.

Q: What did that vandalism involve?

A: Well, we had kids who were kicking off the lock on the basement door. They'd come down, and they'd steal things from tenants' storage cabinets, and they'd also paint on the walls and things like that.

9 By asking Ms. Austern questions about the changes that Metro Appliances made in the water heater, counsel turns potentially damaging evidence to the advantage of the defense. The temperature dial, critical to both the plaintiff's and the defendant's theory of the case, was changed 7 years ago. The changes were made to comply with a new law.

10 Counsel turns the witness' ambiguous answer to the defendant's advantage. Counsel shifts the responsibility away from Garfield House Apartments to Metro Appliances. See *Trial Advocacy* Section 7.8 (D).

11 Counsel uses the transition of "changes" to other "problems" with the water heater, to discuss vandalism.

Riley v. Garfield House Apartments

Defendant's Direct Examination of Connie Austern	Comments/Notes
12 Q: What measures did you take against vandalism? A: I secured all of our equipment in locked enclosures, especially the hot water heater. Q: Why especially the hot water heater? A: Because I recognized that it might present a real temptation for these vandals to tamper with the piece of equipment. Q: Ms. Austern, I'm showing you what has been marked for identification as Defense Exhibit Do you recognize it? A: Yes, I do. Q: What is it? A: It's a picture of a water heater with the enclosure I put up. Q: Was that the water heater at the Garfield House Apartments? A: Yes, it was. Q: How do you recognize it as the heater that was at Garfield House Apartments? A: I took this picture. Q: When did you take this picture?	12 Ms. Austern continues to describe her routine checking of the temperature control setting to establish the fact it is always set at medium. Ms. Austern also describes her routine inspection of the wire enclosure and her vigilance against inadvertent damage and vandalism.

Trial Transcript 122

Riley v. Garfield House Apartments

Defendant's Direct Examination of Connie Austern	Comments/Notes
A: I took it on January 9, just after the Riley child was hurt.	
Q: How can you be sure that that was the date you took the picture?	
13A: Because I added the date on the digital photo using the camera setting, just after I took it.	13Counsel takes Ms. Austern through the appropriate foundation.
Q: Is this photo, which is marked for identification as Defense Exhibit A, a fair and accurate representation of the water heater and the enclosure as you saw it on January 9?	• The photo depicting the water heater is relevant to the case; • Ms. Austern is familiar with the scene; • The photo will assist the jury's understanding of the witness' testimony;
A: Yes, it is.	• The photo is a fair and accurate representation of the scene it purports to depict. See *Trial Advocacy* Section 8.6 (J).
Defendant's Attorney to the Judge:	
Your Honor, I offer Defense Exhibit A.	
Judge:	
It is received.	
Defendant's Attorney:	
Q: When did you first learn of this vandalism?	
A: On January 9.	
Q: What did you do when you saw the vandalism?	
A: I took the picture.	
Q: Ms. Austern, why did you take this picture?	

Trial Transcript 123

Riley v. Garfield House Apartments

Defendant's Direct Examination of Connie Austern	Comments/Notes
14 A: I wanted to show it to the owners of Garfield House because I was concerned. This was the first time vandalism like that had happened to the enclosure around the water heater, and I wanted to make sure they were aware of it. Q: What happened to the enclosure? A: It had been ripped. Q: Had there ever been any other problems with the enclosure? A: Once about two years before that January, I found a hole in the back of the enclosure about the size of an apple, but that didn't look like anything a vandal had done. I figured that was just from wear and tear. Q: And what did you do about that hole? A: I replaced the screening. Q: You've mentioned this picture shows the more recent big rip in the enclosure. What did you do about that? A: I replaced the screen. Q: When did you do that? A: Right after I took the picture.	14 Using the exhibit as a transition, counsel returns to the theme of precautions against vandalism.

Riley v. Garfield House Apartments

Defendant's Direct Examination of Connie Austern	Comments/Notes
Q: The same day?	
A: The same day.	
Q: January 9?	
A: Yes.	
Q: Was that rip in the enclosure there the day before?	
A: No, it wasn't.	
Q: How do you know?	
15 A: Well, because I was working in my shop the day before which is in the same room, and it wasn't there, and that was a big hole. I would have noticed it.	15 Counsel has the witness explain not only what she saw but also how and why she observed what she saw. This information bolsters the witness' credibility. See *Trial Advocacy* Section 7.8 (D).
Q: At the time it was ripped, did you check the water heater at all?	
A: Yes. I looked at the outside, and I also looked at the temperature dial to make sure the setting was still in the same place.	
Q: And was it?	
A: Yes, it was.	
Q: And what was its setting?	
A: It was on medium.	
Q: Had you ever known it to be on any setting other than medium?	
A: No.	

Trial Transcript 125

Riley v. Garfield House Apartments

Defendant's Direct Examination of Connie Austern	Comments/Notes
Q: Ms. Austern, I'd like you to turn your attention to the plumbing, particularly the hot water faucets, at Garfield House. I'm now showing you Plaintiff's Exhibit No. 2. Do you know what it is?	
A: Yes, I do. It's a faucet.	
Q: Do you recognize it?	
A: Yes, I do.	
Q: How do you recognize it?	
A: This is just like the faucet that was in apartment 219 at the Garfield House Apartments before it was remodeled.	
Q: Is that the exact faucet?	
A: No, it is not.	
Q: Do you know what happened to the original faucet?	
A: It was thrown away.	
Q: Why?	
A: The spring following the Riley incident the city historical society provided funds to return the building to its original 1920 appearance and to change the apartments into condominiums. The building was converted. Tenants wishing to move were relocated.	

Riley v. Garfield House Apartments

Defendant's Direct Examination of Connie Austern	Comments/Notes
All condominiums were provided with their own hot water system, and all the fixtures, including plumbing and heating, were replaced.	
16 Q: Ms. Austern, was this faucet like the rest of the faucets at Garfield House Apartments? A: Yes. Q: Ms. Austern, before December 24, did any tenant ever notify you of problems with hot water in the Garfield House Apartments? A: No. Never. Q: Had you ever been notified of problems with hot water by any of your maintenance staff. A: No. Q: Did Mr. or Ms. Riley over complain to you about a problem with hot water? A: Never. Q: Had you yourself known of hot water problems in the apartments?	16 The plaintiff's own exhibit is effectively used by the defense and leads to a reasonable explanation concerning why the heater and control valve were removed.

Riley v. Garfield House Apartments

Defendant's Direct Examination of Connie Austern	Comments/Notes
17 A: No.	17 This is a strong conclusion that supports the defense theory that there was no notice of any problem and the Rileys never complained of any problems. The questions are leading to a specific topic, but do not suggest the answer and are not improper. See *Trial Advocacy* Section 7.6 (B).

Defendant's Attorney to the Judge:

No further questions, your Honor.

Riley v. Garfield House Apartments

Plaintiff's Cross-Examination of Connie Austern	Comments/Notes

Judge:

Cross-examination, counsel?

Plaintiff's Counsel:

Yes, your Honor.

1 Q: Before Rita Riley was burned, you had been maintenance manager at the Garfield House Apartments for six years?

A: That's right.

Q: You were in charge of the physical plant?

A: That's right.

Q: That included the grounds?

A: Yes.

Q: That included the buildings?

A: Yes.

Q: And that included other equipment?

A: Yes.

Q: As part of that equipment you were responsible for the maintenance of the water heaters, weren't you?

1 By repeating some facts raised on direct examination that focus on Ms. Austern's responsibility, plaintiff's counsel effectively and persuasively begins casting doubt on her ability to meet her inspection and maintenance responsibility. See *Trial Advocacy* Section 9.1 (A).

Riley v. Garfield House Apartments

Plaintiff's Cross-Examination of Connie Austern	Comments/Notes
2 A: Yes.	2 Although these questions elicit answers that allow the witness to re-establish part of her direct examination, they are leading questions, and the witness is controlled. Furthermore, Ms. Austern's responsibility for the maintenance of the hot water heater is an element of plaintiff's theory of the case: a breach of duty. See *Trial Advocacy* Section 9.3 (A).

2 A: Yes.

Q: You had a service contract for the maintenance of those water heaters, is that right?

A: Yes.

Q: Ms. Austern, it was your responsibility to see the hot water heater was maintained, isn't that right?

A: You mean fixing it myself?

Q: Yes.

A: No, it wasn't my responsibility.

Q: But you did have the responsibility to make sure other people maintained it?

A: Yes.

Q: You tried to get around on periodic inspections every six to eight weeks, didn't you?

A: Yes, I did.

Q: And when you did those inspections, that included the water heater?

A: Right.

Q: When you were inspecting the water heater, you checked the thermostat to see if it was on the proper setting?

Riley v. Garfield House Apartments

Plaintiff's Cross-Examination of Connie Austern	Comments/Notes
A: Yes.	
Q: And you checked the safety valve?	
A: Yes.	
Q: When you checked the thermostat, you didn't know the exact temperature it was to be set at, did you?	
A: No.	
3 Q: You didn't know how to change the thermostat, did you?	3 This entire line of questioning contains the answers. The questions control the witness by having the witness answer "yes" or "no" without qualification. See *Trial Advocacy* Section 9.3 (B).
A: No.	
Q: You also didn't know what the pressure setting for the safety relief valve should be?	
A: No.	
Q: After that valve was replaced over 7 years ago, you didn't know whether that valve had ever been checked again?	
A: No. I didn't.	
Q: You never read the operating manual for that water heater?	
A: No, I didn't.	
Q: Ms. Austern, you didn't have the operating manual for that water heater?	
A: No, I didn't.	

Trial Transcript 131

Riley v. Garfield House Apartments

Plaintiff's Cross-Examination of Connie Austern	Comments/Notes
Q: And in the six years you had been at Garfield House Apartments, you had never seen the operating manual for that water heater, had you? 4 A: That's right, I had not. Q: Now, the enclosure around that water heater was made out of wire, right? 5 A: Yes. Q: It was basically made of chicken wire, wasn't it? A: It was called chicken wire. Q: And the purpose was to keep people away from the water heater? A: Right. Q: You've mentioned there had been vandalism in the basement of that apartment complex, right? A: Yes. Q: You've also mentioned the enclosure around the water heater had been ripped, isn't that correct? A: That's right. Q: And when that enclosure was ripped, you'd repair it immediately, wouldn't you?	4 Counsel's questions incrementally focus on one point: Ms. Austern's lack of knowledge concerning the water heater. Counsel includes simple facts within each question that force the witness to admit she does not have an operating manual; she has never read such a manual; she has never even seen such a manual during the six years she managed Garfield House Apartments before Rita Riley was burned. This rapid succession of facts reinforces plaintiff's theory of the case. 5 This is a transition to a new topic and a similar series of short, specific questions. See *Trial Advocacy* Section 9.3.

Riley v. Garfield House Apartments

Plaintiff's Cross-Examination of Connie Austern	Comments/Notes

A: Yes, that's right.

Q: You repaired it by putting up the same type of wire that you've had up there previously, right?

A: Yes.

Q: On Jan. 9, you did see the hole in the wire that Ms. Riley made with her broom?

A: Yes.

Q: The thermostat was not moved at all, was it?

A: No.

Q: You never called the maintenance people on January 9 or 10 did you?

6 A: No.

Q: Ms. Austern, you've never kept any records of complaints in the complex, have you?

A: No.

Q: And you never kept any notes about any such complaints?

A: No.

Q: And you have no record of telephone calls of any such complaints?

A: No.

Q: And of course you have no records about any complaints concerning water problems?

6 These questions attempt to neutralize damaging cross-examination of Mary Riley by the defense. Mary Riley may have done a foolish thing by tampering with the enclosure but the thermostat never changed. The water was too hot before and after the child was burned. See *Trial Advocacy* Section 9.4.

Trial Transcript 133

Riley v. Garfield House Apartments

Plaintiff's Cross-Examination of Connie Austern	Comments/Notes
A: None. There was nothing to keep record of.	
Q: Have you kept any records of repairs to that water heater?	
A: No. There were no problems I knew of.	
Q: You have no notes of repairs to that water heater?	
A: No.	
Q: During the year before the accident, you never had the service contract people in, did you?	
A: Not that I know of.	
Q: You never called the service contract people during that time, did you?	
7 A: No.	7 Counsel obtains a series of damaging admissions from Ms. Austern: failure to document complaints by tenants. The tempo and force of these questions and admissions gain momentum. It is tempting for counsel to get carried away. The list of negatives is limited to the critical areas ("you never kept any records"; "you have no notes"; "you never called for service"). The cross-examiner makes a transition to a new topic recognizing that continuing in the same manner would diminish the impact of the questions. This is an effective break and helps retain the attention of jurors. See *Trial Advocacy* Section 9.1 (B).
Q: Now, Ms. Austern you do know who Martin Thomas is, don't you?	
A: Yes, I do.	
Q: You know he is the man hired by the owners of the Garfield House Apartments to check the temperature at the apartment after Rita Riley was burned?	
A: Yes, that's true.	

Trial Transcript 134

Riley v. Garfield House Apartments

Plaintiff's Cross-Examination of Connie Austern	Comments/Notes
8 Q: You took Mr. Thomas to the laundry room in the basement, didn't you?	8 Martin Thomas is clearly identified as defendant's hired expert and is identified as Mr. Thomas, not as Dr. Thomas.
A: Yes. I did.	
Q: You were there when Mr. Thomas checked the temperature of the water in the laundry room, weren't you?	
A: Yes, I was.	
Q: And that temperature was checked at over 200 degrees fahrenheit, wasn't it?	
A: Yes.	
Q: But you didn't know the temperature of the water in the water heater in degrees?	
A: No.	
Q: So you didn't know what the temperature actually was at in the heater, did you?	
A: No.	
Q: When Mr. Thomas checked that temperature, he checked it in the laundry room, isn't that correct?	
A: Yes, he did.	
Q: But he never checked the temperature of the water in the heater, did he?	
A: Not that I know of.	

Riley v. Garfield House Apartments

Plaintiff's Cross-Examination of Connie Austern	Comments/Notes
Q: You do have keys to all the apartments, don't you, Ms. Austern?	
A: Yes, I do.	
Q: But you never took Mr. Thomas around to check the temperature in the different apartments, did you?	
A: No.	
Q: You never checked the temperature in the Riley apartment number 219, did you?	
A: No.	
Q: And you didn't save the water heater or the valve in apartment 219 when the building was remodeled?	9 Counsel's cross-examination is effective because Ms. Austern has been led courteously throughout the entire cross-examination. The questions have been short and simple. The topics have been covered in sequence with transitions between each topic. Counsel has not attacked Ms. Austern but has been politely assertive. The conclusion is strong and shows that the inspection of the premises conducted by Ms. Austern and defendant's expert witness, Dr. Thomas, failed to include inspection of the water in the plaintiff's parents' apartment. This cross-examination supports the conclusion the defendant's expert did not do a thorough job. See *Trial Advocacy* Section 9.1.
9 A: No, they were thrown away.	
Plaintiff's Counsel to the Judge:	
No further questions, your Honor.	

Riley v. Garfield House Apartments

Defendant's Direct Examination of Dr. Thomas	**Comments/Notes**

Judge:

Call your next witness.

Defendant's Attorney:

I call Dr. Martin Thomas.

(Witness sworn by the Clerk).

1 Q: Dr. Thomas, do you live in our city?

A: Yes.

Q: How long have you lived here?

A: Four years.

Q: Are you married?

A: Yes, I am.

Q: What's your wife's name?

A: Diane.

Q: Does she work outside your home?

A: Yes.

Q: Where?

A: She works in a job sharing position as a chemist with the Cornelius Company.

Q: Do you have any children?

A: Yes, I have three children.

1 While the humanizing questions are brief, they do make the witness more real and more believable. See *Trial Advocacy* Section 10.4 (B).

Riley v. Garfield House Apartments

Defendant's Direct Examination of Dr. Thomas	Comments/Notes
2 Q: Where did you obtain your Ph.D.?	2 Counsel demonstrates early on that Dr. Thomas is not a medical doctor but a Ph.D. In addition to personalizing the witness, questions about his education background support his qualifications as an expert. See *Trial Advocacy* Section 10.4 (C).

2 Q: Where did you obtain your Ph.D.?

A: I received my Ph.D. from Notre Dame University in the field of thermodynamics and safety engineering just before I moved here.

Q: Would you tell us where you received any other degrees?

A: I received my master's degree in engineering from the University of Florida with the major field in the study of safety engineering. I received my bachelor's degree from Montana State. My major field of study there was mechanical engineering.

Q: Doctor, where do you work now?

A: Right now, I'm the president of Thomas and Associates. We're a firm of consultants in the safety of heating and ventilation systems, and we specialize in multi-unit dwellings, apartment buildings.

2 Counsel demonstrates early on that Dr. Thomas is not a medical doctor but a Ph.D. In addition to personalizing the witness, questions about his education background support his qualifications as an expert. See *Trial Advocacy* Section 10.4 (C).

Riley v. Garfield House Apartments

Defendant's Direct Examination of Dr. Thomas	Comments/Notes
3 A: When did you start the firm? Q: About 4 years ago. Q: What other work experience do you have in mechanical engineering? 4 A: For 5 years while I was studying for my Ph.D., I also worked for Continental Paper Company in the forestry and paper mill division. Before that I was chief safety inspector for the City of Parkersburg, West Virginia, in the residential division. I inspected apartment buildings and other residential dwellings in the City of Parkersburg and made sure that the appliances and heating systems within those buildings were up to code. And for 2 years, I was assistant manager for the Kanawha County Public Utilities. Most of my work for the utility company was with the steam-generated power plants. Q: Doctor, do you have any publications?	3 Counsel details Dr. Thomas' educational background and achievements in areas of engineering specifically applied to safety. This shows the jury his special expertise in both heating systems and multi-unit dwellings. 4 The development of Dr. Thomas' background reveals the expert's continued application of his specialty. Dr. Thomas has designed heating equipment, managed a utility, inspected residences and apartments. See *Trial Advocacy* Section 10.2 (C).

Riley v. Garfield House Apartments

Defendant's Direct Examination of Dr. Thomas	Comments/Notes
5 A: Yes. I've had three works published. Two articles written specifically for property managers, and one article that was published in the Consumer Information Digest Website.	5 The question about articles allows the expert to further qualify himself as an advisor of property managers and as an advocate of consumer safety.
Q: Do you do any teaching?	
6 A: Yes. Right now I'm teaching a vocational course in the County of Kanawha on heating, vent and air conditioning for licensed electricians. I contribute to a list serve of safety system equipment technicians. I also do some guest lecturing at the state college in the engineering department.	6 The question about teaching not only further qualifies the expert but also humanizes him as a responsible, practical professional entrusted with teaching licensed electricians about heating and invited by academicians to address their engineering students. See *Trial Advocacy* Section 10.5 (C).
Q: Do you belong to any professional associations?	
A: Yes. I'm currently a member of the Commission of Heating and Air Conditioning Accidents.	
Q: Dr. Thomas, do you have any experience dealing with water heaters and with accidents involving water heaters?	

Riley v. Garfield House Apartments

Defendant's Direct Examination of Dr. Thomas	Comments/Notes
7 A: Yes. For 2 years, I worked for General Electric in the appliance design center and I helped design some of their water heaters. I also inspected water heaters in apartments in my role as the chief safety inspector for the City of Parkersburg, and have consulted with attorneys who are involved in accident cases in the proper maintenance and security of water heaters in residential homes and apartment buildings as the president of Thomas and Associates. Q: Have you also been involved in cases where people have been scalded by hot water? A: Yes, I've been involved in scalding cases in my work as a consultant with Thomas and Associates. In fact, most of the cases we are asked to render an opinion on are cases where an individual is burned by hot water coming out of a tap. Therefore, we need to inspect the water heater to ensure it was properly maintained and secured.	7 Using the theme of heating accidents from Dr. Thomas' previous answer, counsel narrows the scope to water heaters. This technique allows Dr. Thomas to amplify his expertise through a chronological outlining of his experience in design, consulting, and in advising persons responsible for safety how to properly inspect and maintain water heaters. See *Trial Advocacy* Section 10.5 (D).

Riley v. Garfield House Apartments

Defendant's Direct Examination of Dr. Thomas

Comments/Notes

8 Q: Doctor, with all your experience in the field of water heater safety and maintenance, and your experience in dealing with scald victims, are you able to determine the temperature of water that causes various degrees of scalding?

A: No, I'm not able to do that.

Q: Why not?

A: I'm not a medical doctor. As an engineer, I would feel unqualified to hypothesize as to the temperature of water that causes various burns.

Q: Have you attempted to determine the temperature of the water that caused the burns to the plaintiff in this case?

A: Yes, I have.

Q: What information did you use to attempt to determine the temperature of that water?

A: Well, I contacted the burn departments of numerous children's hospitals to see if any of the experts there could assist me.

8 Counsel's second question is a hypothetical question with a difference. It seems to call on the witness to agree that he can give his opinion. However, counsel asks whether the expert can determine the temperature of water that causes various degrees of scalding. Dr. Thomas' answer undermines the credibility of plaintiff's expert. Dr. Thomas' deference to physicians allows him to categorize such a determination by non-medical experts as unqualified hypothesis. See *Trial Advocacy* Section 10.5 (D).

Riley v. Garfield House Apartments

Defendant's Direct Examination of Dr. Thomas	Comments/Notes
Q: Is this the type of information that a person in your area of expertise ordinarily relies on to form an opinion?	
A: It certainly is.	
9 Q: What were you able to determine?	9 These questions continue to explore the failure of such a determination. Dr. Thomas was unable to ascertain the temperature of the water that scalded Rita Riley even with the assistance of medical experts. The jury may infer plaintiff's expert's determination of the temperature is invalid. See *Trial Advocacy* Section 10.5 (F).
A: I was given such a wide variance of temperature that would cause scalding, such as the kind that the plaintiff in this case has experienced, that I am unable to even guess as to the temperature of the water that actually caused her burns.	
Q: Now, Doctor, let's discuss water heaters. Based on your training, your education, and your experience in the field of water heater safety and security, do you have an opinion as to why a water heater should be properly secured in an apartment building?	
A: Yes, I do.	
Q: Please tell us why a water heater in an apartment building should be properly secured.	

Riley v. Garfield House Apartments

Defendant's Direct Examination of Dr. Thomas	Comments/Notes
A: Well, a water heater in an apartment building must be properly secured, otherwise vandals will be able to adjust various controls on that water heater. The risk, if this happens, is that they could adjust the thermostat and cause the water produced by that water heater to be excessively hot and cause burns to tenants in the building. The water heater should also be properly secured to protect the water heater itself from damage.	
10 Q: Doctor, do you have a separate opinion based on your training, your experience, and your education, why a water heater in an apartment building should be properly maintained? A: Yes. Q: What is that opinion, Doctor? A: Once again, if the water heater is not properly maintained, it's possible for the water heater to malfunction and cause excessively hot water to come out of the various	10 Dr. Thomas has already testified to the sources of his information. Counsel reminds the jury of the expert's training, education, and experience. See *Trial Advocacy* Section 10.4 (C).

Riley v. Garfield House Apartments

Defendant's Direct Examination of Dr. Thomas	Comments/Notes
faucets within the apartment building and burn the tenants. I also suggest that apartment owners have service contracts on their water heaters so that they have capable professionals who are familiar with the machines available to repair any problems that may come up.	
11 Q: Doctor, based on your training, your experience, and your education, do you have an opinion whether the water heater in the basement of the Garfield Apartments—that specific water heater—was properly secured? Please answer yes or no. A: Yes, I do. Q: What information did you rely upon to come to that opinion? A: Well, in June after this incident, I went to the Garfield House Apartments and ran tests on the water temperature. I also inspected the water heater itself to determine if it was functioning properly. I also read the deposition transcripts of various people involved in this lawsuit.	11 This next series of opinion questions are more specific. The expert narrates the steps managers can take to avert disaster. The theme of the service contract is not lost on the jury. The inference drawn from the two series of opinion questions is that Connie Austern, alert to vandalism and aware of the need for professionals, properly secured and maintained the Rood water heater in the basement. See *Trial Advocacy* Section 10.5 (B).

Riley v. Garfield House Apartments

Defendant's Direct Examination of Dr. Thomas	Comments/Notes
Q: Did you talk to anyone about the water heater? A: Yes. Q: Who? A: Connie Austern, who is the manager.	
12 Q: Doctor, are deposition transcripts and information received from resident managers the type of information an expert, such as yourself, in the field of mechanical engineering and safety engineering normally relies upon to render an opinion when consulting in cases like this? A: Yes, they are. Q: Did you learn if the water heater was in the same condition when you inspected it as it was at the time of the incident in this case? A: Yes. Q: Whom did you learn it from? A: Connie Austern. Q: What did she tell you? A: She told me that it was in the same condition. Q: Do you know what she meant by same condition?	12 Counsel requests the sources of information supporting Dr. Thomas' opinion. This gives the expert another opportunity to bolster his credibility and his qualifications by explaining the tests conducted and attention to deposition testimony. See *Trial Advocacy* Section 10.5 (C).

Riley v. Garfield House Apartments

Defendant's Direct Examination of Dr. Thomas	Comments/Notes
A: Yes. Q: What? 13 A: There had been no adjustments and no repairs. Q: Doctor, was that water heater properly secured on December 24 at the time of this incident? A: Yes, it was. Q: Why do you say that, Doctor? A: Well, it was properly secured because there was a fence around the water heater to keep vandals away from the thermostat and other controls. The fence was also sufficient to keep vandals away from the water heater itself, but still allow the water heater ventilation necessary to properly work. Q: Doctor, once again regarding the specific water heater located in the basement of the Garfield House Apartments, do you have an opinion whether that water heater was properly maintained? A: Yes, I do.	13 This is a weak point in defendant's case. How is the jury to accept the water heater is in the "same condition" after the elapse of six months? Time implies deterioration or possible change. Counsel explains by follow up questions that show "same condition" means no adjustments, no repairs. Opposing counsel may object that the question calls for an answer based on hearsay. However, Connie Austern—a party agent—has testified there were no adjustments or repairs and this information is the kind of information an expert in this field relies upon. See *Trial Advocacy* Section 10.5 (C).

Trial Transcript 147

Riley v. Garfield House Apartments

Defendant's Direct Examination of Dr. Thomas	Comments/Notes
Q: What information did you use to come to that opinion, Doctor?	
A: Well, I used the same information I listed before. I was at the Garfield House Apartments on June 25 and inspected the water heater. I ran tests on the temperature of the water. I relied on information supplied to me by Ms. Austern. I read deposition transcripts of various parties involved	
14 in this lawsuit. And I examined the specifications sheets supplied by Rood Manufacturing. These are the sources I and, other experts in my field use to form our opinions.	14 Note the pattern of questioning that sets out the elements of foundation for an expert witness: Do you have an opinion about the specific water heater? What is the basis of that opinion? Do experts normally base their opinions on such information? What is your opinion? Why is your opinion justified? See *Trial Advocacy* Section 10.5 (B).
Q: Doctor, in your opinion, was that water heater being properly maintained on December 24, the day of this incident?	
A: Yes, it was.	
Q: Why?	
15 A: The water heater was being properly maintained because Connie Austern, the resident manager, was inspecting the water heater on a regular basis. During these	15 Dr. Thomas' answer not only justifies his opinion but bolsters the impression of Connie Austern's responsible routine of inspection and maintenance.

Riley v. Garfield House Apartments

Defendant's Direct Examination of Dr. Thomas	Comments/Notes
inspections, Ms. Austern made sure the water would not become too hot. She also inspected the general condition of the water heater. It was also properly maintained because the owners of the Garfield House Apartments had a service contract with Metro Appliances to inspect and repair the water heater on a regular basis and to come out if there were any problems with the water heater.	
16 Q: Are you familiar with the purpose of a pressure relief valve on a water heater? A: Yes, I am. Q: What does the pressure relief valve do? A: The pressure relief valve is a safety device that is designed to release pressure from the water heater to prevent the water heater from exploding. Q: Was the pressure relief valve working on June 25 when you were at the Garfield House Apartments?	16 There are problems with the pressure relief valve. Candid admission of the problem and a reasonable explanation on direct examination defuses its negative impact during the cross-examination. Counsel continues to explore the weakness. The expert admits surprise that the valve did not activate until 2 degrees below boiling point. This ordinarily adverse admission is mitigated somewhat by the expert's putting it in context of expert testing: at its highest position, the water could not become hotter than 210 degrees. To mitigate further damage, counsel designs a series of questions allowing the expert to establish the pressure relief valve did not cause the accident. See *Trial Advocacy* Section 10.5 (E).

Riley v. Garfield House Apartments

Defendant's Direct Examination of Dr. Thomas	Comments/Notes

A: The temperature of the water reached 210 degrees Fahrenheit and the pressure relief valve did not activate. This surprised me to some degree, but it was not of major concern because the range in which the pressure relief valve was supposed to activate was from 195 degrees to 212 degrees Fahrenheit. There were still 2 degrees left within that range since the water temperature was 210 degrees. Since I tested the water with the thermostat in its very highest position, that water heater could produce water no hotter than 210 degrees; therefore, the fact that the pressure relief valve did not activate at 210 degrees did not concern me.

Q: Would the fact the pressure relief valve did not activate at 210 degrees have any effect on the water produced by the water heater?

A: No. Absolutely not. The purpose of the pressure relief valve is to prevent the water heater from exploding. The pressure relief valve would have absolutely nothing to do with this accident.

Trial Transcript 150

Riley v. Garfield House Apartments

Defendant's Direct Examination of Dr. Thomas	Comments/Notes
17 Q: Dr. Thomas, after inspecting the water heater in the basement of the Garfield House Apartments and the security around that water heater, did you recommend any modifications to the owners of the Garfield House Apartments? A: No, I did not. Q: Why was that?	17 Counsel ends the direct on a strong point. Despite problems with the pressure relief valve, Dr. Thomas recommended no modifications.
18 A: Because the water heater appeared to be working fine, and the security around the water heater was adequate. **Defendant's Attorney to the Judge:** Thank you, Doctor. No further questions.	18 No recommendation means everything was working fine. This tactic further emphasizes the confidence Dr. Thomas had in Connie Austern and the Rood water heater. The tactic also allows Dr. Thomas to reassert that the water heater was "working fine." This is the defense's theory of the case: the water heater was in good operating condition, safe and secured. See *Trial Advocacy* Section 10.2 (A).

Riley v. Garfield House Apartments

Plaintiff's Cross-Examination of Dr. Thomas	Comments/Notes
Judge:	
Cross-examination?	
Plaintiff's Counsel:	
Yes, your Honor.	

Judge:

Cross-examination?

Plaintiff's Counsel:

Yes, your Honor.

1 Q: Doctor, you teach at a vocational school, isn't that correct?

A: Yes, it is.

Q: And when your students complete your course and their other studies at that vocational school, they receive a certificate of completion instead of a college degree, isn't that true?

A: Yes.

Q: You don't teach a college level course, do you, Doctor?

A: No, I don't.

2 Q: And you don't teach a graduate level course either, do you?

A: No.

Q: Now, you've only had three works published, isn't that true?

A: Yes, it is.

Q: And two of those works were published for apartment managers, correct?

A: Yes.

1 The cross-examination of Dr. Thomas is focused on the following areas: (a) credentials (education and experience), (b) specific sources of information for his report on the Garfield House Apartments' water heater, (c) the basis for his expert opinion on security and maintenance for the Rood water heater, (d) the test he conducted, (e) the examination of specification sheets, (f) the function of the pressure relief valve, (g) the failure of the valve to activate until 2 degrees below boiling point, and (h) his decision not to recommend modifications. See *Trial Advocacy* Section 10.6 (B).

2 Dr. Thomas' candor is immediately in issue. On direct exam, Dr. Thomas represented himself as a teacher of professionals. Counsel distinguishes academic from vocational training. Discounting Dr. Thomas' work in vocational training can backfire because the jurors may perceive the attorney is snobbish.

Riley v. Garfield House Apartments

Plaintiff's Cross-Examination of Dr. Thomas	Comments/Notes
Q: And one was published for consumers, isn't that true? A: Yes, it is. 3 Q: None of those works were published in what are known as scholarly journals, were they? A: No, they weren't. Q: In your work with Thomas and Associates, your consulting firm, you specialize in consulting for apartment owners and managers, don't you? A: Yes, I do. Q: In fact, apartment owners and managers supply most of your income, don't they? 4 A: Yes, they do. Q: Nevertheless, you'll work for either plaintiffs or defendants, is that correct? A: Yes, it is. Q: You'll work for whoever hires you to consult on a particular case, correct? A: Yes. Q: And when you consult on a case, you do whatever studies you think are necessary, isn't that true?	3 In referring to "only three works published," counsel should consider the demographics of the jury. Counsel implies that Dr. Thomas' articles are worth less than Dr. Armstead's because Dr. Thomas' audience consists of consumers and managers of multi-unit housing. Trivializing the value of these articles may diminish counsel in the eyes of the jury—a jury selected to determine negligence, not scholarship. See *Trial Advocacy* Section 10.6 (C). 4 In this cluster of questions, counsel seeks to elicit admissions that Dr. Thomas is pro-defense because owners and managers of multi-unit dwellings are the main sources of his income at Thomas and Associates.

Riley v. Garfield House Apartments

Plaintiff's Cross-Examination of Dr. Thomas	Comments/Notes
5 A: Yes, it is. Q: The cost of those studies are paid for by the people who hire you, isn't that true? A: Yes, it is. Q: Any travel expenses involved are paid for by that side also, correct? A: Yes. Q: And then after doing the studies that you think are necessary, you issue a report? A: Yes, I do. Q: And render an opinion in that report, correct? A: Yes. 6 Q: And you testify at trial if necessary? A: That's true. Q: And your fees for issuing the report, for doing the tests, and for testifying at trial are all paid for by the attorney who originally hired you, isn't that true? A: Yes, by the client. Q: When you render an opinion, you base that opinion on various facts and assumptions, don't you?	5 Counsel seeks to show that defendant's expert is a hired gun and indiscriminate: he will work for anyone and everyone who pays. The effectiveness of this line of questions is doubtful. The jury may just as readily conclude that Dr. Thomas is open-minded and bases his opinions on facts, not prejudices. The pattern of these questions parallel the questions asked on cross-examination of the plaintiff's expert. See *Trial Advocacy* Section 10.6 (B). 6 Another tactic to impugn the credibility of the expert witness is a frequent appearance in lawsuits. The jury is supposed to infer that the opposing expert's testimony lacks objectivity.

Riley v. Garfield House Apartments

Plaintiff's Cross-Examination of Dr. Thomas	Comments/Notes
A: Well, I base it more on facts than assumptions.	
Q: Well, in this particular case, you based it on at least one assumption, didn't you?	
A: I don't know what you're referring to.	
7 Q: Well, you were told by Ms. Connie Austern, weren't you, that the water heater was in the same condition on June 25 as it was on December 24, weren't you?	7 This series of questions points out the biased sources of the information and the fact that the opinion is based on assumptions. The biased source and the possible flaw in the assumptions makes the opinion less credible. Dr. Thomas' opinion requires that the Rood water heater was in the "same condition" from December to June. See *Trial Advocacy* Section 10.6 (C).
A: Yes, I was.	
8 Q: But, you have no first-hand knowledge of that fact, do you?	
A: No.	8 Through a series of simple, short leading questions, counsel questions the validity of Dr. Thomas' investigation. The expert admits that different facts may alter the conclusion. The jury recalls that Dr. Thomas has the liberty to conduct any tests. The fact that he failed to conduct more than one implies he failed to test other causes of the accident. Counsel then enumerates all the tests that might show different temperatures in different areas.
Q: The only knowledge that you have that the water heater was in the same condition was what Connie Austern told you, isn't that correct?	
A: Yes, it is.	
Q: When you render an opinion, you also base that opinion on various facts, don't you?	
A: Yes, I do.	
Q: And the more facts that you have when you make an opinion, the more likely the opinion will be accurate, isn't that correct?	

Trial Transcript 155

Riley v. Garfield House Apartments

Plaintiff's Cross-Examination of Dr. Thomas	Comments/Notes

A: Yes, it is.

9 Q: And if some of the facts you based your opinion on were changed, it's possible the opinion itself might change, isn't that true?

A: Yes, that's possible.

Q: Now, in this particular case you went to the Garfield House Apartments, didn't you?

A: Yes, I did.

Q: Now, while you were at the Garfield House Apartments, it would have been possible for you to test the temperature of the water in the bathtub where little Rita Riley was burned, wouldn't it?

A: Yes, I could have done that.

Q: And you could have tested the temperature of the water in the kitchen sink in that same apartment, couldn't you?

A: Yes, I could have.

Q: And you could have tested the temperature of the water in that apartment with a washing machine on in the basement, to see if that would have any effect, couldn't you?

9 An effective technique is to change the basis of the expert's opinion. See *Trial Advocacy* Section 10.6 (B).

Riley v. Garfield House Apartments

Plaintiff's Cross-Examination of Dr. Thomas	Comments/Notes

A: Yes, I could have.

Q: And you could have tested that temperature while flushing a toilet in the apartment, to see if that would change the temperature, couldn't you?

A: Yes, I could have.

Q: But you didn't run any of those tests in the apartment did you?

A: No, I didn't.

Q: The only test that you ran was the test in the laundry room, right next to the water heater?

A: Yes.

Q: And when you tested the water, it came out at 210 degrees Fahrenheit, didn't it, Doctor?

A: Yes, it did.

Q: Of course the boiling point of water is 212 degrees, correct?

A: Yes.

Q: So that the temperature of the water you tested was only two degrees less than boiling hot water, true?

Trial Transcript 157

Riley v. Garfield House Apartments	
Plaintiff's Cross-Examination of Dr. Thomas	**Comments/Notes**

A: Yes, that's true.

Q: You told us that you examined the specification sheets of the Rood water heater, isn't that true?

A: Yes, I did.

Q: And on that specification sheet it stated that the range of temperatures for that water heater was between 140 and 180 degrees, didn't it?

A: Yes, that's what was listed on the specification sheet.

Q: And, in fact, the American Gas Association states the appropriate range for temperatures of water produced by a hot water heater is between 140 and 180 degrees, isn't that true, Doctor?

A: Yes, it is.

Q: The water in the apartment building was 30 degrees higher than the highest possible temperature recommended by the American Gas Association, isn't that correct?

Riley v. Garfield House Apartments

Plaintiff's Cross-Examination of Dr. Thomas	Comments/Notes
10 A: Yes, it is.	10 This area of the cross-examination is effective because Dr. Thomas must acknowledge that the temperature is 30 degrees more than the recommendation of both the manufacturer and the AGA. Even a lay jury, unschooled in engineering, can question Dr. Thomas' judgment in failing to recommend modifications when he had knowledge that the water exceeded the range. See *Trial Advocacy* Section 9.1 (A).

Q: Now, you are familiar with the pressure relief valve, aren't you?

A: Yes, I am.

Q: And the pressure relief valve is an important safety device on a water heater, wouldn't you agree?

A: Yes, I would.

Q: In fact, the purpose of the pressure relief valve is to prevent the water heater from exploding in case the water should get too hot, isn't it?

A: Yes, that's its function.

Q: And even though the temperature of that water was 210 degrees Fahrenheit, the pressure relief valve didn't activate, did it?

A: No, it did not.

Q: In fact, that surprised you, didn't it?

A: Yes, it did.

Q: It surprised you because even though the range that the temperature relief valve was supposed to kick in was between 195 and 212 degrees, two degrees is an extremely small amount when we're

Riley v. Garfield House Apartments

Plaintiff's Cross-Examination of Dr. Thomas	Comments/Notes
talking about water that hot, isn't it? A: Yes, it can be. 11 Q: In your experience consulting with apartment resident managers, you advise them to activate that pressure relief valve to make sure it's working, don't you? 12 A: Yes, I do. Q: And if the resident manager does activate that pressure relief valve, you found that it will work when it is supposed to, isn't that true? A: Yes, it is. Q: And isn't it true that it has been your experience that when a new pressure relief valve is installed after a water heater has been manufactured, it's done so because there have been problems with the water heater, isn't that true? A: That is a reason. Q: And isn't it true that a new pressure relief valve on the Rood water heater in the basement of the Garfield House Apartments was installed nine years after that water heater was manufactured?	11 Counsel concludes the cross-examination on a strong point—the weakness of the defendant's excuse for the pressure relief valve. Dr. Thomas admits that the valve did not activate even though the water reached a temperature two degrees below boiling. Dr. Thomas admits that the valve should activate between 195 and 212 degrees Fahrenheit and it did not. See *Trial Advocacy* Section 10.6 (C). 12 Counsel has the expert admit past practice: ordinarily Dr. Thomas advises resident managers to activate the pressure relief valve as part of their routine inspection and he did not in this case.

Riley v. Garfield House Apartments

Plaintiff's Cross-Examination of Dr. Thomas	Comments/Notes
A: Well, it was installed after the water heater was manufactured, and it had been installed after the water heater had been in the basement of the Garfield House Apartments. But I'm not sure of the precise date when it was installed.	
13 Q: The only way that the water heated by that water heater could come out at 210 degrees Fahrenheit was if there was a malfunction in the control system of that water heater, isn't that correct, Doctor?	13 This is only the second time in the cross-examination that the witness has been called "Doctor." The other time was in the first question. The use of the title here is in contrast to the mistake in judgment made by the witness.
A: Yes, that's true.	
Q: But even though there was a malfunction in the control system of that water heater that caused the water to come out at 210 degrees Fahrenheit, you made no recommendations for modifications to the water heater in the basement of the Garfield House Apartments, did you?	
A: No, I did not.	
Q: And even though the pressure relief valve failed to activate at 210 degrees Fahrenheit, you still made no recommendations for corrections or improvements?	

Riley v. Garfield House Apartments	
Plaintiff's Cross-Examination of Dr. Thomas	**Comments/Notes**
A: No, I didn't.	
Plaintiff's Counsel to the Judge:	
14 I have no further questions.	14 These strong last two questions are based on discovery documents. They are not risky because they are based on solid facts and are an excellent way to conclude a cross-examination. See *Trial Advocacy* Section 10.6.

Riley v. Garfield House Apartments

Defendant's Summation	Comments/Notes
Judge:	
Counsel, please approach the bench.	
Colloquy at the Bench:	
Counsel, yesterday we conferred and discussed all of the jury instructions. Do either of you have any questions or requests for changes?	
Defendant's Attorney:	
I have none, your Honor.	
Plaintiff's Counsel:	
I don't have any either, Judge.	
Judge:	
1 All right, we will proceed with summation. Defendant's attorney may now argue to the jury.	1 In this case, the plaintiff has the final summation. In many jurisdictions the plaintiff goes first and may make a short rebuttal following the defendant's summation. See *Trial Advocacy* Section 11.1 (A).

Riley v. Garfield House Apartments

Defendant's Summation	Comments/Notes
Defendant's Attorney:	2 The defense and the plaintiff draw different inferences and arrive at different conclusions from the same facts. Because the defendant does not have the burden of proof, defendant will have no opportunity to save part of the closing argument for rebuttal. Defense counsel must therefore structure the closing argument so that the plaintiff's inferences and conclusion are less credible and less consistent with common sense and life experiences. See *Trial Advocacy* Section 11.4 (A).
2 Your Honor, ladies and gentlemen: This case is a tragedy. The accident to Rita Riley would not have happened if Mary Riley had not left her daughter alone. It would never have happened if she had told Connie Austern about the problem she had with the water.	
3 It is so tragic a young child has been hurt. It is even more tragic that her mother, the person who loves her so much, is responsible for her being burned. The people who owned and managed the Garfield House Apartments are not responsible for what happened to Rita Riley. They did not cause her injuries.	3 Counsel makes no preliminary remarks. Instead, counsel seizes the plaintiff's theme from the opening statement—tragedy—to develop a series of inferences leading the jury away from assigning liability to the defendant. Counsel assigns the tragedy to Mary Riley with the irony that the person who loves Rita so much has caused her suffering.

Riley v. Garfield House Apartments

Defendant's Summation	Comments/Notes
4 The plaintiff has the burden of proof in this case. They had to show that the owners of Garfield House Apartments were responsible for the injuries to that baby. The plaintiff could not and did not do that. They had to prove four things listed on this chart: First of all, they had to prove that the owners of Garfield House Apartments had a duty to Rita Riley. Second, they had to prove that the owners of Garfield House Apartments breached that duty and somehow failed to fulfill their responsibilities. Third, they had to prove the actions of the people at Garfield House Apartments were the direct cause, the proximate cause, of the injuries. And fourth, they had to prove damages and actual money costs. The plaintiff had to prove all four of these things, not just one or two, but all four. They weren't able to do that.	4 Defense counsel sets out plaintiff's burden of proof and clearly explains that the plaintiff failed to meet that burden. Counsel refers to the "plaintiff" as "they"—even though not grammatically correct—to emphasize that Rita's mother is also responsible and that Rita's parents will benefit from a plaintiff's verdict in this case. Defense counsel uses a visual aid to list the four duties to help the jurors understand and to provide an outline for summation. See *Trial Advocacy* Section 11.5 (G).

Trial Transcript 165

Riley v. Garfield House Apartments

Defendant's Summation	Comments/Notes
5 The owners and employees of Garfield House Apartments did have a duty to provide a reasonably safe residence for the tenants of that apartment complex—a reasonably safe place to live. And they did that. They have a reasonable duty, and there are limitations on that duty. They do not have a duty to protect tenants from their own carelessness. They don't have a duty to protect tenants from their own negligence. They do not have a duty to protect tenants from themselves. And in this particular case, they did not have a duty to protect Rita Riley from her own mother's carelessness.	5 The word "duty" is a good transition to the main theory of the case. Counsel admits that defendant had a duty. Immediately after that admission, counsel qualifies that duty. The duty is narrowed to providing a reasonably safe place to live, not to protect the little girl from her own mother's carelessness.
6 Plaintiff could not prove the people at Garfield House Apartments breached their duty. Plaintiff did not prove the people of Garfield House failed to fulfill their obligations. The people at Garfield House Apartments had properly inspected and maintained that water heater, and they had adequately protected it.	6 Defense counsel tells the defendant's side in a positive credible manner. See *Trial Advocacy* Section 11.2.

Riley v. Garfield House Apartments

Defendant's Summation	Comments/Notes
7 Connie Austern told you that she had constructed an enclosure around that water heater and that whenever it was in any type of disrepair, she took care of it, immediately. She knew when that enclosure was in disrepair because it was only a few feet from her workroom. She passed it every working day. In fact, even though there had been vandalism in the apartment building, she told you there had been no significant repairs required before the injuries to Rita Riley. There had been a small hole, about the size of an apple, in the wiring, but she repaired it. She took the screen down and put a new one up. The only real damage to the enclosure didn't occur until some time after the little girl was injured. Isn't it interesting that it happened about two weeks after the injuries to Rita Riley? During the time	7 While plaintiff's case stressed the insubstantial wire and vandalism, the defense stresses the daily routine of observing the enclosure and the history of immediate repairs, the most significant being the one that occurred after Rita's accident. Counsel further turns this fact to the defense's advantage by posing a rhetorical question. See *Trial Advocacy* Section 11.5 (D).
8 when her mother was down there poking around that heater.	8 Counsel moves from the after-the-fact inference to the real liability inference:

Riley v. Garfield House Apartments

Defendant's Summation	Comments/Notes
Connie Austern also told you she conducted periodic inspections of that water heater, and when she did she would check to see that the thermostat was set properly.	Rita's parents' failure to report excessively hot water is consistent with Mary Riley's irresponsible tampering with the gauge and her possible involvement with damaging the enclosure. The jury can blame the victim's parents. These are irresponsible people who leave a baby unattended, who fail to report problems, and who even create hazards.
9 She also told you the truth, even if it showed that she did not know everything. She told you that she didn't know how to check to see if the thermostat was accurately recording the temperature; she didn't know how to change the thermostat; she didn't know how to handle the safety relief valve on the water heater. She hadn't had any training in the maintenance of the water heater, and none of her staff had any training. But, what she told you was it all wasn't necessary. It wasn't necessary for her to know about that water heater. The reason it wasn't necessary was because Garfield House Apartments had a maintenance service contract with a company in town. That maintenance service contract included, among other	9 Defense counsel shows how plaintiff's apparently strong facts—Connie Austern's lack of training, or experience do not create a strong argument. Counsel turns the facts in the defense's favor—acknowledged need for expertise and the precaution of the service contract. Counsel then shows how the protection of a service contract did not benefit Rita because of her parents. Had they complained, the experts would have corrected any problem. See *Trial Advocacy* Section 11.4 (C).

Riley v. Garfield House Apartments

Defendant's Summation	Comments/Notes
things, a periodic inspection of the heater. In addition, the maintenance people were on call to come out and service it whenever necessary, whenever there were any complaints. But there had been no complaints. Mary Riley didn't report any problems with hot water. No one reported any problems with hot water to Connie Austern, the maintenance manager, to any of the people who worked for her, to the resident manager of that complex, or to the owners of the complex. There had been no reason to have any problems repaired under the service contract because no one had indicated that there were any problems.	
10 The plaintiff was also unable to prove the actions of the people at the Garfield House Apartments were the direct cause of the injuries to that little girl. It was Mary Riley, the little girl's mother, who had a duty to protect her baby. But she left the little girl alone in that bathtub.	10 Counsel moves from one element of negligence—breach— to the next—direct cause—by the conclusory language, "plaintiff was also unable to prove. . .." This supports the structure of the argument: plaintiff cannot prove, therefore, plaintiff cannot recover. See *Trial Advocacy* Section 11.4 (A).

Riley v. Garfield House Apartments

Defendant's Summation	Comments/Notes
11 She was comfortable leaving her alone. Her mind was on the holidays, her husband coming home, Christmas with	11 While plaintiff's counsel must acknowledge Mary Riley's carelessness, defense counsel shows that no matter how forthright the concession, there is no reasonable explanation for what she did.
12 her parents, gift-wrapping, food preparation, cleaning house, picking up clothes,	12 Defense counsel retells the story of the accident capitalizing on the plaintiff's case weaknesses. The story of Mary Riley's failed duty is given a different explanation—preoccupation with holiday preparations. See *Trial Advocacy* Section 11.5.
13 and the various holiday activities. She told you when she was standing in the closet and she heard the water come on, and she heard her baby cry, she knew what had happened. She knew what had happened because she	13 Counsel uses the impact words, like "comfortable," which were brought out in cross-examination of Mary Riley to illustrate her preoccupation due to gift-wrapping, picking up clothes, and preparing food when she knew about the danger.
14 left the baby alone when she was aware of the problems with the hot water. Mary Riley left her baby alone knowing she was physically capable of pulling herself up, she could move around, she could grab onto things, and she could turn things on. Mary Riley told us she knew of problems with hot water in the apartment, but she'd never told anyone. If Mary Riley had told someone at Garfield House Apartments about the hot water so that they could have done something about it, and	14 Again, using words from the cross-examination, counsel can emphasize the theory of liability. Rita Riley would "pull herself up" and "grab" the faucet and "turn" it. These verbs accurately reflect the facts and the reasonable

Riley v. Garfield House Apartments

Defendant's Summation	Comments/Notes
if she had not left her baby alone in the tub, Rita Riley would not have been burned on Christmas Eve.	inference, an inference Rita Riley's mother drew herself when she heard the water running.
15 You will receive instructions from the judge concerning how the plaintiff must prove the actual cost of the injuries. That's called the damages. Those damages may only be proved by the facts— not by sympathy, not by conjecture, and not by speculation.	15 Ordinarily after arguing against defendant's liability, it is often difficult for the defense to admit damages. In this case, disfigurement is a physical fact. Medical expenses are documented and in evidence. The purpose is not to dispute the physical injury, but to attack the amount plaintiff claims is required. See *Trial Advocacy* Section 11.5 (C).
16 The plaintiffs have tried to prove damages for pain and suffering, by using speculation, conjecture, and sympathy to arrive at some figure they will request as compensation. They have not proved actual money damages by relying on the real facts. No one can predict the future. No one can predict how Rita will handle her injuries or how well she will heal. No one can know how well doctors will treat her, or what new medical technology will become available. They can't predict, they can't prove, they can only assume just as	16 Plaintiff will be asking for a significant amount of money for intangible damages. Defense counsel casts doubt on the justification for the figure by suggesting, at best, damages are mere approximations. Defense counsel reminds the jury of all the other inaccurate assumptions in the plaintiff's case.

Riley v. Garfield House Apartments

Defendant's Summation	Comments/Notes
Mary Riley assumed Garfield House Apartments wouldn't do anything about the problem, and just as she assumed her baby would be safe in the bathtub. The compensation they have requested for pain and suffering is based only on assumptions, without a real factual basis.	
17 It is very unfortunate that Rita Riley was injured. It is natural to be saddened by what she has had to go through. It is impossible not to sympathize with the Riley family. Sympathy cannot govern the decision making taking place here today. No mother wants to accept blame for the injuries to her daughter. It is difficult for her to live with. But, she can't shift the responsibility. This case must be decided	17 Counsel reminds the jury their duty is to decide based on the evidence, not sympathy.
18 on the evidence you've heard here today and the instructions you receive from the judge. The judge will tell you what the law is. Based on the evidence and the law the plaintiff was not able to prove the people at Garfield House Apartments were negligent.	18 Concluding the argument, counsel reminds the jury whatever emotions are created by the facts, their sympathy cannot outweigh the rational requirements of the law. Unless plaintiff proves all four elements of negligence, plaintiff cannot prevail. See *Trial Advocacy* Section 11.4 (D).

Riley v. Garfield House Apartments

Defendant's Summation	Comments/Notes
19 In summary, the people of Garfield House Apartments met their duty to provide a safe and habitable residence. Their duty did not include any obligation to protect Rita Riley from her mother's carelessness. The plaintiff could not prove any breach or failure to fulfill that responsibility because the people at Garfield House Apartments had adequately protected the water heater and had properly inspected and maintained it. Plaintiff also couldn't prove the actions of the people at Garfield House were the direct cause of the injuries to the little girl because it was her mother, who says she knew of the problems with hot water, who says she knew what her little baby was capable of, who left her baby there alone. The plaintiffs couldn't prove the extent of damages in actual dollars. The plaintiffs couldn't prove what they had to prove, and you must return a verdict in favor of the people at Garfield House Apartments.	19 Counsel's conclusion summarizes the argument: • Rita's mother cannot shift responsibility to remedy her carelessness—no duty. • The water heater was properly inspected and maintained—no breach. • The mother left the child alone and the mother knew the water could get excessively hot. The mother was responsible—no direct cause. • The magnitude of the child's injury has not been proved—little damages.

Riley v. Garfield House Apartments

Plaintiff's Summation	Comments/Notes

Judge:

You may now give your summation.

Plaintiff's Counsel:

Thank you your Honor.

1 What happened to Rita Riley on Christmas Eve three years ago is a devastating tragedy. It is a tragedy a little one-year-old baby has to

1 Counsel uses the first moments of summation to take advantage of the jury's peak attention and chooses not to thank the jury for fulfilling their civic duty attentively and faithfully. See *Trial Advocacy* Section 11.1.

2 experience terrible pain. It is a terrible tragedy the little girl is going to have to experience the physical and emotional

2 Counsel begins not with the events leading to the tragedy, but to its aftermath—damages.

3 suffering she will in the future. She is going to experience great physical pain as a result of the many skin grafts she's going to have to undergo in the future. She is going to experience emotional pain as a result of the scars and disfigurement. She is going to experience a great deal of hurt and pain in her mind and in her heart as she develops from a little girl to a young woman to a mature adult.

3 Counsel repeats the word "tragedy" three times, and uses the word "experience" three times as a preface. This form of repetition, if reasonably done, can be effective.

Riley v. Garfield House Apartments

Plaintiff's Summation	Comments/Notes
4 What really makes this a tragedy is those injuries never should have happened. They need never have occurred. The defendant corporation had a duty to provide a safe and livable residence for the tenants of the apartment complex. They didn't do it. They had an obligation to provide a water heater that worked properly. And they just didn't do it. As a result of its failure to fulfill its obligations, the little girl was burned and scalded over more than one-third of her body, and she's going to have to live with the physical and mental scars of that incident for the rest of her life.	4 After briefly refreshing the jury's recollection of Rita Riley's medical expenses and pain and suffering, counsel turns from the tragic effect to its causes. Repetition of the word "tragedy" allows counsel to support plaintiff's damages by emphasizing the sources of liability: Defendant's negligent omissions. See *Trial Advocacy* Section 11.5 (A).
5 We have met our burden of proof—what the law calls and what the judge will explain as the preponderance of the evidence, which proves that the defendant was negligent by the greater weight of the evidence. We have proved, in other words, that it's more likely than not that what we say happened, did happen.	5 Counsel decides to briefly mention the burden of proof and leave it for the judge to describe in more detail.

Riley v. Garfield House Apartments

Plaintiff's Summation	Comments/Notes
6 We had to prove four things, and we did. This chart lists what we proved. We proved the defendant corporation had a duty, an obligation, to that little girl. We proved it breached that obligation. It failed to fulfill its duty. We proved its failure to fulfill its obligation was the proximate cause, the direct cause, of the injuries to that little baby. And last, we proved she was hurt, she suffered pain, she was damaged. We proved those four things, and we didn't rely on sympathy. We didn't have to. We relied on the facts.	6 Plaintiff clearly sets out the elements and explains how each has been proved. Counsel also uses a visual aid during summation to hold the jurors' attention and to make it easier for counsel to talk to the jurors without relying on notes. See *Trial Advocacy* Section 11.5 (B).
7 Now, the defendant corporation was in the business of renting apartments to tenants who had reasonable expectations. They had every right to expect that those premises were safe. Defendant corporation has admitted it had a duty to maintain the apartment in a safe and habitable condition. In addition, because of the vandalism that it was aware of at the apartment complex, it	7 Counsel forcefully summarizes the evidence which proves the first element of the defendant's negligence, which is duty. The fact words parallel the evidence: Defendant was "in the business" of renting and defendant admitted its "duty" to "maintain" the safety of the premises. The conclusory words parallel the reasonableness of the plaintiff's theory: Defendant

Riley v. Garfield House Apartments

Plaintiff's Summation	Comments/Notes
had a duty to ensure the safety of the water heater. The defendant had a duty to ensure the safety of the tenants, the guests of the tenants and, in this particular case, that little baby. We proved the defendant corporation breached its duty and it failed to fulfill its obligation because it didn't properly inspect, maintain, and adequately protect that water heater.	failed to protect the premises from vandals; defendant failed to inspect and maintain the water heater; therefore, defendant breached its duty. Counsel uses words based on reason, not emotion or exaggerated facts.
8 Dr. Armstead, an expert safety analyst, told you it was her opinion, because she had seen similar kinds of incidents, that an enclosure constructed out of two-by-fours and chicken wire mesh was not adequate to protect the water heater from vandals tampering with or damaging it. Even though the wire was replaced when damaged, the replacement was still inadequate.	8 The story of liability is brought out through summaries of the lay and expert testimony and exhibits— inadequate safeguards against a known problem, vandalism, the service contract and Connie Austern's responsibility, and her lack of knowledge and training. See *Trial Advocacy* Section 11.5.
The defendant also failed to properly inspect and maintain the water heater.	
Connie Austern told you even though there was a	

Riley v. Garfield House Apartments

Plaintiff's Summation	Comments/Notes
service contract with the company in town providing maintenance on the water heater, she still is primarily responsible. She didn't know when the water heater	
9 had been inspected last. She didn't know if anyone had been called to do a service check or do anything to the water heater. She was responsible and didn't know. Connie Austern was incapable of performing the necessary maintenance herself. She didn't have an operator's manual and she hadn't read any. In fact, she hadn't even seen the manual in the six years she had worked in the apartment complex. She had no training. No one working for her had any training in the maintenance of the water heaters. She told you she would check the thermostat on the water heater to see that it was at the proper setting, but she didn't know whether the thermostat was accurate in recording the temperature in the water heater. She didn't know how	9 To explain the relationship of the evidence to inadequate methods of inspection and maintenance, counsel draws on all the negatives in Connie Austern's testimony: no manual available, no manual ever read in the past, or even seen; no training; no ability to check for accurate temperature readings; no way to adjust an inaccurate dial, to change a safety valve, to even know the proper setting. See *Trial Advocacy* Section 11.3 (C).

Riley v. Garfield House Apartments

Plaintiff's Summation	Comments/Notes
to change it if it wasn't working. She didn't know how the pressure setting was supposed to be set. Connie Austern didn't know whether the water heater had been inspected or maintained and, even though she had the responsibility of making sure it was done, she personally didn't know very much about the water heater.	
We next proved the defendant's failure to fulfill its obligation was a direct cause of the injuries to	
10 Rita Riley. Maybe Mary Riley shouldn't have left her little baby in the bathtub. With 20–20 hindsight, we might be sure she shouldn't have done that. But she had no reason to expect hot water was going to come surging out of the faucet, particularly when the arrow was on medium. If the defendant corporation had adequately protected the water heater, and if the defendant corporation had properly inspected and maintained that water heater, that	10 Counsel reduces the impact of the mother's negligence. Counsel acknowledges her misjudgment without calling it a mistake and then offers a reasonable explanation: the mother had no reason to expect scalding water to surge out, particularly if the lever were pushed to medium. The "hot water" serves as a transition and counsel turns the blame back on the defendant for improper inspection and maintenance of the source of the hot water. See *Trial Advocacy* Section 11.3 (D).

Riley v. Garfield House Apartments

Plaintiff's Summation	Comments/Notes
baby girl wouldn't have been burned with water at a temperature of 210 degrees Fahrenheit—just two degrees below boiling, even if she turned the faucet on in the hot position. Water that hot should never come out of a household faucet and no hot water should ever come out when a faucet is on medium. It is reasonable for the defendant to foresee that children may be alone in a bathtub. It is reasonable to expect the defendant to have a water system that will work. It is reasonable to expect the defendant to have a water system that will not scald a child when the water setting is on medium.	
11 Finally, we proved damages. There were medical expenses, and there was pain and suffering. Mary Riley told you that she has documented $157,875 in medical expenses so far. It is going to cost much more to treat Rita Riley over the next ten to fifteen years.	11 After linking defendant with the causes of the tragedy, counsel returns to the aftermath—Rita's damages. Damages are used to create the psychological impact compelling the jury's verdict for plaintiff. Counsel argues permissible elements of damages such as actual medical expenses, future medical expenses, disfigurement, mental anguish,

---

Riley v. Garfield House Apartments

Plaintiff's Summation	Comments/Notes

All the money in the world will not restore Rita Riley's normal life to her. Money will never take away her scars. If only we could make her whole again. But, we cannot. All we can say to her is "You have suffered, and it's the defendant's fault." That is all the law can do. We can and must tell her that her life, the pain she suffers, the scars she has, do have a value. We can and must tell her she has a value. We are asking you to compensate her in the amount of one million nine hundred and fifty-seven thousand dollars. That amount of money is substantial, but it's not too much to compensate that little girl for the pain she's gone through in the past, what she's going through now, and what she'll go through every day for the rest of her life. Rita is a very young little girl. If she lives a reasonable life, say sixty-five or more years, that amount makes a lot of sense. We suggest to you that $357,000 of that amount will pay for past and present medical expenses,

past pain and suffering, present and future pain and suffering. The jury may balk at a large amount for intangible damages. Counsel acknowledges that the amount is large, but uses concrete damages to parallel the great pain Rita suffered and will suffer all her life: six months of hospitalization, skin that came off in her mother's hands, physical disfigurement, and consequent emotional scarring that will affect her relationships all her life. Counsel uses the phases of Rita's future life and casts them in terms of adverse human relationships: mocking children, painful adolescence, marred social interaction. This emotional cluster illustrates Rita's intangible damages. Significantly, not all of Rita's pain is emotional. Her disfigurement has caused real physical limitations on her activities. See *Trial Advocacy* Section 11.5.

Riley v. Garfield House Apartments

Plaintiff's Summation	Comments/Notes
for all the operations Rita has needed and will need over the next ten to fifteen years. We suggest that $1,600,000 of that amount will compensate Rita for the staggering pain and suffering she has had to and will endure the remainder of her life. When you consider that over one hundred and fifty thousand dollars is for medical costs already spent and there will be enormous medical bills, then a million, six hundred thousand dollars is a reasonable amount of money to compensate her for her pain, disfigurement, emotional suffering, and loss of a normal life. She will suffer for nearly seventy years and one million, six hundred thousand dollars will compensate her less than twenty-five thousand a year for her terrible loss. Mere money can never be enough, but this is a reasonable amount. That little girl went through tremendous pain from the very instant she was scalded. She has experienced the kind of pain	

Riley v. Garfield House Apartments	
Plaintiff's Summation	**Comments/Notes**

that takes extensive medical treatment before she could even leave the hospital, pain that is so intense that when her mother came to help her out of that hot water, the skin came off in her mother's hands. That's only an example of the pain that little girl has suffered in the past.

You saw her when she came to this courtroom yesterday. She will suffer great physical and emotional pain in the future. She's going to go through a great deal in terms of living with those scars. As a youngster, other children are going to treat her differently because of her disfigurement. As a teenager, she's not going to be able to engage in the activities her friends do, such as swimming, because she's going to be more susceptible to burns and more susceptible to further injuries. More importantly, she's not going to be able to engage in many of those activities because of the humiliation and embarrassment that come

Trial Transcript 183

Riley v. Garfield House Apartments

Plaintiff's Summation	Comments/Notes
from her disfigurement. As an adult, she's always going to wonder whether she's going to get hurt in terms of her relationships with others because of the way they perceive and react to her scars. The testimony you've heard here and the instructions you'll receive from the judge prove that there must be a verdict in favor of Rita Riley. You will be given a verdict form that you are to complete during your deliberations. I have the verdict form on this screen, and you see that it contains five questions you will need to answer. I will briefly go through these five questions with you and suggest how they should be answered.	
12 The first question reads, and you can read silently along with me: Was defendant Garfield House Apartments or its employee, Connie Austern, negligent? Yes__ No__	12 Counsel has had the verdict form enlarged on a monitor so all the jurors can see and read the questions. It also appears on the laptop so counsel can enter in the answers to the questions. This visual aid helps the jury understand what they must do during deliberations and increases the chances that the jury will properly complete the form. See *Trial Advocacy* Section 11.3 (E).

Riley v. Garfield House Apartments

Plaintiff's Summation	Comments/Notes
The answer to this question, based on all the evidence, is "yes," and you should write in the word "yes" on this line. The second question reads:	

Was Mary Riley negligent?

Yes__ No__

The answer to this question is no. Rita's mother acted reasonably in the circumstances and ought not to be responsible for the defendant's negligence. You may have a doubt about whether Mary Riley made the best decision in leaving Rita in the bathtub, but her conduct was not negligent.

The third question reads:

If you answered "yes" to both questions 1 and 2, then answer this: Taking the combined fault which contributed to the accident as 100%, what percentage do you attribute to:

A. Garfield House

Apartments ____ %

B. Mary Riley ____ %

Total 100 %

Riley v. Garfield House Apartments

Plaintiff's Summation	Comments/Notes
13　You need not answer this question if you only answered "yes" to question No. 1, and "no" to question No. 2, and you can move on to questions regarding damages. There are amounts of money you will need to write in to answer Questions 4 and 5. Question 4 deals with damages Rita has already suffered, and Question 5 deals with damages she will suffer in the future. Question 4 reads: What sum of money will fairly and adequately compensate Rita Riley for damages up to the date of this verdict for: A. Medical expenses $_____$. B. Embarrassment, emotional distress, pain, disability, and disfigurement $_____$. You have heard the undisputed evidence in this case that the present medical expenses are $157,875. And that is the amount you should put on this line.	13　With regard to Questions 2 and 3, counsel decides not to suggest to the jury that Mary Riley may have been partially negligent. Other lawyers may have argued: "Some of you may have a doubt about whether Mary Riley acted properly in leaving Rita in the bathtub. But, her actions should not be used as an excuse—which the defendant has argued—to avoid the duties and responsibilities of Garfield Apartments. You may find Mary Riley, perhaps, 10% negligent, but not any higher percentage. The defendant caused this accident, and its efforts to shift the blame to Mary Riley is yet another effort to avoid its responsibility." See *Trial Advocacy* Section 11.3 (D).

Riley v. Garfield House Apartments	
Plaintiff's Summation	**Comments/Notes**

Plaintiff's Summation

Earlier I suggested that a total of $1,600,000 is reasonable compensation for Rita for all her pain and suffering. Of that amount, Rita has suffered $350,000 up to the time of this trial, and that amount should be placed on this line, as I am doing now.

The damages Rita will suffer in the future are included in Question 5, which reads:

What sum of money will fairly and adequately compensate Rita Riley for such future damages as are reasonably certain to occur for:

A. Medical expenses $_____

B. Embarrassment, emotional distress, pain, disability, and disfigurement $_____.

A reasonably certain amount of medical expenses Rita will incur in the future is $200,000. That amount is a conservative figure, and the skyrocketing medical costs could easily double or triple that figure over the next ten to fifteen years. A reasonably certain amount for pain and

Riley v. Garfield House Apartments

Plaintiff's Summation	Comments/Notes
suffering is $1,350,000 for the rest of Rita's life. Again, while that is a large amount of money, it is a conservative amount.	
14 No amount of money can ever compensate Rita for what she will have to live with as a result of this accident. The law provides that the only way Rita can be compensated in a tragic case like this is with money. The law holds those responsible for causing Rita these terrible injuries to pay her for this tragic accident. You, as guardians of the law, must hold the defendant Garfield House Apartments responsible for such negligence. The only way that can be done is for you to return a verdict for Rita Riley. A verdict based on the law and the evidence in this case. A verdict based on justice.	14 Counsel has covered all the essential elements and because the argument is simple, straightforward, and short, counsel can maintain the jury's attention. See *Trial Advocacy* Section 11.6.

Riley v. Garfield House Apartments

Judge's Final Instructions to the Jury	Comments/Notes
1 In defining the duties of the jury, let me first give you a few general rules: It is your duty to find the facts from all the evidence in the case. To the facts as you find them, you must apply the law as I give it to you.	1 These sources of jury instructions are from jury instruction guides. See *Trial Advocacy* Section 12.2.
2 The questions you must decide will be submitted to you in the form of a special verdict consisting of five questions. You must answer these questions by applying the facts and the law.	2 Some judges read the instructions rapidly while others take more time. A great deal of information is being given to the jurors, and there is some question as to how much the jurors can retain from these complex instructions. Many judges provide the instructions to the jurors in writing so they can review them during their deliberation.
3 You must follow the law as I give it to you, whether you agree with it or not. That means you must decide the case solely on the evidence before you. In following my instructions, you must follow all of them and not single out some and ignore others. They are all equally important. You must not read into these instructions, or into anything the court may have said or done, as a suggestion from the court as to what the verdict should be or how special verdict questions should be answered.	3 The clear explanation of the role of the jury in regard to the law and facts is important and should be spelled out in all instructions. The relation of the law to the facts and the importance to be placed on the instructions must be defined precisely.

Riley v. Garfield House Apartments

Judge's Final Instructions to the Jury	Comments/Notes
You must consider these instructions as a whole and regard each instruction in the light of all the others. The order in which the instructions are given is of no significance.	
Deciding questions of fact is your exclusive responsibility. In doing so, you must consider all the evidence you have heard and seen in this trial, and the reasonable inferences to be drawn from that evidence. You must do your duty as jurors regardless of any personal likes or dislikes, opinions, prejudices, emotions or sympathy.	
4 Attorneys are officers of the court. It is their duty to present evidence on behalf of their clients, to make such objections as they deem proper, and to argue fully their client's cause. However, the arguments or remarks of the attorneys are not evidence in this case.	4 All judges give some type of instruction concerning comments and actions of the courts and the attorneys, the meaning of objections and rulings by the court, circumstantial evidence and the criteria to use to weigh credibility and testimony of each witness. Attorneys often refer to these instructions during summation. See *Trial Advocacy* Section 12.2 (B).

Riley v. Garfield House Apartments

Judge's Final Instructions to the Jury	Comments/Notes
If the attorneys have made, or if I have made or should make, any statement as to what the evidence is, which differs from your recollection of the evidence, then you should disregard the statement and rely solely upon your own memory. If the attorneys' arguments contain any statements of the law different from the law I give you, you should disregard the attorneys' statements. During the trial, I have ruled on objections to certain testimony and exhibits. You must not concern yourselves with the reasons for my rulings since they are controlled by rules of law. Objections to questions are not evidence. Lawyers have an obligation to their clients to make an objection when they believe evidence being offered should not be admitted under the rules of evidence. If the objection is sustained, ignore the question. If it is overruled, treat the answer like any other.	

Riley v. Garfield House Apartments

Judge's Final Instructions to the Jury	Comments/Notes
By receiving evidence to which an objection was made, I did not intend to indicate the weight to be given such evidence. You are to disregard all evidence ordered stricken. A fact may be proved by either direct or circumstantial evidence, or by both. The law does not prefer one form of evidence over the other. A fact is proved by direct evidence when, for example, it is proved by witnesses who testify to what they saw, heard, or experienced, or by physical evidence of the fact itself. A fact is proved by circumstantial evidence when its existence can be reasonably inferred from other facts proved in the case. You are the sole judges of whether a witness is to be believed and the weight to be given to the testimony of each witness. There are no hard and fast rules to guide you in this respect. In determining the believability of	

Trial Transcript 192

Riley v. Garfield House Apartments	
Judge's Final Instructions to the Jury	**Comments/Notes**

the witnesses and weight to be given to their testimony, consider the following:

- Their interest or lack of interest in the outcome of the case.

- Their relationship to the parties.

- Their ability and opportunity to know, remember, and relate the facts.

- Their manner, appearance, and experience.

- Their frankness and sincerity.

- The reasonableness or unreasonableness of their testimony in the light of all the other evidence in the case.

- Any impeachment of their testimony.

- Any other factors that bear on believability and weight.

You should in the last analysis rely upon your own experience, good judgment, and common sense.

A witness who has special training, education or experience in a particular science, profession or calling is allowed to express an opinion.

Trial Transcript 193

Riley v. Garfield House Apartments

Judge's Final Instructions to the Jury	Comments/Notes
In determining the believability and the weight to be given such opinion evidence, you may consider, among other things: • The education, training, experience, knowledge and ability of the witness. • The reasons given for the witness' opinion. • The sources of the witness' information. • Factors already given you for evaluating the testimony of a witness. Such opinion evidence is entitled to neither more nor less consideration by you than the fact evidence presented.	
5 A special verdict form has been prepared for you. You must complete it. It states: 1. Was defendant Garfield House Apartments or its employee, Connie Austern, negligent? Yes __ No __ 2. Was Mary Riley negligent? Yes __ No__ 3. If you answered "yes" to both questions 1 and 2,	5 Special verdict forms permit the jurors to focus on the issues and permit the judge to determine the allocation of the award of damages that may be required because of insurance settlements or other considerations required by law in the particular jurisdiction. See *Trial Advocacy* Section 12.2 (C). This verdict form is a condensed form. In many jurisdictions, additional questions

Riley v. Garfield House Apartments

Judge's Final Instructions to the Jury

Comments/Notes

then answer this: Taking the combined fault which contributed to the accident as 100%, what percentage do you attribute to:

    A.   Garfield   House Apartments _____ %

    B. Mary Riley _____ %

    Total 100 %

4. What sum of money will fairly and adequately compensate Rita Riley for damages up to the date of this verdict for:

    A. Medical expenses? $____

    B.   Embarrassment, emotional distress, pain, disability and disfigurement? $____

5. What sum of money will fairly and adequately compensate Rita Riley for such future damages as are reasonably certain to occur for:

    A. Medical expenses? $____

    B.   Embarrassment, emotional distress, pain, disability and disfigurement? $____

would be asked whether the negligent acts were a direct cause of the injuries. In some jurisdictions, the damage questions would be further subdivided according to the different types of damages.

Trial Transcript 195

Riley v. Garfield House Apartments

Judge's Final Instructions to the Jury

	Comments/Notes
In order to answer any question "yes," the greater weight of the evidence must support such an answer, otherwise you should answer the question "no." Greater weight of the evidence means all of the evidence produced must lead you to believe it is more likely the claim is true than not true. If the evidence does not lead you to believe it is more likely the claim is true than not true, then the claim has not been proven by the greater weight of the evidence. The greater weight of the evidence does not necessarily mean the greater number of witnesses or the greater volume of testimony. Any believable evidence may be a sufficient basis to prove a fact.	

Riley v. Garfield House Apartments

Judge's Final Instructions to the Jury	Comments/Notes
6 Negligence is the failure to use reasonable care. Reasonable care is that care which a reasonable person would use under like circumstances. Negligence is the doing of something which a reasonable person would not do, or the failure to do something which a reasonable person would do, under like circumstances. But, an act or omission is not negligence if no risk of injury could have been reasonably anticipated or foreseen.

The law requires negligence be apportioned among those parties found to be at fault in causing the plaintiff's injuries. If by your answers to questions 1 and 2 you have determined two are negligent and their negligence was a direct cause of plaintiff's injuries, you must apportion negligence among them. A direct cause is a cause which had a substantial part in bringing about the injury either immediately or through happenings which follow one after another. | 6 This instruction begins the instruction on the law specific to this case. This type of instruction is typical; however, the law applicable to cases of this type will vary from jurisdiction to jurisdiction. See *Trial Advocacy* Section 12.2 (A). |

Riley v. Garfield House Apartments

Judge's Final Instructions to the Jury	Comments/Notes

In answering questions 4 and 5, you are to determine the amount of money which will fairly and adequately compensate Rita Riley for her past and future injuries, giving consideration only to such of the following items as shown by the evidence to have resulted from the accident.

The reasonable value of medical supplies and hospital and medical services of every kind, necessary for treatment including the reasonable value of the services of attendants required for Rita Riley's care.

Any pain, disability, disfigurement, embarrassment, or emotional distress experienced by reason of Rita Riley's injuries up to the time of trial. There is no yardstick by which you can value these items exactly. They are not necessarily determined on a per diem or per hour basis. You should consider the nature, extent, and severity of the injuries, how painful they were, what the treatment

Trial Transcript 198

Riley v. Garfield House Apartments

Judge's Final Instructions to the Jury	Comments/Notes
was and the pain connected with it, how long the injuries persisted, and such other factors as, in your judgment bear upon the matter.	
The reasonable value of necessary medical supplies and hospital and medical services including the services of attendants required for Rita Riley's care that are reasonably certain to be required in the future.	
Such pain, disability, disfigurement, embarrassment or emotional distress as Rita Riley is reasonably certain to experience in the future.	
When you retire to the jury room, you will select one of your number to act as foreperson to preside over your deliberations.	
7 The final test of the quality of your service will be in the verdict which you as a jury return to this court. You will make a definite contribution to the efficient administration of justice if you arrive at a just and proper verdict.	7 These instructions have been condensed and represent generally applicable instructions. The attorneys must review the precise details of the instructions well in advance of trial. Instructions that are generally given in a case in the jurisdiction in which the case is going to be tried affect how the attorneys approach the presentation of their case and their argument. See *Trial Advocacy* Section 12.2.

Trial Transcript 199

Riley v. Garfield House Apartments

Jury Deliberations and Verdict	Comments/Notes
Judge to the Clerk:	
Please swear the bailiff to take charge of the jury during their deliberations.	
Jury Deliberations	
Foreperson:	
8 Thank you all again for putting me in charge. I would like to go around the table and ask each one of you to tell us, whether you think the defendant Garfield House Apartments was responsible, whether you think Ms. Riley was responsible, and also whether the little girl should get any money and how much.	8 There is no typical jury deliberation. This dialogue is an example based on reviews of video recorded jury deliberations in simulated cases. See *Trial Advocacy* Section 12.3.
Will you go first, Maria?	
Maria Alvarez:	
Ms. Riley was negligent, but I have left my kids alone for awhile and that faucet should never have been so hot, so I say 30% for Ms. Riley and Connie Austern was 70% at fault. I don't think that Connie Austern will have to pay anything because the owners of the apartment building are the defendants. I think the little	

Riley v. Garfield House Apartments

Jury Deliberations and Verdict	Comments/Notes
girl was really hurt and her burns were bad, but I do think they will get better, so I think she should get maybe a million dollars.	

Foreperson:

Ann, how about you?

Ann Bier:

Well, I do think Ms. Riley should have been more careful, but if we vote she is really negligent, little Rita won't get anything, so I'll say 80% for the defendant. I also think the injuries are really bad, but I just can't go along with a million dollars. I'll never make that much in my whole life. I think $500,000 is plenty. If she puts it in a bank, I'll bet she could get $50,000 a year.

Foreperson:

Chris, what do you think?

Chris Gard:

I'd like to see the baby get some money, but I think we have to follow the law. I think the mother had warning and should have known better. I'd say 90% negligence for

Riley v. Garfield House Apartments

Jury Deliberations and Verdict	Comments/Notes

Ms. Riley, and I'll split the difference on money and say $750,000.

Foreperson:

Garret, how about you?

Garret Raymond:

Well, I just don't know . . ..

The Verdict

Judge:

The record will reflect that all counsel and all parties are present in the court. Members of the jury have you reached a verdict?

Foreperson:

Yes, we have your Honor.

Judge:

Will you please give the verdict form to the clerk, who will give it to me.

I will now read the verdict and I will ask if this is your true and correct verdict, so please listen carefully. The verdict reads as follows . . . .

What is your verdict? And why? Critique the lawyers. How well did they do? Why?

SECTION FOUR

ARBITRATION HEARING TRANSCRIPT

BINGHAM v. ECOTRONICS

A video of this arbitration appears at
http://software.westacademic.com/lawyering-skills/.

ARBITRATION

Bingham v. Ecotronics
TRANSCRIPT

The following transcript presents an arbitration hearing. The case demonstrates advocacy strategies, tactics, and techniques discussed in the companion *Trial Advocacy Before Judges, Jurors, and Arbitrators* text. Comments appear in the transcript explaining the advocacy approaches. This case illustrates how lawyers try an arbitration case, how the various stages of a case interrelate, how evidence is introduced, how case theories are presented, and how strategies and tactics affect the decision of a case. A video of this arbitration appears at http://software.westacademic.com/lawyering-skills/.

This arbitration involves a claim of age discrimination and a breach of employment contract brought by Lester Bingham against Ecotronics, his former employer. Ecotronics asserts that Les Bingham was an at will employee and that he was terminated because his position at the company was eliminated and he did not perform his duties appropriately.

The arbitration transcript contains an edited version of a complete arbitration hearing, although not all of the witnesses who would normally have testified appear, and includes the following:

- Introductory remarks by the Arbitrator

- Opening Statements by the Claimant and Respondent

- Direct and Cross-Examination of Claimant Lester Bingham

- Direct and Cross-Examination of Jessica Martindale for the Respondent

- Summations by Respondent and Claimant

- Closing remarks by the Arbitrator

As you read through the transcript, consider the various strategies, tactics, and techniques presented and analyze the effectiveness of these lawyers and what you would have done similarly or differently to produce a favorable award. Section references in this *Supplement* refer to sections in *Trial Advocacy Before Judges, Jurors, and Arbitrators*.

Bingham v. Ecotronics

Arbitrator Preliminary Instructions?	Comments/Notes
Arbitrator:	
1 Good morning. This is the arbitration of Les Bingham as a Claimant, and Ecotronics Incorporated, the Respondent. My name is Jerry Blackwell, and I will be arbitrating this matter today. I see I have counsel present here at the table with a couple of persons accompanying each of you. Why don't I take just a moment to have you tell me who you are, who you represent and who you have brought along with you at the table today.	1 Generally, arbitrators make some kind of introductory remarks to the people present at the arbitration. Those remarks vary depending on what the participants need to know. The Arbitrator, Mr. Blackwell, addresses his remarks both to the Attorneys and to the parties. In effect he is telling them how he expects the arbitration to proceed. See *Trial Advocacy* Section 2.2 (E).
Claimant's Attorney:	
Thank you, Mr. Blackwell. My name is Tyrone Bujold. I am the attorney for Les Bingham, the Claimant. He is seated next to me.	
Arbitrator:	
Good morning, Mr. Bingham.	

Arbitration Transcript 3

Bingham v. Ecotronics

Arbitrator Preliminary Instructions?	Comments/Notes
Respondent's Attorney: Mr. Blackwell, my name is Karen Kingsley. I am representing Ecotronics. Here with me today is Jessica Martindale. She is the personnel manager for Ecotronics. **Arbitrator:** Good morning, Ms. Martindale. Before we get into the specifics of the arbitration itself, I want to give you an overview of the process. Having seen both attorneys at other arbitrations, I know that you both are very experienced with the process. But for the benefit of the persons sitting with you, I would like you to know I have had an opportunity to read all of the papers and submissions you have given to me.	

Arbitration Transcript 4

Bingham v. Ecotronics

Arbitrator Preliminary Instructions?	Comments/Notes
2 They are all well done. I appreciated them. The information is most helpful to me.	2 By this statement, Arbitrator Blackwell informs everyone that he has read the documents, that he understands the factual and legal issues, and that he is prepared. See *Trial Advocacy* Section 1.3 (B).
3 Because this is an arbitration, I will give you far more latitude with respect to admissibility of evidence than you would have at a regular trial in a case like this. Having said that, if I hear certain evidence and it appears to me that it is not relevant or reliable, even for purposes of this process, I'll have to deem it not admissible. Is that all right?	3 The rules of evidence are ordinarily relaxed in arbitrations. However, the effective use of the evidentiary rules assist in a more persuasive presentation. The rules are practical tools to assist the attorneys. The Arbitrator makes clear that there are limits that he will enforce: irrelevant and unreliable evidence will be excluded. See *Trial Advocacy* Section 4.1 (B).

Respondent's Attorney:

That's fine.

Claimant's Attorney:

Certainly. Understood.

Arbitrator:

I'll give each of you a full and fair opportunity to present your full case. I want to hear all the facts and the law that you feel will be

Arbitration Transcript 5

Bingham v. Ecotronics

Arbitrator Preliminary Instructions?	Comments/Notes
relevant and helpful to me in making a decision at the close of this arbitration. I would request that each of you begin with a brief opening statement. While	4 In many arbitrations, considerable discussion between the attorneys and the arbitrator has occurred before the beginning of the case. In these cases a thorough opening statement may not be necessary. In this case, Arbitrator Blackwell expects the attorneys to make a presentation that will provide him information setting out the extent and limits of the dispute. See *Trial Advocacy* Section 3.11 (A).
4 I do not always expect opening statements; in this case I would like to have a brief opening statement from each attorney. The purpose is to give me a good idea of the critical facts in this matter and to give me a good overview of the law that I	
5 will need to reach a decision at the close of this matter.	5 In an opening statement before a jury, a discussion of the law is generally not permitted. In an arbitration, where there is a debate as to the application of the law and a debate as to the facts, it is important to make both a vigorous legal and factual opening statement that will set groundwork for the presentation of the evidence. See *Trial Advocacy* Section 6.1 (B).
I think both of you have come prepared to make an opening. Is that right?	
Respondent's Attorney:	
That's right.	
Claimant's Attorney:	
Yes, that is correct.	

Bingham v. Ecotronics

Arbitrator Preliminary Instructions?	Comments/Notes
Arbitrator:	
Following the opening statements from each of you, Mr. Bujold, as the Claimant, has the burden of proof here. You will present your case first. And what that will mean is that you will be calling certain witnesses who will testify in support of the claims you have made in this matter. After you have presented your witnesses, for example, Mr. Bingham, Ms. Kingsley will have an opportunity to cross-examine him	
Claimant's Attorney:	
Yes.	
Arbitrator:	
6 Following Ms. Kingsley's cross examination, you may have an opportunity to conduct a redirect examination of the same witness and in turn she may then conduct a re-cross exam. I don't think we will need to go much further than that for this	6 In arbitrations the order of argument and presentation of witnesses may vary considerably. The law of the applicable jurisdiction will determine who has the burden of proof. Normally, the party with the burden of

Bingham v. Ecotronics	
Arbitrator Preliminary Instructions?	**Comments/Notes**

7 type of a case.

Once the Claimant's case is put in, then Ms. Kingsley may present the Respondent's case. It will be the same process. You call each of your witnesses. You have a chance to conduct a direct examination. Mr. Bujold will have a chance to conduct a cross-examination.   Finally, once again there will be an opportunity for very limited redirect exam, and recross-examination.

Ms. Kingsley, once you have presented your case, Mr. Bujold will have a chance to present rebuttal evidence for the Claimant. This will be to rebut whatever new facts that were elicited during the Respondent's case, and you will have an opportunity to do the same, Ms. Kingsley.

proof will give the first opening statement, present witnesses first and will either have the first closing argument—followed by the other side's closing—and then a rebuttal, or, as in this case, will present the last final argument. See *Trial Advocacy* Section 2.12.

In this case, the law and the employee contract require the Claimant, Mr. Bingham, to prove that he was unlawfully fired. Therefore, the Claimant gives the first opening statement and will argue last.

7 The scope of redirect and recross examination is limited. The redirect examination is limited to new matters brought out in cross-examination.   Recross-examination is limited to new matters brought out in the redirect. The Arbitrator will not permit the Attorneys to continue to present the same information. See *Trial Advocacy* Section 3.6 (G).

Arbitration Transcript 8

Bingham v. Ecotronics

Arbitrator Preliminary Instructions?	Comments/Notes
Following all of the witness presentations, once all the evidence is in, and I've heard all that you both think I need to hear from witnesses, you will each have a chance to make a closing argument. The closing arguments are simply summations of the evidence you presented. I expect you to argue the facts and the relevant law to give me, in a nutshell, what it is you think I'll need to take away with me from this proceeding to make a decision. Okay?	
Respondent's Attorney:	
That's fine.	
Claimant's Attorney:	
Yes, thank you.	
Arbitrator:	
8 Feel free at any time to ask any questions as we proceed along here.	8 In arbitrations, as opposed to trials there is often a give and take between the arbitrator and the attorneys. Arbitrator Blackwell emphasizes this and demonstrates his interest in a less formal proceeding. See *Trial Advocacy* Section 2.8 (F).

Arbitration Transcript 9

Bingham v. Ecotronics

Arbitrator Preliminary Instructions?	Comments/Notes
9 I may, from time to time, ask questions of your witnesses. Now if I ask those questions, it won't be to assist any party in presenting its case. It won't be to necessarily bring out any facts that weren't otherwise elicited. It will simply be for purposes of my own clarification. If I didn't understand exactly what the witness was saying, I may ask some questions.	9 In bench trials, some judges will occasionally involve themselves in the taking of evidence. However, in arbitrations the practice may vary. In this case Mr. Blackwell makes it clear that should he feel a matter is not clear, he will ask clarification questions. See *Trial Advocacy* Section 3.7 (F).
10 In regard to other just general housekeeping matters before we get started here, have there been any stipulations in regard to any of the facts or exhibits that we'll be hearing today or seeing today? **Respondent's Attorney:** Mr. Blackwell, we stipulated to foundation for some of the documents, specifically the employment records, which will come in with the proviso that it's just as to foundation. Obviously, any questions as to	10 In many cases, the attorneys come to some agreement about the admissibility of certain evidence that can be entered into evidence through stipulation. While the attorneys in this matter have agreed that the documents are all accurate, Ms. Kingsley, the

Arbitration Transcript 10

Bingham v. Ecotronics

Arbitrator Preliminary Instructions?	Comments/Notes
the relevancy of the document, that type of thing will be addressed later.	Respondent's Attorney, makes it clear to Arbitrator Blackwell there are certain documents that the attorneys argue are not relevant. She is preserving her right to object should she consider some documents not relevant. See *Trial Advocacy* Section 3.11 (B).
Arbitrator:	
So all objections are preserved then.	
Claimant's Attorney:	
That is correct.	
Arbitrator:	
11 Now, with respect to the exhibits, I've seen copies of them. I take it all of the exhibits have been pre-marked already?	11 It is good practice to pre-mark all exhibits. It reduces confusion and saves time during the hearing.
Respondent's Attorney:	
Yes.	
Claimant's Attorney:	
Yes, they have.	
Arbitrator:	
12 Now, I had copies of your witness lists. Ms. Kingsley. I see that you have four witnesses on your list.	12 It is commonly expected in arbitrations, as well as in trials, that evidence lists be exchanged prior to the hearing.

Arbitration Transcript 11

Bingham v. Ecotronics

Arbitrator Preliminary Instructions?	Comments/Notes
Do you intend to call four witnesses? **Respondent's Attorney:** 13 Yes, I do. In addition, one of the witnesses I have listed is the Claimant. It's Mr. Bingham. We do intend to call him as a witness unless he will be called in the Claimant's case in chief. **Arbitrator:** All right. Mr. Bujold, you are planning to call Mr. Bingham, aren't you? **Claimant's Attorney:** Yes; certainly. **Respondent's Attorney:** Since Mr. Bingham will be called as a witness by Mr. Bujold, we will likely not call him as a witness. **Arbitrator:** When we are midway through the proceeding, in the morning,	13 Ms. Kingsley, the attorney for the Respondent, has listed the Claimant, Lester Bingham, as a witness on her witness list. She is indicating that should Mr. Bujold not call Mr. Bingham as a witness, she intends to call him as an adverse party and cross- examine him. See *Trial Advocacy* Section 3.6.

Arbitration Transcript 12

Bingham v. Ecotronics	
Arbitrator Preliminary Instructions?	**Comments/Notes**
close to lunch time, we'll take a break. As I said, anytime you want to ask a question or seek a clarification, or if at some other point in time you would like to take a break, just let me know, and we'll do that.	

Arbitration Transcript 13

Bingham v. Ecotronics

Opening Statement – Claimant	Comments/Notes
Arbitrator:	
Mr. Bujold, are you ready to proceed with your opening?	
Claimant's Attorney:	
1 Yes, thank you. Mr. Blackwell.	1 Both Mr. Bujold, for the Claimant, and Ms. Kingsley, for the Respondent, vigorously set out their positions. Each begins and concludes with their theme. Each sets out a brief outline of their positions, followed by the details which allows the Arbitrator to see the case in context. Both are short, succinct, clear, and understandable. See *Trial Advocacy* Section 6.3 (B)
2 Les Bingham was fired by Ecotronics after 15 years of service last November. He was fired improperly. He was fired because Ecotronics thought he was too old. He was only 54 years of	
3 age when they fired him. When he was 39 years of age, he was recruited by Ecotronics to work as a manager of marketing. Now Ecotronics is a company that is in the business of cleaning up after ecological and pollution problems such as oil spills or contaminated ground problems. Mr. Bingham's responsibility over his 15 year career included first, negotiating and closing contracts, second, supervising site staffing decisions, third,	2 The claimant's attorney, Mr. Bujold, does not hesitate to boldly set out the theme of this case that Mr. Bingham was improperly fired because the Respondent, Ecotronics, thought he was too old.
	3 Following the bold statement of his theme, the Attorney provides a

Arbitration Transcript 14

Bingham v. Ecotronics

Opening Statement – Claimant	Comments/Notes
negotiating contracts with sub-contractors, and fourth, finally, managing follow up with clients.	brief background in which he brings out information that may not be relevant to the case but personalizes Mr. Bingham, particularly in the areas of his job, and the fact that he has not been able to find other employment.
At age 54, Mr. Bingham has now found it impossible to gain employment in the field for which he was trained. In fact, the evidence will show, rather than being in the younger class of up and coming managers that he was when he was recruited by Ecotronics at 39, they say he is now in a class called "retirement."	
4 Ecotronics says that Les Bingham was fired because he was an employee at will. Ecotronics says it needs no justification for firing Les Bingham.	4 In the following statements the attorney sets out the four improper reasons for which Mr. Bingham was fired. His failure to enter into an improper early retirement program, age discrimination, the subterfuge concerning his employment history and the company's failure to follow its own rules.
Ecotronics says it did not discriminate against Les Bingham because of his age. However the facts show something different.	

Arbitration Transcript 15

Bingham v. Ecotronics

Opening Statement – Claimant	Comments/Notes
Ecotronics tried to get Mr. Bingham to retire, but he refused, and so he was fired. The real reason he was fired was because his boss viewed him as a "fossil," a "has-been," a "back number." Ecotronics says he was too vocal at marketing meetings, and also too insistent that clients discuss any contract issues him, and not Ecotronics' engineering personnel. They say he did not fit in. Ecotronics had rules for making a decision to fire someone and they did not follow their own rules.	This is an effective organizational approach. See *Trial Advocacy* Section 6.3.
5 Now let me help to put in focus the factual issues and the legal issues that are before you, in light of this controversy. There are at least four governing legal principles in this case. First, Mr. Bingham is clearly an employee at will under the law of this jurisdiction.	5 Following Arbitrator Blackwell's request concerning the law, Mr. Bujold combines the facts and the law and sets out the legal principles upon which he will rely. He blends these legal principles with the facts. See *Trial Advocacy* Section 6.4 (M).

Arbitration Transcript 16

Bingham v. Ecotronics

Opening Statement – Claimant	Comments/Notes
This means that under the law of this jurisdiction, he can be fired for any reason. He had no written contract that stated differently. But, he could not be fired for an improper reason. However, under the second legal principle, Ecotronics had an employee handbook that created certain fixed rights upon which Mr. Bingham relied and which were violated by Ecotronics. Ecotronics could not "make up" a false work history and they had to follow their own rules before they could fire him. Because of these rights, Mr. Bingham has a right to damages because he was wrongfully fired. The third controlling legal principle is if Mr. Bingham was fired because of his age—that is Ecotronics, as a matter of policy, wanted people in	

Bingham v. Ecotronics	
Opening Statement – Claimant	**Comments/Notes**

Mr. Bingham's age group out. Or because Mr. Bingham's boss, Jack Fenster, wanted him out because he, Mr. Bingham, was a "relic" at the age of 54, then Ecotronics violated the law and Mr. Bingham is entitled to redress.

And the fourth legal principle is as follows: Ecotronics claims that before it fired Mr. Bingham, it asked him to sign up for a so-called voluntary retirement program, which he refused to do. He refused to sign up for that so-called voluntary program. In <u>Mathers v. Folley Particulate</u>, the court in this jurisdiction held that if such a program, such a voluntary program, is in reality, and I'm quoting now from the decision, "a subterfuge to evade this jurisdiction's prohibition against discrimination on the basis of

Arbitration Transcript 18

Bingham v. Ecotronics

Opening Statement – Claimant	Comments/Notes
age"—and I close quotes—the Mathers court said that is a subterfuge and the employee may bring an age discrimination claim.	
6 In the context of those four legal principles, let me turn to the facts. Ecotronic did not follow its own employee handbook. The handbook gave Les Bingham rights and set up procedures and the company violated those rights and procedures, and clearly fired Les Bingham because of his age.	6 After he outlined his positions and described the legal principles, the Attorney now provides facts in a more expanded version. The brief introduction provided Arbitrator Blackwell with the context for the more detailed statements that follow. See *Trial Advocacy* Section 6.4 (B).
The employees' handbook, on which Mr. Bingham relied, addressed termination of an employee. The handbook states that an employee may be terminated and I'm quoting now from the handbook: ". . . for violating a rule of conduct or acting adversely to the interest of the company."	
The employees' handbook sets up a requirement that there be	

Bingham v. Ecotronics	
Opening Statement – Claimant	**Comments/Notes**
three episodes of that kind of conduct within a 24 month period, that each episode be a "same or similar offense," and that there be a warning by the employer after each claimed offense. After the third warning, the employee has to persist in engaging in the same or similar offense before he can be fired. Under those circumstances, the employees' handbook sets out the procedures that have to be followed. The handbook says the warnings must be given by the employer, and only if the conduct continues after the third warning, can the employee be terminated. Under those rules Ecotronics could not fire Les Bingham. Three similar or substantially similar acts of rule violation or acts adverse to the interests of the company did not occur.	

Arbitration Transcript 20

Bingham v. Ecotronics

Opening Statement – Claimant	Comments/Notes
Furthermore, after the third required warning, there is no evidence that Mr. Bingham did anything that the company could complain about, Nothing! We intend to show that after a third warning there was no improper conduct. Yet he was fired—He was fired in violation of the company's own rules.	
7 The real reason for Mr. Bingham's discharge is set out in a document called the "Fenster Memorandum." Forty-two days before he was fired, Les Bingham's boss, Mr. Fenster, wrote a memorandum to Jessica Martindale who is the personnel manager. In that memorandum Fenster described Les Bingham as "old dog," "fossil," "has been," "back number," and "relic."	7 It is an effective technique to use the exact words from the written records. Attorney Bujold combines that with vigorous language of his own when he says, "Now this ageist language, shocking in its vitriol was contained in a three paragraph memo." He then clearly sets out how the Respondent's witnesses were involved with that memo. See *Trial Advocacy* Section 6.4 (G).
This ageist language, shocking in its vitriol, was contained in a	

Arbitration Transcript 21

Bingham v. Ecotronics	
Opening Statement – Claimant	**Comments/Notes**
three paragraph memo from Mr. Fenster to Ecotronics' personnel manager, Jessica Martindale, who is seated here. In that same memo, Mr. Fenster, concluded "we need light, we need new blood, we need youth, we don't need Bingham. Jessica, get rid of him."	
8 This urgent petition from Mr. Fenster was received by Ms. Martindale at a time when her own views were totally receptive to a policy of clearing out the aging underbrush of the corporation. She will acknowledge that her fundamental philosophy as personnel manager for Ecotronics was that the "older executives still tend to make decisions without careful consideration of the legal consequences."	8 By tying the memo to Ms. Martindale, the age discrimination is transferred from Mr. Fenster to the company.
9 Les Bingham was improperly fired.	9 This restatement of the factors ties the narrative together.

Arbitration Transcript 22

Bingham v. Ecotronics

Opening Statement – Claimant	Comments/Notes
<ul><li>The policies, procedures and requirements of the employee handbook were ignored by Ecotronics.</li><li>The poor job performance was fabricated.</li><li>The so-called voluntary retirement program submitted to Mr. Bingham was a subterfuge to cover Ecotronics real motivation for ending Mr. Bingham's 15-year career.</li><li>Mr. Bingham's termination was driven by unlawful motivations, and</li><li>The company's policy to clear out aging employees and Vice President Fenster's desire to be freed of, as he said, an "old dog" who stood in the way of the company's prosperity is wrong.</li></ul>All are improper reasons for firing Les Bingham.	

Arbitration Transcript 23

Bingham v. Ecotronics

Opening Statement – Claimant	Comments/Notes
10 Based on the law and these facts, we will show you that Les Bingham was improperly fired. Because he was improperly fired, his claims should be granted.	10 At the conclusion of his opening statement, Mr. Bujold returns to his introductory theme and once again boldly states his position. See *Trial Advocacy* Section 6.3 (B) (3).

Arbitration Transcript 24

Bingham v. Ecotronics

Opening Statement – Respondent	Comments/Notes
Arbitrator:	1 Respondent's attorney, Ms. Kingsley does not hesitate to meet Mr. Bujold's opening statement head on. In Mr. Bujold's opening he does not deny that Les Bingham is an employee at will. By using Mr. Bujold's own words, Attorney Kingsley strongly sets out the respondent's position. That position is that Lester Bingham is an employee at will and can be fired for any reason. Attorney Kingsley then clearly sets out the two reasons why Lester Bingham was fired. Those two reasons are described briefly giving Arbitrator Blackwell a table of contents for what is to follow. See *Trial Advocacy* Section 6.3 (B) (1).
Ms. Kingsley, are you prepared to proceed with the Respondent's brief opening?	
Respondent's Attorney:	
1 Yes, I am Mr. Blackwell. I agree with one thing Mr. Bujold said, in that we do strongly agree that Mr. Bingham was an at will employee and as indicated, being an employee at will means that you can be fired for any reason. Mr. Bingham was fired for two reasons. One was his conduct, and we'll briefly discuss that and we'll talk about what the testimony will show. The other reason is just the changing needs of the company. Now let's look at his conduct.	
2 Over the last two years, Lester Bingham became increasingly difficult to deal with in his relations with his co-workers.	2 In very precise detail, respondent's attorney puts people into the case and sets out facts that demonstrate that Les

Bingham v. Ecotronics

Opening Statement – Respondent	Comments/Notes
You will hear testimony from Hannah Pohl, the chief site engineer, Ms. Martindale, the personnel manager, and John Fenster, the Marketing Vice President, who is the supervisor for Mr. Bingham. Les Bingham's job was marketing. An integral part of that job is keeping up relationships between the company and the clients. The testimony is going to show that Les Bingham told one of the company's clients—and a very prominent client for the company—that he was not to deal with Hannah Pohl, that he advised against it. And she was one of the company's chief site engineers. We will also look at other conduct. Les Bingham complained to the clients of the company about the company. He expressed his grievances to them. He also complained about the quality of work on a	Bingham was not doing his job appropriately. See *Trial Advocacy* Section 6.4 (F).

Arbitration Transcript 26

Bingham v. Ecotronics

Opening Statement – Respondent	Comments/Notes
project that Hannah Pohl was responsible for. Those complaints led to an investigation by both the company and the EPA and those complaints were found to be groundless. It was found that the quality of work was indeed up to par. Other conduct by Bingham also caused concern over the last few years. You'll hear about incidents at personnel meetings and marketing meetings. Les Bingham, in front of other employees, used a derogatory term when referring to his own supervisor—in fact, in a meeting in front of other employees, referred to Mr. Fenster, his supervisor, as a "gutless ass." This was in front of the other employees. Mr. Bingham was increasingly flying off the handle in these meetings.	

Bingham v. Ecotronics

Opening Statement – Respondent	Comments/Notes
3 Importantly, he has had three written reprimands. You've heard about the company handbook. The company handbook provides that if a person is given three reprimands, that is cause for termination. And indeed, Mr. Bingham was ultimately terminated. One reason Les Bingham	3 Ms. Kingsley states her client's interpretation of the three violation rule in the handbook.
4 was let go was because of his conduct.	4 The failure of an employee to perform the job appropriately is a valid reason for termination. In addition, so is downsizing or eliminating positions in a company.
5 The other reason he was let go was the changing needs of the company. This is a company in transition. The job descriptions are changing. The need for particular types of employees has been changing. Mr. Bingham was a site executive. That position has become less and less necessary. Over time the clients have become more comfortable with other site engineers and have expressed the wish to deal directly with the engineers instead of	5 The Attorney justifies the second legitimate reason for terminating Bingham by showing the company's changing needs. See *Trial Advocacy* Section 6.4 (J).

Arbitration Transcript 28

Bingham v. Ecotronics

Opening Statement – Respondent	Comments/Notes
the executives. Mr. Bingham has no engineering background. That's not the job he is in. He is in a marketing position. This is the type of job that's become unnecessary in recent years. Originally there were six site executives. One of them recently left for health problems and that person wasn't replaced. That's evidence of the fact that that portion of the company is being downsized.	
6 Les Bingham was offered an early retirement package. At this point in time, because of downsizing, he was asked whether be would be interested in an early retirement package, and some continuing wage benefits were offered to him. He declined. The company did everything it could to accommodate Les Bingham.	6 The early retirement offer is shown to be the sign of a "caring" company. See *Trial Advocacy* Section 6.4 (C).

Arbitration Transcript 29

Bingham v. Ecotronics

Opening Statement – Respondent	Comments/Notes
7 This wasn't simply the case where, you know, two problems and you're gone. At that time there had already been two written reprimands. This followed two years of increasing tensions between Mr. Bingham and other employees, specifically with his supervisor, Mr. Fenster. That's a very important working relationship, as is his relationship with Hannah Pohl, and with other people there. With increasing tensions, he is given two written reprimands.	7 The claimant relies on a violation of handbook rules. Respondent's attorney provides a reasonable alternative interpretation of the handbook.
8 Some mention was made of the <u>Mathers</u> case before. There is no subterfuge going on here. If you look at the fact that they were already downsizing the department, that there were serious problems with his conduct, it all indicates that the <u>Mathers</u> case and the proposition that it stands	8 These two sections provide the detail justifying the firing of the at will employee. Attorney Kingsley makes short work of the legal discussion by the claimant's attorney by stating that the law concerning subterfuge just doesn't apply. See *Trial Advocacy* Section 6.4 (M).

Arbitration Transcript 30

Bingham v. Ecotronics

Opening Statement – Respondent	Comments/Notes
for is really not applicable in this case.	
9 There were valid reasons for letting Mr. Bingham go. After deciding to decline this offer, he was again involved in an incident which resulted in a written reprimand. There was a marketing meeting at which Mr. Bingham's temper flared. Some inappropriate comments were made, things got a little out of hand. He violated the rules of conduct in the employees' manual. The rules talk about treating other people with respect and acting professionally. He did not do so. He therefore received his third reprimand or notice of inappropriate conduct, and he was terminated pursuant to the guidelines which were set out in the handbook.	9 Respondent's attorney justifies an interpretation of the handbook that permits termination under the circumstances.
10 We'll show that Mr. Bingham was terminated	10 Just as the claimant's attorney did, Ms. Kingsley

Arbitration Transcript 31

Bingham v. Ecotronics

Opening Statement – Respondent	Comments/Notes
because of his insubordination, because the company was changing, and there was less need for that position. The position was being phased out. The termination was not based upon his age. It was not based upon the memo, that was referred to, by Mr. Fenster. That termination was based upon his conduct and upon the changing needs of the company. The termination should be upheld.	returns to her introduction and vigorously states her theme and repeats her position. See *Trial Advocacy* Section 6.3 (B) (3).

Arbitration Transcript 32

Bingham v. Ecotronics

Direct Examination – Les Bingham	Comments/Notes
Claimant's Attorney:	
1 Q: Please tell us your full legal name. A: My name is Lester Bingham. Q: Mr. Bingham, how old are you? A: I'm 54. Q: Please tell the arbitrator very briefly your life work experience. A: I've spent fifteen years working for Ecotronics. Q: Before you worked for Ecotronics, were you generally in the field of waste management or related fields? A: Yes I was. I had been assistant manager for byproducts and waste management at another company called M.C.C. Manufacturing.	1 While this direct examination begins chronologically, it soon moves to a thematic approach to address the major issues. See *Trial Advocacy* Section 7.6 (B) (1).
2 Q: While you were working for Ecotronics, was there in existence a so-called employees' handbook?	2 Within a matter of a few questions, Attorney Bujold introduces the handbook and the characterization of the handbook by using the word "so-called." This characterization could illicit an objection.

Arbitration Transcript 33

Bingham v. Ecotronics

Direct Examination – Les Bingham	Comments/Notes
A: Yes there was.	
3 Q: Let me show you what I have had marked as Petitioner's Exhibit 3, it is a handbook. Identify that for the arbitrator please?	3 Although the admission of the documents have been agreed through stipulation, Attorney Bujold does lay some foundation for the exhibit to establish the witness' credibility and to make the exhibit more persuasive in its relation to this witness' testimony. See *Trial Advocacy* Section 8.5 (B).
A: Yes, this is the employee handbook.	
Q: And is that the handbook that was furnished to you from the beginning of your employment right up until the day that you were fired?	
A: Yes it was.	
Q: Did you, Mr. Bingham, rely upon the various provisions contained in that handbook as you served as an employee of Ecotronics?	
A: Yes I did.	
Q: I offer in evidence Petitioner's Exhibit 3.	

Arbitration Transcript 34

Bingham v. Ecotronics

Direct Examination – Les Bingham	Comments/Notes
Arbitrator: Is there any objection? **Respondent's Attorney:** No objection. *Portions of this examination have been deleted, and the Attorney continues.* 4 Q: Did you ever tell a client not to work with site engineer Hannah Pohl? A: I merely told the client that it was our policy that client requests for activity and action go through me so that we can keep the line of communication clear. 5 Q: Mr. Bingham, when you told that client that the communications to the company should go through you, and not Hannah Pohl, did you feel that you were violating any rule of the corporation?	 4 In the next series of questions the Attorney has the witness explain the underlying facts that preceded the reprimands from his employer. 5 As you read the next series of questions, observe that the questions ask for yes or no responses. While these questions are very directive, they do give the witness a choice of answers. These "Did you" questions may elicit a "leading" objection. There is a fine line between appropriate directive preliminary questions and inappropriate leading questions. These questions lead up to the

Arbitration Transcript 35

Bingham v. Ecotronics	
Direct Examination – **Les Bingham**	**Comments/Notes**
A: No. I certainly did not. Q: Did you feel that you were acting adversely to the interests of Ecotronics when you did that? A: Quite to the contrary. I was working on behalf of them. Q: Now in the face of your giving that communication to the client, did you receive some type of warning back in July from Ecotronics' people? A: Yes, I did.	open-ended question which is "what was the nature of the warning?" See *Trial Advocacy* Section 7.7 (A).
6 Q: What was the nature of that warning? Do you recall it? A: Well, I recall that I objected to it. Q: Would it help you to refer to the warning itself? A: Yes. Yes it would.	6 In this segment the witness does not recall the warning. Witnesses do forget facts, even those with which they are quite familiar. The present recollection of a witness can be refreshed by providing the witness a document, by asking short leading questions, or by providing the witness with anything that would refresh recollection. See *Trial Advocacy* Section 7.7 (B) (13).

Bingham v. Ecotronics

Direct Examination – Les Bingham	Comments/Notes
Claimant's Attorney to Arbitrator: May I show the reprimand to Mr. Bingham to refresh his recollection? **Respondent's Attorney:** I have no objection. **Arbitrator:** You may show him the reprimand. 7 Please look at the document. Q: You need not read it in any detail, but if it will help you to refresh your recollection summarizing the nature of the warning that you got, please tell the arbitrator about that. A: Well, they raised the question that I wasn't generally acting as a team player, and I remember, as I now refresh it here, that my teamwork was perfectly adequate. It was well within my job description, and	7 While some arbitrators require that a memory refreshing document needs to be marked and introduced as an exhibit, the general rule is that the "memory refresher" is not an exhibit, is not evidence, will not be received as evidence, and need not be marked as an exhibit. See *Trial Advocacy* Section 8.5 (B) (7).

Arbitration Transcript 37

Bingham v. Ecotronics

Direct Examination – Les Bingham	Comments/Notes
it says right here "he was warned that his team work skills needed improvement." I don't think there was any proof of that. I was never, there was never any concern with the way I performed my job with the client, on the site, with the projects. They all worked well. Q: When you told the client last July that any communication should go through you, did you feel that you had a duty to do that? A: Very much so. That was very much part of my job.	
8 Q: Mr. Bingham, I would like to talk to you about an incident that occurred last September and specifically, a second warning that you received. Did you, in fact, receive such a warning, and if so, tell the arbitrator about the circumstances?	8 In this next series of questions the witness is permitted to testify in a narrative. In every examination, the witnesses are permitted some leeway in testifying about factual situations in some reasonable length. A mix of questions that require short answers and those that illicit longer answers

Arbitration Transcript 38

Bingham v. Ecotronics

Direct Examination – Les Bingham	Comments/Notes
A: Yes, I did. Well, the circumstances were supposedly that I blew up at Jack Fenster at a meeting. Well, marketing meetings are that way. There is a lot of controversy that goes on and a lot of discussion back and forth. They are open meetings. That's what the company is all about. That's what makes it a good company, or at least I thought it was. What was even more remarkable about it, the notice said it was my final notice, which I knew just goes against the handbook anyway. I mean it had nothing to do with my work, had nothing to do with other than the fact that I happened to blow up at Jack Fenster. I've done that for years.	makes the testimony more interesting. However the narrative answers must be limited in scope. See *Trial Advocacy* Section 7.7 (C).
Q: That was my next question. Tell the arbitrator whether the marketing meetings were characterized by frank and vigorous discussions.	

Arbitration Transcript 39

Bingham v. Ecotronics

Direct Examination – Les Bingham	Comments/Notes
9 A: Well, they certainly were. I guess anybody that knows me knows from time to time I've got a quick trigger, and if I hear something I really just don't go along with, I express myself. Q: Have you observed situations where others have also been equally as vigorous in the presentation of their views at these meetings. A: Well, certainly. Not as many as should have maybe, but certainly that is true. Q: Now when you have been vigorous in your presentation of views on other occasions, did you receive any warnings from the company in that respect? A: No. Q: Do you know of any warnings being issued to other people who have been forthright and vigorous in the presentation of their ideas at these meetings?	9 This next series of questions again call for short yes or no answers. It would be difficult to illicit this testimony from a witness without these types of questions. They are very focused and are directed to specific facts. Note that the witness starts responding to the questions with short answers, but then goes beyond a mere yes or no with some descriptive testimony. The witness' answers are not inappropriate and fit the questions. The answers are not improper. See *Trial Advocacy* Section 7.8 (B).

Arbitration Transcript 40

Bingham v. Ecotronics	
Direct Examination – **Les Bingham**	**Comments/Notes**
A: I have no knowledge of that.	
Q: When you, as you say, "blew up" in the process of being vigorous and forthright with the other people at the meeting, did you feel that you were violating a company rule?	
A: Good Lord, no. I mean that's—I'm just disagreeing with someone. I hope to God I could disagree with somebody.	
Q: And when this disagreement occurred, did you feel that you were acting adversely to the interests of the company?	
A: No. Quite to the contrary. I'm expressing my feeling about what is in the interests of the company.	
Q: Finally, let me proceed to a final event which occurred in	

Arbitration Transcript 41

Bingham v. Ecotronics

Direct Examination – Les Bingham	Comments/Notes
November. Did you receive another warning in that month? A: Well, yes, I did. Q: Will you please tell us about that particular warning? 10 A: Well, this particular one—I should have seen it coming—I mean Jack Fenster was just going on and on and talking about things that frankly were going to drive this company in the wrong direction—taking us down the wrong way, against where this company needed to go if it's going to succeed. And frankly, I couldn't sit there and take it. I mean he was turning his back on everything that we have been building for as much time as I have been in the company and he has been in the company, and I blew up at him. Q: Have you seen instances where other people have blown up, as you say, in the course of these marketing meetings?	10 The short series of introductory questions leads to the longer more explanatory narrative.

Bingham v. Ecotronics

Direct Examination – Les Bingham	Comments/Notes
A: Certainly.	
Q: Are they typically meetings at which there is a frank exchange and an open exchange of views, sir?	
A: Yes.	
Q: And you received a warning after that event did you?	
A: Well, yes, I did.	
Q: Once again, did you feel that you had either violated a company rule or acted adversely to the interests of the company?	
A: No, I might have been a little too loud, but other than that, I certainly didn't move against the company.	
Q: When did you receive your termination notice?	
A: Two days later.	

Arbitration Transcript 43

Bingham v. Ecotronics	
Direct Examination – **Les Bingham**	**Comments/Notes**
Q: When did you first see the memorandum signed by Mr. Fenster dated September 29 that he sent to Jessica Martindale? A: Just recently, a few weeks ago.	
11 Q: Did you read in that memorandum where Mr. Fenster says to Ms. Martindale that he believes that it is impossible to teach—referring to you—"an old dog new tricks." A: Yes I did. Q: And did you see that you are described as a "fossil," a "has been," a "back number," and a "relic." Do you see those words in there? A: Yes. Q: Had you ever heard Fenster say those things about you before? A: No.	11 In the next series of questions, the Attorney uses Mr. Bingham to introduce the memorandum from Mr. Fenster to Ms. Martindale demonstrating that the witness had not seen this information before his termination. The language setting out age discrimination is brought to the attention of the Arbitrator in the claimant's case. See *Trial Advocacy* Section 7.8 (C) (2).
12 Q: I would like to ask you this, sir, how did you feel when you first saw Mr. Fenster's	12 While this last question is not relevant to the age discrimination

Arbitration Transcript 44

Bingham v. Ecotronics

Direct Examination – Les Bingham	**Comments/Notes**
description of you in those terms? A: It was like what I'd done for 15 years wasn't worth anything. Q: Thank you. That's all I have.	claim, it is a summary of the damage done by the company to Mr. Bingham. See *Trial Advocacy* Section 7.8 (D) (3).

Bingham v. Ecotronics

Cross Examination – Les Bingham	Comments/Notes
Arbitrator: Ms. Kingsley, are you ready to proceed with your cross-examination? **Respondent's Attorney:** Yes, sir. Thank you very much. 1 Mr. Bingham, I've got a few questions for you, based on your direct examination. Now in response to questions from counsel, you talked about a November marketing meeting. You do recall that series of questions? 2 A: Yes. Q: Now, you testified that in that November marketing meeting you disagreed with Mr. Fenster? A: Yes. Q: You testified that you were upset with Mr. Fenster's views in this meeting? A: Yes. I was. I think I said that I disagreed with the direction that he was forming for the company.	 1 This introduction focuses the witness and the Arbitrator on the specific area of the cross-examination. Ms Kingsley is challenging the witness' interpretation of the facts. See *Trial Advocacy* Section 9.3 (A). 2 In a series of focused questions, Ms. Kingsley doesn't waste any time setting up each of the areas in order of position. In the first series with only four questions, she demonstrates that Mr. Bingham clearly knows that Mr. Fenster, the man with whom he had the disagreement, had the authority for making the marketing decisions for the company. See *Trial Advocacy* Section 9.3 (B).

Arbitration Transcript 46

Bingham v. Ecotronics

Cross Examination – Les Bingham	Comments/Notes
Q: Mr. Fenster is your boss, isn't he? A: Yes. Q: And isn't it true that it is his job to formulate the direction for the company within the marketing area? A: Certainly. 3 Q: Now I'd like to ask you some questions about your relationship with Ms. Pohl. Now, earlier you testified that you reported to your superiors that you believed a clean up job that was handled by Ms. Pohl was handled incorrectly. Do you recall making that testimony? A: Yes, I do. Q: That clean up dealt with your former company, called M.C.C. Manufacturing, isn't that correct? A: Yes. They're our client.	3 Ms. Kingsley now moves to the relationship with Ms. Pohl in which she quickly demonstrates that the Environmental Protection Agency did not uphold his complaint about Ms. Pohl's work, and then demonstrates Mr. Bingham's bad relationships by bringing out his continuing negative feelings towards Ms. Pohl. See *Trial Advocacy* Section 9.3 (E).

Arbitration Transcript 47

Bingham v. Ecotronics

Cross Examination – Les Bingham	Comments/Notes
4 Q: M.C.C. Manufacturing became a client of Ecotronics? A: Yes. Q: Now, it's true, is it not, that following your complaint to your superiors that the EPA investigated your complaint? A: That was some time afterwards, yes. Q: But they did investigate it. A: Oh, sure. . . . Q: Even after the EPA said the work was okay you continued to complain about that investigation, didn't you? A: Well, I complained about the way Mrs. Pohl conducts her work. That's right, yes. Q: You're upset even today about the fact that the EPA upheld Ms. Pohl's work, aren't you? A: No, I'm not upset about that. I'm upset about the fact that	4 In the following series, the Attorney controls the witness with short, simple questions. See *Trial Advocacy* Section 9.3 (D).

Arbitration Transcript 48

Bingham v. Ecotronics	
Cross Examination – **Les Bingham**	**Comments/Notes**
my honesty is being questioned in the matter. When I objected, her work was incomplete. Q: Based on your reaction to my questions, your current relationship with Ms. Pohl is a very negative one, isn't that correct? A: There is tension between us. I don't know that negative is right. Q: Well, isn't it true that you believe that Ms. Pohl cuts corners on clean up in derogation of standards? A: I wouldn't characterize it that way, no. Q: You have circulated opinions like that in the work place, have you not? A: No. Only specific to a moment and specific to a product. I don't carry around any case against Mrs. Pohl.	

Bingham v. Ecotronics

Cross Examination – **Les Bingham**	**Comments/Notes**

Q: Well, your opinion of Ms. Pohl is known throughout the company, isn't it?

A: Well, probably more because of what's happened to me than because of anything that I've said, I'm sure.

Q: So—anything that's happened with respect to Ms. Pohl is all somebody else's fault. Is that what your point is?

A: No. No. No. I've said things about Ms. Pohl, and I'm sure it's gotten around here and there. But nothing I've ever said has been incorrect when it dealt with what she did or didn't do on the job. That's my job.

Q: Well, let me follow that up. Isn't it true that you were disciplined for telling a client not to deal with Ms. Pohl?

A: I was disciplined, but the fact is they were . . .

Arbitration Transcript 50

Bingham v. Ecotronics

Cross Examination – Les Bingham	Comments/Notes
Respondent's Attorney:	
5 Objection. Non-responsive.	5 The question Attorney Kingsley asked Mr. Bingham called for a yes or no response. In the previous three answers, the witness had not answered the question yes or no, and was not responsive. Generally, it is the examiner who has the right to object to a non-responsive question. Here, instead of arguing with the witness, the Attorney asks the Arbitrator for assistance in controlling the witness. See *Trial Advocacy* Section 9.3 (D) (6).
Arbitrator:	
Sustained.	
Respondent's Attorney:	
Q: When you instructed a client not to deal with Ms. Pohl, that was not the situation that we've earlier discussed about your former company was it?	
A: I'm not sure.	
Q: Your former company was M.C.C. Manufacturing?	
A: Yes.	
Q: M.C.C. Manufacturing— that was the company that was involved in your complaint to superiors about whether the clean up met standards, is that right?	
A: Right, that's exactly right.	

Arbitration Transcript 51

Bingham v. Ecotronics

Cross Examination – Les Bingham	Comments/Notes
Q: But it was a different client that you instructed not to communicate with Ms. Pohl, isn't that correct?	
6 A: To tell you the truth, I can't recall right now.	6 The witness here is clearly being evasive. Instead of arguing with the witness, the Attorney continues with the questioning and gets the response she wants. The fact that the witness here is being evasive hurts his credibility. See *Trial Advocacy* Section 9.3 (D) (6) (b).
Q: You do know that you did tell some client not to communicate with Ms. Pohl?	
A: Yes	
Q: Now, with respect to that instance in telling the client not to communicate with Ms. Pohl, your testimony was that you were warned about that conduct, isn't that correct?	
A: Well, yes, and I also said that was part of my job.	
Respondent's Attorney:	
7 Objection, non-responsive. He answered yes.	7 Once again the witness is not responsive and the Arbitrator, clearly irritated by the witness' failure to answer the questions,

Arbitration Transcript 52

Bingham v. Ecotronics

Cross Examination – Les Bingham	Comments/Notes
Arbitrator:	gives a rather sharp reprimand to Mr. Bingham. Since it is the Arbitrator who is making the factual determinations, this type of behavior by a witness could be very damaging to his case. See *Trial Advocacy* Section 9.3 (D) (6) (h).
Sustained. Let me remind you, Mr. Bingham, to please listen to the questions, and answer only the questions that are asked of you. If you need to go into a lot of detail to explain your answer, your lawyer will have an opportunity, when he questions you later, to bring out the additional things you have to say.	
Respondent's Attorney:	
Q: The client in this situation, with Ms. Pohl, told you that she wanted to deal with Ms. Pohl?	
8 A: I don't think that's true at all.	8 Rather than argue with the witness the Attorney can call Ms. Pohl as a witness to contradict him.
Q: Now you did talk to Mr. Fenster about whether this particular client should communicate through you or through Ms. Pohl?	
A: I believe I probably did, yes.	

Arbitration Transcript 53

Bingham v. Ecotronics	
Cross Examination – **Les Bingham**	**Comments/Notes**
Q: And isn't it true that Mr. Fenster said that the customer is always right? A: Yes. *The remaining cross-examination of the witness has been deleted.*	

Arbitration Transcript 54

Bingham v. Ecotronics

Direct Examination – Jessica Martindale	Comments/Notes
The Direct and Cross-examinations of the other Claimant's witnesses were deleted.	
Respondent's Attorney continues:	
Introductory and background questions of Respondent's witness were deleted. Respondent's Attorney continues.	
1 Q: Okay Jessica, I'd like to ask you about some specifics about your dealings with Mr. Bingham. First, I want to ask you some questions	1 Rules of decorum may not permit the attorney to address a witness by their first name. The use of the first name here is designed to personalize the witness. The rule is designed to prevent a showing of a personal relationship between attorney and witness. See *Trial Advocacy* Section 7.4.
2 about a meeting which took place about eight months ago. It's my understanding that you and Mr. Fenster stopped by Mr. Bingham's office about eight months ago, is that right? A: That's right.	2 If not overdone, this short introduction is permissible as it helps focus the testimony.
3 Q: First of all, what was the purpose of that meeting?	3 The next series of questions call for short narrative responses that

---

Bingham v. Ecotronics

Direct Examination – Jessica Martindale	**Comments/Notes**
A: We wanted to go and offer Les Bingham the opportunity to retire with what we thought was a pretty good package, and I further explained to him how our company was changing and that it was a good idea that our company pare down. We wanted to give him an option to do what would be most comfortable for him.	in the context of this Arbitration are completely appropriate. See *Trial Advocacy* Section 7.8 (G).
Q: Before this meeting, had you talked about this at all with Mr. Fenster?	
A: Yes, I did. We talked in depth about it. Our company is changing very much right now. In fact, Mr. Fenster and I are having many meetings trying to discuss different options we have to go along with our changing company, and Les Bingham was an issue. We thought that we would	

Arbitration Transcript 56

Bingham v. Ecotronics

Direct Examination - Jessica Martindale	Comments/Notes

offer him the most comfortable way to leave the company.

Q: You say he was "an issue." What do you mean by that?

A: Our company doesn't have such a strong need right now for his position. It's focusing more on the engineering aspect of the site clean ups. And we wanted to let him know that the focus of the company was changing, and the best option that we saw for him was to offer him early retirement rather than try to incorporate him, because of his lack of knowledge of engineering, in our company and the changing needs.

4 Q: Well, first of all, set the stage for me in the meeting a little. This took place on a Friday, is that right?

A: Right.

Q: What time of the day was it?

A: I believe it was about 2:30, 3:00.

4 This leading question is appropriate as it is introductory and deals with a matter that is not in controversy. See *Trial Advocacy* Section 7.7 (B) (3).

Bingham v. Ecotronics

Direct Examination – Jessica Martindale	**Comments/Notes**
Q: Okay and were you in Mr. Bingham's office?	5 The Arbitrator has determined that there are close evidentiary issues. It is not unusual for an arbitrator to ask for an explanation to help understand the attorney's position before ruling. See *Trial Advocacy* Section 4.4.
A: Yes, we both entered his office and sat down, and Mr. Fenster gave the offer. And then I further explained the reasons why, and then offered him the half salary for the next year.	
Q: When you say Mr. Fenster gave him the offer, do you recall specifically what he said?	6 While the Attorney's response to this objection is that the arbitration proceedings relax the rules of evidence, there are other arguments that could be made in regard to the admissibility of this evidence. In the first place, it may not be hearsay because it is not being offered for the truth of the matter asserted. It may also be admissible because it merely puts in context the conversations at the meeting between Mr. Bingham and the other parties. Mr. Bingham was at that meeting and the validity of those comments can be challenged. In addition, without these statements by
Claimant's Attorney:	
Objection. Hearsay.	
Arbitrator:	
5 What's your response?	
Respondent's Attorney:	
6 Your Honor, this is an arbitration proceeding. It's my understanding the rules are a little bit lax here.	
Arbitrator:	
I agree. Overruled. Go ahead.	

Arbitration Transcript 58

Bingham v. Ecotronics

Direct Examination – Jessica Martindale	Comments/Notes
Respondent's Attorney:	Mr. Fenster the statements made by Mr. Bingham would not make any sense. See *Trial Advocacy* Section 4.8 (F) (2).
Q: You may answer.	
A: Okay. He just said "Les, I'd like you to retire and the reasons are as follows," and then he went into depth as to why we were offering him this retirement package.	
Q: And what did you say?	
7 A: I just basically said—I was explaining the changing of our company, and I thought that given his personality, he is not one who takes change very well, and he wasn't changing with the company and meeting the needs of the company any longer because he still expected to operate as it did ten years ago, and it's a completely different atmosphere right now. I just explained that the most comfortable thing for him to do would be to accept an early retirement.	7 In a very concise way, the respondent's attorney permits the witness to demonstrate that the early retirement offer was a legitimate offer and not a subterfuge.

Bingham v. Ecotronics

Direct Examination – Jessica Martindale	Comments/Notes
8 Q: What was his response to that? A: He didn't seem all that thrilled about it. Although that's par for the course for Mr. Bingham. However, he just said that he would think about it. Q: Okay and did the meeting end just then? I mean, was there anything else said at that time? A: No. I thought it was a fairly professional meeting. We got up, and after he said that "I would think about it," we just said "thank you," and we left.	8 Statements of Mr. Bingham are not hearsay because they are statements of a party opponent. See *Trial Advocacy* Section 4.8 (F) (3) (a).
9 Q: At that point in time had any other site executives left the company? A: One executive had retired for health reasons in December. Q: And had that executive ever been replaced? A: No. We did not replace him. Q: Did you have any intentions to replace him?	9 In a step-by-step progress, respondent's attorney deals with all of Mr. Bingham's claims to demonstrate that his termination was based on job performance and downsizing rather than on age. See *Trial Advocacy* Section 9.1 (A).

Arbitration Transcript 60

Bingham v. Ecotronics	
Direct Examination – **Jessica Martindale**	**Comments/Notes**
A: No, because of the paring down of that particular position, we don't feel the need that we had to replace him. Q: Did you have any set course at that time. Had you made any decisions to further reduce the site executives? A: That is our long term goal. And again, that goes in line with restructuring the company because of the changing needs of our company. Q: Okay. I want to ask you now about a marketing meeting which took place, and it's my understanding it took place last November about two days before Mr. Bingham was fired, is that right? A: Right.	

Arbitration Transcript 61

Bingham v. Ecotronics	
Direct Examination – **Jessica Martindale**	**Comments/Notes**
Q: And you were present at that marketing meeting? A: Yes. Q: Are you generally present at marketing meetings? A: Not generally. As of late, I attend probably about one marketing meeting a month, and that is because our policies are changing quite a bit. And being the personnel manager, I need to be aware of all the policies and make sure that all of our employees understand the policies, because we are constantly changing our company policies to change the fitting needs of our company. So that particular one was one that I did attend. Q: There's been characterizations made about what these meetings are like. Tell us about the general tenor of these meetings.	

Arbitration Transcript 62

Bingham v. Ecotronics

Direct Examination – Jessica Martindale	Comments/Notes
A: They are—we do give people the opportunity to talk freely. We like to hear ideas. We are definitely not closed to ideas. However, there is some structure. We are professionals. There is no shouting. It's not something that we accept. In the two years that I have been with the company, I've never been in a meeting that's wreaking havoc. So they are very professional, but very open to bettering the company.	
10 Q: Would you say—have you ever seen blow ups in these meetings? A: Only with Les Bingham. Q: You've never seen blow ups with any other employees? A: No. Absolutely not. Q: This meeting that took place in November, can you describe for us, what was the purpose of that meeting?	10 The following give and take between the Attorney and the witness is very structured. The questions are short and the responses vary from very short to short narratives. See *Trial Advocacy* Section 7.8 (G) (2).

Arbitration Transcript 63

Bingham v. Ecotronics	
Direct Examination – Jessica Martindale	**Comments/Notes**
A: The purpose of the meeting was to let the people know that we were going to go forward with changing the structure of the company. We were going to use the engineers a lot more to oversee the site clean ups. And we were going to focus for the marketing site executives to deal basically with getting the clients and dealing with that side rather than the actual technical stuff that they deal with on the on site clean up.	
Q: Were there other site executives besides Mr. Bingham there at the meeting?	
A: Yes, the other four.	
Q: Did any of the other site executives voice any objections?	
A: No. They were very open. Everything that we were describing was making perfect sense. The discussion was good.	

Arbitration Transcript 64

Bingham v. Ecotronics	
Direct Examination – **Jessica Martindale**	**Comments/Notes**
There was a good exchange of ideas about the different roles of site engineers. We explained that site executives would still be useful, just used in a different capacity. Q: Tell me about Mr. Bingham's reaction at this meeting. A: He completely blew up. He felt like we were singling him out, and he stood up and yelled at Mr. Fenster and called him a "gutless ass." That was completely unacceptable. We are professionals. His behavior was not acceptable. He was just irate. There was really no dealing with him after that point. Q: Do you have an employee handbook that deals with things like the derogatory reference Mr. Bingham made to Mr. Fenster? A: Yes, we do.	

Arbitration Transcript 65

Bingham v. Ecotronics	
Direct Examination – Jessica Martindale	**Comments/Notes**
Q: And are there guidelines in the handbook for what type of behavior is and is not acceptable?	
A: Definitely.	
Q: Was his behavior acceptable?	
A: His behavior was not acceptable.	
Q: Why?	
A: The handbook says that people should show respect to other employees and be a part of a team effort. Bingham was not respectful and not part of the team	
Q: Okay. How did that meeting resolve? I mean, did people just leave or was there a confrontation?	
A: It was a very tense moment. Everybody was just appalled. I felt that the morale was very, very damaged. I think he started to get some of the site executives thinking a little more negative towards the change. The change is very	

Arbitration Transcript 66

Bingham v. Ecotronics

Direct Examination – Jessica Martindale	Comments/Notes
positive. We are doing a wonderful business. Our company has gone from 20 employees to 120 employees. **Claimant's Attorney:** 11 Objection, your Honor. This is unresponsive. **Arbitrator:** Sustained. If you would listen carefully to the questions and answer just the question that is asked. **Respondent's Attorney:** A: Okay. Q: Any repercussions from that meeting? Was anything done as a result of Mr. Bingham's behavior? A: Yes. He was written up again. Q: When you say he was "written up," who wrote him up? A: I do the write ups.	11 In this situation, the "non responsive" objection is a shorthand way of saying that the question was answered, there is no question in front of the witness, and the witness' extra commentary is not appropriate because information is being elicited without the opposing attorney having an opportunity to know what is coming and to object. The Arbitrator wants to control the hearing and the witness' behavior. See *Trial Advocacy* Section 4.6 (C).

Arbitration Transcript 67

Bingham v. Ecotronics

Direct Examination – Jessica Martindale	Comments/Notes
Q: And what were your comments about his behavior?	
A: I just said that he was insubordinate. He was not benefitting the company at all, and fundamentally, our company creed is that we need to be a team player, and he was not demonstrating that at all.	
12 Q: Now, let me just ask one other thing. Did Mr. Bingham's age have anything to do with your decision to terminate him?	12 This emphatic last question returns to the main issue and restates the Respondent's theme. See *Trial Advocacy* Section 6.4.
A: None whatsoever.	
Q: Thank you. I have no further questions.	

Arbitration Transcript 68

| **Bingham v. Ecotronics** | |
| **Cross Examination –
Jessica Martindale** | **Comments/Notes** |

Arbitrator:

Mr. Bujold you may cross-examine.

Claimant's Attorney:

Q: Ms. Martindale, you have been with Ecotronics two years?

1 A: Yes.

Q: Mr. Bingham has been an employee for over 15 years, hasn't he?

A: For 15 years, yes.

Q: And during those 15 years, the first reprimands that he had ever received are ones that you wrote up?

A: Yes.

Q: Before that, his personnel file did not reflect any issues with respect to his employment, did it?

A: No.

Q: And in fact, each of the reprimands that were in his file are ones that you participated in writing?

1 The Attorney uses short, succinct leading questions to control the witness and demonstrates that Mr. Bingham had an unblemished record until Ms. Martindale entered the picture. This supports the claimant's position that poor job performance is a fabrication and an invalid reason for Bingham's termination. See *Trial Advocacy* Section 9.3 (A).

Arbitration Transcript 69

Bingham v. Ecotronics

Cross Examination – Jessica Martindale	Comments/Notes
A: Yes.	
Q: You say that there was a meeting approximately eight months ago that occurred on a Friday afternoon with Mr. Bingham regarding an early retirement program?	
A: That's right. Yes.	
2 Q: Mr. Bingham was the only employee you had spoken with that day regarding early retirement? A: That day, he was the only one.	2 This series of questions demonstrates that the early retirement program offered to Mr. Bingham was not a real program and was a subterfuge. The facts brought out in this cross-examination are consistent with the legal position stated in the opening statement. See *Trial Advocacy* Section 6.1 (B).
3 Q: Well, Ms. Martindale, you didn't speak to other employees that day, or any other day about early retirement? A: No. Not at the time. Q: Not at that time, or anytime? A: That's right.	3 In this series the Attorney follows up with precise questions. The Attorney listens to the responses, and pins the witness down. See *Trial Advocacy* Section 9.3 (D).

Bingham v. Ecotronics

Cross Examination – Jessica Martindale	Comments/Notes
Q: So Mr. Bingham was the only person you talked to about early retirement? A: Right.	
4 Q: You indicated that—that Mr. Bingham was insubordinate and not, as you say, demonstrating the attitude of a "team player"?	4 This transition to a new idea requires the Attorney to change delivery through movement, tone or pacing to demonstrate a new topic. See *Trial Advocacy* Section 7.5 (A).
5 A: Exactly. Q: You say he was quite antagonistic? A: Right. Q: And again, the only references to these matters that are reflected in his personnel file are those that you generated? A: Yes. But there was never another personnel director in the company before. Q: There were personnel records and files that would have been available for managers to reflect any employee performance issues, weren't there?	5 The Attorney has demonstrated that he is listening to the answers and has control of the questioning. The witness now answers the questions and does not ramble. See *Trial Advocacy* Section 9.3 (D) (5).

Arbitration Transcript 71

Bingham v. Ecotronics	
Cross Examination – Jessica Martindale	**Comments/Notes**
A: Right.	
Q: There has never been any issue with respect to the competence at which Mr. Bingham performed his duties before those that you wrote out, correct?	
A: No.	
Q: Do you remember a memo you received last September from Mr. Fenster relating to Lester Bingham?	
A: Refresh my memory.	
Q: Let me show you what has been marked here as Exhibit 3. Is that a memo of September 29 directed to you from Jack Fenster?	
A: Yes, it is.	
Q: Does that refresh your recollection of having received it?	
6 A: Yup, shortly after his last blow up, or the second blow up rather. Q: In that memo, Mr. Fenster stated that Lester Bingham's	6 This last series of questions mirrors the questions asked Mr. Bingham on direct examination in regard to the memo written by

Bingham v. Ecotronics

Cross Examination – Jessica Martindale	Comments/Notes
day had "come and gone" with respect to Ecotronics, correct? A: Yes. Q: And further, that we cannot "teach this old dog new tricks," correct? A: Yes. Q: And further referred to Les Bingham, and I quote, "as a fossil," a "has been," and a "back number"? A: Yes. Q: He, Mr. Fenster, told you that, in his opinion, Ecotronics needed new blood, that they needed youth. Isn't that correct? A: Yes. Q: And he stated, "we don't need Bingham." A: Those are the words he used, yes. Q: And he stated to you in the memo: "Jessica, get rid of him."	Mr. Fenster to this witness about Mr. Bingham. The Attorney was able to bring out this series of responses both on the direct examination of his witness and on the cross-examination of the witness for the other side. See *Trial Advocacy* Section 9.1 (A).

Arbitration Transcript 73

Bingham v. Ecotronics	
Cross Examination – **Jessica Martindale**	**Comments/Notes**

A: Yes.

Claimant's Attorney:

I have no further questions.

Arbitration Transcript 74

Bingham v. Ecotronics	
Redirect – Jessica Martindale	**Comments/Notes**

Arbitrator:

Redirect?

Respondent's Attorney:

Yes, Mr. Blackwell. Just a few questions. Ms. Martindale, I want to ask you a few questions about the memo that you've been shown. First of all, do you know the circumstances surrounding what brought that memo up?

1 A: Yes, I do. It was right after he had been insubordinate in a meeting again. He blew up at Mr. Fenster. Jack was very, very upset. It was more of a memo out of rage and just frustration than anything.

Q: Did that memo have any factor in your decision-making process to terminate Mr. Bingham?

A: Not at all.

Respondent's Attorney:

Thank you. I have nothing further.

1 Redirect examination is limited to those new matters brought out on cross-examination. Here the witness is asked to explain the very damaging words in the Fenster memo. See *Trial Advocacy* Section 7.9.

Bingham v. Ecotronics

Re-Cross – Jessica Martindale	Comments/Notes
Arbitrator:	
Mr. Bujold, do you have a brief recross-examination?	
1 Q: Yes, I do. Ms. Martindale, the memorandum that we have been referring to by Jack Fenster, it does not mention in any of the three paragraphs anything about the meeting that you've referred to, does it?	1 Recross examination is limited to those new items brought out in redirect examination. Attorneys on redirect and recross are not permitted to raise items that have already been brought out on the direct or cross-examination. See *Trial Advocacy* Section 9.2 (I).
A: No.	
Q: That's all.	
Arbitrator:	
Anything further from you, Ms. Kingsley?	
Respondent's Attorney:	
No.	
Arbitrator:	
Thank you very much.	
The Direct and Cross-Examinations of the other respondent's witnesses have been deleted.	

Bingham v. Ecotronics	
Arbitrator Asks for Rebuttal	**Comments/Notes**

Arbitrator:

Now that both parties have put on all their witnesses and presented all of the evidence, is either party interested in putting on any rebuttal evidence? Counsel?

Claimant's Attorney:

Nothing.

Respondent's Attorney

No, Sir.

Arbitration Transcript 77

Bingham v. Ecotronics

Final Argument / Summation – Respondent	Comments/Notes

Arbitrator:

Ms. Kingsley, are you prepared to proceed with Respondent's summation?

Respondent's Attorney:

Yes sir. Thank you very much.

Arbitrator:

Please proceed.

Respondent's Lawyer:

1 Mr. Blackwell, based on the evidence that you've heard today, it's clear that Claimant has failed to prove either of his claims. First, with respect to the contract claim, the substantial evidence here shows that the Claimant is an at will employee. Now, they've claimed that the handbook constitutes a contract. The testimony of Ms. Martindale showed that the handbook does not cover every possible reason to terminate somebody.

1 In this arbitration the Claimant has the burden of proof. Rather than saying that the Respondent has the responsibility of proving anything, the Respondent's Attorney makes it clear that the Claimant has failed in meeting the burden of proof. By relying on the fact that the Claimant is an at will employee, all the Respondent need show is that there is a reasonable basis for termination other than age. See *Trial Advocacy* Section 11.5 (G) (1).

Arbitration Transcript 78

Bingham v. Ecotronics	
Final Argument / Summation – Respondent	**Comments/Notes**
2 Certainly, if Mr. Bingham, for example, committed sexual harassment, he could be terminated even though it's not covered by the handbook. The handbook merely prescribes guidelines. Even if the handbook does rise to the level of a contract, Ecotronics met the terms of the guidelines in the handbook. The guidelines say that after three disciplines, three warnings, if you may, the employee can be terminated. Mr. Bingham was indeed warned three times.	2 The Respondent's Attorney demonstrates that the handbook rules are not as clear as the Claimant wants the Arbitrator to believe. The rules in the handbook are guidelines rather than rising to the level of a contract.
3 Moving to the age case. In order to prevail on the age discrimination claim, the Claimant must show first, that he is a member of the protected age group; second, that he was performing to the employer's legitimate expectations; third, he was discharged; and fourth, younger, similarly situated	3 In the next segments the Attorney argues very concisely that Mr. Bingham was terminated because of his lack of appropriate performance and that, rather than age discrimination, termination was based on the changing needs of the company. See *Trial Advocacy* Section 11.5 (B).

Bingham v. Ecotronics

Final Argument / Summation – Respondent	Comments/Notes
employees were treated more favorably. Claimant's case fails on two of these elements. First, the evidence shows that his performance was not up to the standards of his employer. The most significant incident with respect to this element is Mr. Bingham's undermining of Ms. Pohl with one of his clients. This incident could not help but cast Ecotronics in a bad light. And certainly that's part of meeting the expectations of an employer, especially when you have a person in a marketing area. Mr. Bingham, in a marketing situation, is expected to be sensitive to those kinds of employer-client relationships, and he certainly breached that relationship and situation. His disruptive shenanigans at work certainly fall short of legitimate expectations.	

Arbitration Transcript 80

Bingham v. Ecotronics

Final Argument / Summation – Respondent	Comments/Notes
Plaintiff's case on age discrimination also fails in a fourth element that younger employees were treated more favorably. Testimony shows that Ecotronics' business is changing and a marketing background is no longer appropriate or necessary for the future of this company. Therefore, younger employees who are similarly situated with marketing backgrounds will have no place with the company in the future.	
4 Ecotronics has shown by over whelming testimony, legitimate non-discriminatory reasons for his discharge. Ms. Martindale and Mr. Fenster testified to clear incidents of insubordination on the part of Mr. Bingham. Under the law, insubordination, even one incident, if it's bad enough, is a sort of misconduct that	4 Although the Respondent does not have the burden of proof, the Attorney demonstrates that Ecotronics not only relies on its defense of the failure of the Claimant to prove its case, but has gone further and provided strong testimony demonstrating the non-discriminatory reasons for Mr. Bingham's discharge. See *Trial Advocacy* Section 11.5 (A).

Arbitration Transcript 81

Bingham v. Ecotronics

Final Argument / Summation – Respondent	Comments/Notes
justifies discharge. Mr. Bingham's discharge is also justified by his disruptive behavior and his attitude. His contempt of his boss, Mr. Fenster, was completely unconcealed. Everyone in the company knew that he had feuded and continued to feud with Hannah Pohl. A company that depends on teamwork cannot function with the negative and disruptive influence like Mr. Bingham in its midst.	
5 Now, a couple of particular points. Counsel for Mr. Bingham has focused on a memo from Mr. Fenster to Ms. Martindale in which he referred to Mr. Bingham in unflattering terms, including a "has been." As Mr. Fenster explained, this reference was not to Mr. Bingham's age, but rather to his continued role at Ecotronics. At one time, clean-	5 In the final segment of this summation, the attorney deals with one of the more difficult aspects of its case, the Fenster memorandum. The statements in the memorandum are particularly damaging. This is a very difficult piece of evidence. The placement of this portion of the argument is very important. The Attorney could not avoid it.

Arbitration Transcript 82

Bingham v. Ecotronics

Final Argument / Summation – Respondent	Comments/Notes
up work was subcontracted out, and his marketing background and experience was necessary and useful. This business changed. It wasn't the fault of Mr. Bingham. It wasn't the fault of Ecotronics. That's how it worked. It certainly is sad when somebody gets discharged, but that doesn't mean the law has been violated. Mr. Bingham became a "has been" because circumstances changed. Rock stars can become "has beens" at 25 when the tastes of teenagers change. The Fenster memorandum does not prove that Jessica Martindale fired Mr. Bingham because of his age. She did not rely on that memo. Age had nothing to do with his firing at all. Now counsel has brought up earlier the case of the	In the argument, the Attorney first dealt with the Claimant's failure to prove its case, then with the Fenster memorandum, followed by a return to the positive arguments. Primary and recency are important doctrines, what the Arbitrator hears first and last may have the greatest impact. See *Trial Advocacy* Section 11.2.

Arbitration Transcript 83

Bingham v. Ecotronics

Final Argument / Summation – Respondent	Comments/Notes
6 <u>Mathers v. Folley Particulate</u> case. This case only comes into play if there is a violation of the age discrimination act. Since we've already shown that Ecotronics did not discriminate against Mr. Bingham on the basis of age, the <u>Mathers</u> case really has no applicability.	6 Rather than dealing with the Mathers case directly, contesting each individual component of that case, the Attorney restates what she said in her opening statement and that is that the Mathers case doesn't apply and need not be considered.
7 The claimant has failed to prove that the firing of Mr. Bingham was improper. Bingham was fired for legitimate reasons. He was an at will employee who did not do his job and did not meet the needs of the company. His termination must be sustained. I have nothing further, your Honor. Thank you.	7 In the final segment of the summation the Attorney restates the theme, and strongly and simply states the Respondent's position. See *Trial Advocacy* Section 11.4 (D).

Arbitrator:

Thank you, counsel.

Arbitration Transcript 84

Bingham v. Ecotronics

Final Argument / Summation – Claimant	Comments/Notes
Arbitrator:	
Mr. Bujold, are you prepared to proceed with Claimant's summation?	
Claimant's Attorney:	
I am.	
Arbitrator:	
Please proceed.	
Claimant's Attorney:	
1 At the age of 54, Lester Bingham had devoted 15 years of his professional life to Ecotronics—the most productive years of his career. He had developed many new clients in his position within the marketing of the company. He had expanded existing client relationships. In all of that, he was a true partner with Ecotronics in their growth these last 15 years. His reward for that was to be terminated. A termination that was unjustified.	1 The Claimant's closing argument parallels the opening statement. The attorney begins with a positive statement of Lester Bingham's performance followed with a statement setting out the basis for the unjustified termination. The company discriminated against Mr. Bingham because of his age and did not follow its own rule. The company's reasons were fabricated. See *Trial Advocacy* Section 11.1 (C).

Arbitration Transcript 85

Bingham v. Ecotronics

Final Argument / Summation – Claimant	Comments/Notes
A termination that violated their own policies and procedures and a termination that was illegal. Illegal because the truth is, it was based on his age, not his performance and not his contribution to this company.	
2 There is no issue here with respect to Mr. Bingham's competence. No issue has been raised and there is no evidence that he was not competently performing the duties within the marketing department. A review of his personnel file shows that for the last 15 years, there were no indications of any problems until some 18 months ago when Ms. Martindale came on board. It was at that time that this issue of voluntary retirement was raised. Voluntary retirement—a program that was offered to no one but Mr. Bingham. There is no evidence to show that	2 Following the introduction to the summation, the detailed structure of the summation is straightforward: • The personnel file shows no history of poor performance. • The retirement program was a subterfuge. • And the words of the Fenster memorandum show that Mr. Bingham was fired because of age. See *Trial Advocacy* Section 11.4 (A) (5).

Arbitration Transcript 86

Bingham v. Ecotronics

Final Argument / Summation – Claimant	Comments/Notes
there was any program in force or that any person other than Lester Bingham was to be a participant in that program. The facts clearly are that there was no program—no voluntary retirement program, that that was simply used to try to terminate him.	
3 And the facts here clearly also demonstrate that Ecotronics violated their own policies. The employee handbook shows the policies that were in force and should have been followed if a termination was to be given to this gentleman because of what has been alleged here as insubordination and failure to participate in accordance with the policies of the company. And that was not followed. We have shown that through the testimony of all the witnesses. The only undisputed fact is	3 These facts are not a random restatement of evidence. The details follow the introduction outline and are stated strongly to support each of the Attorney's positions. See *Trial Advocacy* Section 11.4 (A).

Arbitration Transcript 87

Bingham v. Ecotronics

Final Argument / Summation – Claimant	Comments/Notes
the memorandum of Jack Fenster, and it is that memorandum of September 29 that clearly sets forth the real reason for Mr. Bingham's termination. There has been no explanation offered by any of the witnesses to show that it is anything other than based on his age. The memorandum is clear. The memorandum shows that Mr. Bingham was determined by Mr. Fenster and Ms. Martindale to be an old man that had to leave. He was specifically referred to as an "old dog," a "fossil," a "has been," and a "back number," and that as of September 29, Jack Fenster and Jessica Martindale determined that, because of the age and because of his desire to get youth within the company, to move ahead, to further their objectives within this company, that they	

Arbitration Transcript 88

Bingham v. Ecotronics	
Final Argument / Summation – Claimant	**Comments/Notes**
had to get rid of him. And that's what they proceeded to do. The case that applies and controls is the <u>Mather's</u> case. A case that states that if there is to be a voluntary retirement program, it cannot be a subterfuge to evade the jurisdiction's prohibition against discrimination based on age. That's what this all comes down to. Clearly age was the motivating factor. The desire for youth and the desire to get rid of Mr. Bingham because he just was no longer, in the eyes of Mr. Fenster and Ms. Martindale, young enough to further their objectives within the company. The issues with respect to his insubordination and his behavior have been blown clearly out of proportion. If, indeed he was such a troublesome employee, someone who had such difficulty as a team player,	

Bingham v. Ecotronics

Final Argument / Summation – Claimant	Comments/Notes
how did he get along for 15 years before that with no issues?	
4 Les Bingham's complaint to the EPA simply showed a man who cared about his company, who felt that he had an obligation to the company to call its attention to an issue. That issue was investigated, the company made a decision, and the EPA confirmed that decision. But that should not be a basis for terminating him when one of his obligations in his position is to make sure that client relationships and the projects themselves are carried out in accordance with the policies and procedures of this company.	4 The Attorney turns seemingly negative facts into positive facts. Rather than being a negative, the complaint to the EPA presents Mr. Bingham in a positive light. It shows a person who cares about the company and its clients. It does not show an unhappy person. See *Trial Advocacy* Section 11.5 (A).
5 So when you sift through all of that and you get to the only piece of evidence that no one has been able to refute, the only piece of evidence that was documented at a time prior to	5 The most powerful evidence is the Fenster Memorandum. By saving it for the end, the Attorney ends the argument with the strongest point.

Arbitration Transcript 90

Bingham v. Ecotronics

Final Argument / Summation – Claimant	Comments/Notes
the termination to show exactly what motivated that termination, was the memorandum of September 29—a memorandum that clearly shows the basis for this termination to be age related.	
6 The termination was unjust and Mr. Bingham's claims should be granted.	6 Following the same structure as the opening statement, the Attorney "bookends his summation" and clearly restates his theme. The termination was based on age which was an improper and illegal ground for termination. See *Trial Advocacy* Section 11.4 (E).

Bingham v. Ecotronics	
Arbitrator Concluding Remarks	**Comments/Notes**

Arbitrator:

7 Now that the summations are completed in this case, I'll tell you what the process is from this point forward. You can expect a ruling from me based on all of the things that you have provided to me before the arbitration and the testimony today and the exhibits I've seen. Expect a ruling within ten days. As I understand it, neither side will be submitting any post-arbitration brief is that right?

Claimant's Attorney:

Correct.

Respondent's Attorney:

That is correct.

Arbitrator:

This arbitration is concluded.

7 **And what is your decision in this case and why? How effective or ineffective were the advocates? What would you have done differently to win?**

Arbitration Transcript 92

SECTION FIVE

ADMINISTRATIVE HEARING TRANSCRIPT

MR. SCRATCH v. JABEZ STONE

ADMINISTRATIVE LAW HEARING

Mr. Scratch v. Jabez Stone

TRANSCRIPT

This transcript presents an administrative hearing, from opening statement to summation. The case demonstrates advocacy strategies, tactics, and techniques discussed in the companion *Trial Advocacy Before Judges, Jurors, and Arbitrators* text. Comments appear in the transcript explaining the advocacy approaches. This case illustrates how lawyers try an administrative law case, how the various stages of a case interrelate, how evidence is introduced, how case theories are presented, and how strategies and tactics affect the decision of a case.

This case is based in large part on a short story, *The Devil and Daniel Webster*, written by Stephen Vincent Benet. The story presents a fascinating tale. A farmer named Jabez Stone signs a contract with Mr. Scratch, the devil. This variation on the ancient theme has Mr. Stone agreeing to give his soul to the devil after a period of seven years, during which time the devil promises to provide him with good fortune. Prior to this arrangement, Mr. Stone had suffered bad luck for many years while his neighbors had prospered. After he signed the infamous document, his fortunes improve and he becomes successful. At the end of the term, the devil seeks to enforce the contract. Stone pleads for more time, and Scratch grants him a 3 year extension of more good fortune. At the conclusion of this time period, Mr. Scratch returns to claim another soul and Mr. Stone demurs.

The State of Summit, the locale of this case, has a statute which validates a contract to sell or barter one's soul if the contract has sufficient consideration and if a fraud was not perpetrated by one of the parties. The statute also provides that any dispute regarding the validity and enforceability of this type of contract involving a soul is to be submitted to a state administrative agency with a hearing conducted by an administrative judge who is to decide the case. The claimant devil now seeks to enforce the terms of the contract. The respondent farmer claims that the document is null and void based on fraud and insufficient consideration. Section references in this *Supplement* refer to sections in *Trial Advocacy Before Judges, Jurors, and Arbitrators*.

We have created a transcript to reflect how the case may have been tried today. Parts of this hearing have been condensed. Not all legal strategies and tactics are presented, and not all evidence is introduced. Only the parties are called as witnesses.

As you read through the transcript, consider the various strategies, tactics, and techniques presented and analyze the effectiveness of these lawyers and what you would have done similarly or differently to produce a favorable decision.

Mr. Scratch v. Jabez Stone

Preliminary Remarks	Comments/Notes
Judge:	
1 This administrative law case is entitled Mr. Scratch, who is the Claimant, appearing here now with his lawyer, versus the respondent, Jabez Stone, who is also present with his lawyer.	1 The administrative law judge begins with an introduction of the parties and lawyers and an explanation of the procedures. The procedural explanation tells the parties what will happen. There are a variety of administrative hearing procedures. In some types of cases, the judge asks questions first followed by the lawyers. In other types of cases, the attorneys may present all the evidence. In still other cases, the judge or judges may ask most of the questions. And there may or may not be an opportunity to make an opening statement. See *Trial Advocacy* Section 2.2 (D)
The Claimant shall proceed first and make an opening statement followed by Respondent. I will then ask a few questions of the Claimant and Respondent, and I may ask more questions later. Claimant will then offer evidence and testify, to be cross-examined by Respondent, who shall then follow and present evidence and be cross-examined by Claimant. Both sides will have a closing opportunity to present summations.	
Counsel, you may make your opening statement.	

Administrative Law Case 3

Mr. Scratch v. Jabez Stone

Opening Statement for Claimant Scratch	Comments/Notes
Claimant's Attorney:	
2 Your Honor, this is a very straightforward and simple contract case. Over ten years ago, Mr. Scratch and Mr. Stone entered into a contract—a written contract signed by both Mr. Scratch and Mr. Stone. In that contract, Mr. Scratch agreed to provide great good fortune to Mr. Stone for seven years, and Mr. Scratch later agreed to extend that good fortune for an additional three years. Mr. Scratch in fact did provide him with that good fortune for ten years; and in return, Mr. Stone agreed to give his soul to Mr. Scratch.	2 This opening is concise, clear, and persuasive. Its simplicity is intended to reflect the position of the Claimant that the case is a straightforward case. The first paragraph briefly summarizes the essential facts. The second paragraph introduces the primary theory of the case, and minimizes a bad aspect of the Claimant's case. The third paragraph explains in more detail the supporting facts. The concluding paragraph restates reasons why the Claimant should win and what decision the judge needs to make. Overall, it is a very good example of an effective opening. See *Trial Advocacy* Section 6.1 (B).
Your Honor, this contract is like any other contract. The terms of the contract agreed to by Mr. Scratch and Mr. Stone are binding. Mr. Scratch did what he agreed to do, and now	

Administrative Law Case 4

Mr. Scratch v. Jabez Stone

Opening Statement for Claimant Scratch	Comments/Notes
Mr. Stone must do what he agreed. Yes, Mr. Scratch is the devil, and what he may well be is deceitful, a liar, and a scallywag. But his character and the character of Mr. Stone are not relevant to this enforcement of this contract. Here's what happened.	
Mr. Stone had been a very unfortunate man. He had suffered ill fortune all his life. While plowing one day, a large rock appeared to fly up from the earth wrecking the transmission of his Harvester tractor. And, as he stood looking at the tractor, the engine caught on fire destroying the tractor. Worse, his two children were down with the measles, his wife was ailing, and he had a sore on his thumb. And then he said	

Administrative Law Case 5

Mr. Scratch v. Jabez Stone	
Opening Statement for Claimant Scratch	**Comments/Notes**
aloud: "I vow"—and he looked around for help—"I vow it's enough to make a man want to sell his soul to the devil! And I would, too, for two cents!" Hearing that, Mr. Scratch approached Mr. Stone the next day and presented him with the contract which was signed behind his barn, signed by Mr. Stone in his own blood.	
You will conclude—based on the evidence and the law of the State of Summit—that the contract is valid and enforceable. The ten years of good fortune were more than sufficient consideration. There was no fraud for Mr. Stone knew what he was doing and who he was dealing with. Mr. Scratch fulfilled his part of the contract. Jabez Stone must now be held to fulfill his obligation under the terms of that contract and honor his word and commitment.	

Administrative Law Case 6

Mr. Scratch v. Jabez Stone

Opening Statement for Defendant Stone	Comments/Notes
Respondent's Lawyer:	
3 The claimant is deceitful, a liar, and a scallywag. Yes, those are the very words of Claimant's able counsel. Those words and the evidence you will hear in this case will convince you that this contract is not binding but is only a worthless piece of paper.	3 The opening by the Respondent begins with an explanation of the theories of the case and why Respondent should win. The second paragraph uses three parallel phrases to highlight the strengths of the Respondent's cases and to neutralize its weaknesses. The next two paragraphs summarize the salient facts portraying events differently than the story told by the Claimant. The final two paragraphs reiterate why the Judge should rule in favor of Claimant. Overall, this opening is a very good example of a compelling opening that weaves together the facts and legal theories. See *Trial Advocacy* Section 6.4.
It is true that Mr. Stone, an honest but unfortunate and now wiser man, signed that piece of paper in blood behind his barn. And it is true that Mr. Stone did not know the extent of the terms of the supposed contract and thought it was all a bad dream. It is also true that Mr. Stone signed that worthless piece of paper because of the misrepresentations made by the claimant. The claimant, the devil, took advantage of the misery of the defendant.	

Administrative Law Case 7

Mr. Scratch v. Jabez Stone

Opening Statement for Defendant Stone	Comments/Notes
Jabez Stone was a desperate man. He had never prospered. His neighbors around him always had fortune much greater than his own. While he worked and struggled, everything that could go wrong went wrong. While his neighbors' fields grew lush, his withered. When his neighbors' cattle grew fat, his grew thin. When his neighbors' children were rosy cheeked, healthy, and smart, his were sickly and dull. While a few of his other neighbors had some bad luck, occasional failed crops or poor livestock, and once in a while, sick children, it seemed to Jabez Stone that somehow his luck was poorer than those others. So yes, in desperation, one day he did say for two cents he would sell his soul to the devil.	

Administrative Law Case 8

Mr. Scratch v. Jabez Stone	
Opening Statement for Defendant Stone	**Comments/Notes**
And yes, while the fortunes of Jabez Stone improved over the next ten years, they only improved to the extent that his neighbors had the same improved good fortune.	
The evidence will show that the claimant cannot prove that Jabez Stone received anything beyond that which his neighbors regularly received. Claimant cannot prove that he provided consideration to Jabez Stone as a result of the terms of this unenforceable contract. And the testimony will establish that the devil—who in is his own desperation, wanted and needed souls— defrauded and deceived Mr. Stone.	
No contract exists here, and the laws of Summit do not validate this worthless piece of paper. At the end of this case, I will ask you to render an award against the devil, Mr. Scratch, and in favor of Jabez Stone.	

Administrative Law Case 9

Mr. Scratch v. Jabez Stone

Opening Statement for Defendant Stone	Comments/Notes
Judge:	

Judge:

4 I will now swear the witnesses and ask some preliminary questions. Please raise your right hands.

Do you affirm that you will tell the truth, the whole truth, and nothing but the truth, and this you will do under the penalties of perjury?

Mr. Scratch:

I do.

Mr. Stone:

I do.

To Mr. Scratch:

Q: Mr. Scratch, you are the Claimant in this case?

A: I am.

Q: Is it your contention that a contract exists between you and Mr. Stone to sell his soul?

4 This evidentiary part of this case begins with the administrative law judge asking questions to establish key facts and summarizing the issues presented by the parties. It is common for administrative judges to review the exhibits to establish relevance, foundation, and authenticity in an effort to determine what is in issue. Or a judge may ask the parties to stipulate to uncontested exhibits. The Judge here also summarizes the issues. This is helpful to make sure that the Judge understands what decisions need to be made and that the lawyers know what they must prove. This approach also helps a subsequent reviewing court understand the case. See *Trial Advocacy* Section 2.8 (E).

Administrative Law Case 10

Mr. Scratch v. Jabez Stone

Opening Statement for Defendant Stone	Comments/Notes
A: Yes. There is a contract.	
Q: I hand you what has been marked as Exhibit No. 1. Tell us what it is.	
A: It's the contract Mr. Stone and I signed.	
Q: Is this the document you are seeking to enforce?	
A: Yes, I am.	
Q: Is this your signature on Exhibit No. 1?	
A: Yes. I proudly signed it.	
To Mr. Stone:	
Q: I show you Exhibit No. 1, tell me what it is.	
A: It's a piece of paper that means nothing.	
Q: Is this the document you claim is not enforceable?	
A: It is not enforceable, sir.	
Q: Did you sign this Exhibit here?	
A: Sadly, I did.	

Administrative Law Case 11

Mr. Scratch v. Jabez Stone

Opening Statement for Defendant Stone	Comments/Notes

Judge:

I understand that the Claimant seeks a decision ordering Mr. Stone to give his soul to Mr. Scratch.

Claimant's Attorney:

That's correct, your Honor.

Judge:

And I understand that Respondent contends that there is no or insufficient consideration supporting an agreement and that Claimant defrauded and deceived Respondent.

Respondent's Lawyer

Yes, sir, that is what happened.

Judge:

Exhibit No. 1 is in evidence. Counsel for Claimant you may proceed.

Claimant's Attorney:

I call Mr. Scratch.

Administrative Law Case 12

Mr. Scratch v. Jabez Stone

Direct Examination of Mr. Scratch	Comments/Notes
Claimant's Attorney	
5 Q: Mr. Scratch, who are you? A: I am the devil. Q: Where do you live? A: I currently live in the place of darkness and misery. Q: Why did you not swear to God to tell the truth? A: I cannot take that oath. Everyone understands that. Q: But you are telling the truth?	5 Objections to the form of questions can be made in administrative hearings. Leading questions, though they may be efficient, do not permit the witness to tell a story. See *Trial Advocacy* Section 4.1 (B).
Respondent's Lawyer: Objection. Leading.	
Judge: Sustained.	
6 Q: What are you telling us now? A: I took an affirmation to tell the truth. So be it. Q: There are those who say you are deceitful, a liar, and a scallywag. A: I can assure that what I am about to say in this case actually happened. It happens all too frequently.	6 The beginning of the direct reaffirms the devil is telling the truth, an apparent weakness, and has the devil explain why he is telling the truth in this case in an effort to defuse an obvious concern. See *Trial Advocacy* Section 7.6 (A).

Administrative Law Case 13

Mr. Scratch v. Jabez Stone

Direct Examination of Mr. Scratch	Comments/Notes
7 Q: Mr. Scratch, when did you first become aware of Mr. Stone?	7 This preliminary background sets the stage for the introduction of the heart of the direct examination story. A direct needs to be structured so that the witness can easily testify and the fact finder can easily follow the story and be able to apply the law to the facts presented. See *Trial Advocacy* Section 7.8 (A).

7 Q: Mr. Scratch, when did you first become aware of Mr. Stone?

A: I have always known him.

Q: Why is that?

A: As part of my job, I am aware of everyone. I had watched Mr. Stone from a distance throughout his entire life.

Q: What had you observed?

A: I had observed that he was extremely unlucky and had bad fortune.

Q: Mr. Scratch, are you able to hear people when they talk even when you are not present?

A: Yes.

Q: How?

Respondent's Lawyer:

Objection. Improper opinion and speculation.

Judge:

Overruled.

A: It's just one of my talents.

Administrative Law Case 14

Mr. Scratch v. Jabez Stone

Direct Examination of Mr. Scratch	Comments/Notes
Q: What had you observed about Jabez Stone?	
A: I knew that he had a rocky field, a broken tractor, two children with measles, an ailing wife, and a whitlow on his thumb.	
Q: What's a whitlow?	
A: A very bad sore.	
Q: Did you have anything to do with this bad fortune?	
A: I did not!	
Q: Did you hear what Mr. Stone said while he was plowing some eleven years ago?	
A: Yes.	
Q: What did he say?	
A: He said "I vow it's enough to make a man want to sell his soul to the devil! And I would, too, for two cents!"	
Q: And why do you remember that so exactly?	

Administrative Law Case 15

Mr. Scratch v. Jabez Stone

Direct Examination of Mr. Scratch	Comments/Notes

A: It is something I had been waiting to hear for some time.

8 Q: What did you then do?

A: I appeared on his farm.

Q: What time did you arrive?

A: Around supper time.

Q: What did you do?

A: I approached him, and he went with me behind his barn.

Q: How did you look that day?

A: The same as I appear today.

Q: Same horns?

A: Yes.

Q: Same red facial features?

A: Yes.

Q: Same tail?

A: Yes.

Q: And how did Mr. Stone appear and act.

A: He seemed to recognize me and looked normal and relieved.

8 These answers introduce the parties, the contract, and the exact promises. The description of the parties establishes a contract setting. The simple, clear terms of the agreement constitute consideration. A direct examination must include facts that support the claims that rebut the opponent's contentions. The story presented here avoids any references to extraneous theories of confusion, desperation, or deceit to reduce the time and emphasis spent on those allegations. See *Trial Advocacy* Section 7.8 (G).

Administrative Law Case 16

Mr. Scratch v. Jabez Stone

Direct Examination of Mr. Scratch	Comments/Notes
Q: What did you do there? A: I showed him a document. Q: Mr. Scratch, I have just given you Exhibit No. 1. Earlier, you testified that this Exhibit is the contract you seek to enforce, correct? A: Yes. Q: Is this contract in the same condition now as it as when it was signed? A: It looks and is the same. Q: Were there any other terms discussed besides those written in the contract? A: None. Q: Please read the contract. A: "I, Jabez Stone, agree to sell my soul to the devil in return for great good fortune." "I, Mr. Scratch, agree to provide Jabez Stone with great good fortune for at least seven years in return for his soul."	

Administrative Law Case 17

Mr. Scratch v. Jabez Stone

Direct Examination of Mr. Scratch	Comments/Notes
9 Q: Mr. Scratch, after that day in May when did you next contact Mr. Stone? A: Seven years later to the day. Q: During those seven years, did you do anything in regard to Mr. Stone. A: Yes. Q: What did you do? A: I oversaw his life. Q: What do you mean? A: I saw to it that he had good crops, healthy children, a happy marriage, was successful in the community, and that he always prospered. Q: How were you able to do this? A: I am the devil. I can do those things. Q: When you met Jabez Stone, what did you do?	9 This chronology sets forth the essential facts Claimant must prove to show consideration and an enforceable contract. This direct is structured and presented to reflect what the Claimant claims: this is a simple case seeking to enforce a valid contract. See *Trial Advocacy* Section 6.3 (A).

Administrative Law Case 18

Mr. Scratch v. Jabez Stone

Direct Examination of Mr. Scratch	Comments/Notes
A: We met and I came to collect his soul.	
Q: What did Mr. Stone do?	
A: He begged and pleaded for an extension.	
Q: Did you give it to him?	
A: Yes, I did.	
Q: For how long?	
A: Three years.	
Q: What did you do for Jabez Stone during those three years?	
A: I continued to provide for his great good fortune.	
Q: What happened at the end of those three years?	
A: I came to collect his soul.	
Q: Did you collect his soul?	
A: No. He refused to give it to me as he had promised.	
Claimant's Attorney:	
I have no further questions of this witness.	

Administrative Law Case 19

Mr. Scratch v. Jabez Stone

Cross-Examination of Mr. Scratch	Comments/Notes
Respondent's Lawyer:	
10 Q: Mr. Scratch, you are a liar? A: Yes. Q: You are a deceiver? A: I am. Q: You are a scallywag? A: Of course. Q: You could never swear an oath before God to tell the truth? A: That is true.	10 The cross begins with a strong point to which the witness has to and may even want to agree with. The cross questions are all leading, short, and fact based which is the best way to obtain answers to these questions. See *Trial Advocacy* Section 9.3 (A).
11 Q: In the time before you met Mr. Stone, you were aware of the bad fortune of Jabez Stone? A: Yes, I was. Q: And you also knew that many farmers in his community had very good fortune during that same time? A: Yes. Q: You also knew that many other farmers had some bad fortune during this time?	11 These carefully crafted questions require the witness to agree even if he wanted to disagree. The answers to these questions establish favorable evidence for the Respondent and support the key defense of lack of consideration. See *Trial Advocacy* Section 9.1 (A).

Administrative Law Case 20

Mr. Scratch v. Jabez Stone	
Cross-Examination of Mr. Scratch	**Comments/Notes**
A: Yes I did.	
Q: You knew that when his crops failed they were no worse than some other farms in the area?	
A: Yes, that's true.	
Q: Some neighbors had poor live stock just like Mr. Stone?	
A: Yes.	
Q: Others had sick children too?	
A: That's correct.	
Q: Some nearby farmers had similar bad luck over the years?	
A: I agree.	
Q: You knew that Jabez Stone worked as hard or harder than all the other farmers, didn't you?	
A: I did.	
12 Q: You said on direct examination that you first approached Mr. Stone at his farm, correct? A: Yes.	12 The Cross-examiner picks up the pace and intensity of the exam and asks more pointed and difficult statements for the witness to agree with.

Administrative Law Case 21

Mr. Scratch v. Jabez Stone

Cross-Examination of Mr. Scratch	Comments/Notes
Q: You did not tell him you were the devil, did you? A: Of course not. Q: You went to Mr. Stone to get him to sign a contract for his soul. A: Sure. Q: You knew he was desperate. A: Isn't everyone? Q: My question to you, Mr. Scratch, was: You knew Mr. Stone was desperate. A: He had reason to be. Q: And you knew he was desperate? A: Yes. Q: And he was depressed? A: He was sad. Q: You knew he was feeling depressed. A: I felt that in him. Q: And you knew he thought he was having a bad dream.	As a result, the witness attempts to avoid direct answers. The Advocate obtains responsive answers by repeating the question and by insisting on responses. This approach both controls the witness and establishes the helpful facts. A witness who knows that a lawyer will continue to pursue a question is more likely to be responsive and less likely to be evasive. See *Trial Advocacy* Section 9.3 (D).

Administrative Law Case 22

Mr. Scratch v. Jabez Stone

Cross-Examination of Mr. Scratch	Comments/Notes
A: He said something about a dream.	
Q: You know what dreams he, or anyone else, is having, right?	
A: Sure.	
Q: And then you told him to sign the paper.	
A: He wanted to sign it.	
13 Q: Because he thought the nightmare would end, right?	13 In an effort to pursue information, the Advocate asks objectionable questions. While this may be in reaction to non-responsive answers or a growing frustration, the Advocate should focus on asking relevant and fact based questions. A witness who refuses to answer an obvious question is likely to lose credibility as a witness. Here, of course, the witness is the devil and the Cross-examiner need not be as compassionate toward this witness as a typical witness. See *Trial Advocacy* Section 4.7.
A: I don't know.	
Q: You know everything, don't you?	
A: Only God does.	
Q: You went to Mr. Stone to take advantage of him.	
A: No.	
Q: Well, you went to him to get his soul?	
A: Definitely.	
Q: Because you lost your soul many millennia ago.	

Administrative Law Case 23

Mr. Scratch v. Jabez Stone	
Cross-Examination of Mr. Scratch	**Comments/Notes**

Claimant's Attorney:

Objection. Argumentative.

Judge:

Sustained.

14   Q: Mr. Scratch you drafted the terms of Exhibit No 1?

A: I wrote the terms.

Q: You brought this piece of paper with you when you first met Mr. Stone.

A: Yes.

Q: You had this Exhibit already written out before you saw Mr. Stone.

A: Yes.

14   Ordinarily, an Advocate should always refer to an exhibit by its marked number or letter to avoid any confusion and to maintain an accurate record. Here, there is only one documentary exhibit. See *Trial Advocacy* Section 8.5.

15   Q: Now after Mr. Stone signed that document, he had good fortune?

A: Yes, he did.

Q: During that time that he had good fortune, his crops were no better than many other farmers' crops in the area?

15   The Cross-examiner returns to a line of questioning establishing lack of consideration. The structure of this cross is designed to have the fact finder easily understand and follow the established facts. See *Trial Advocacy* Section 9.2 (F).

Administrative Law Case 24

Mr. Scratch v. Jabez Stone	
Cross-Examination of Mr. Scratch	**Comments/Notes**
A: This is true.	
Q: His cattle were no better than the best cattle in the area?	
A: This is true.	
Q: His wife and children were no more healthy than other healthy families in the area?	
A: This is true.	
Q: And Mr. Stone was no more respected than other very respected people in the area during that time?	
A: This is also true.	
16 Q: During the initial seven year period, you never talked to Mr. Stone, did you?	16 The Judge understands the potential relevancy of this line of questioning. If the Judge has sustained the objection, the Advocate could ask to be heard and explain the relevancy. Administrative judges often use a more restrictive scope of relevancy than judicial judges and administrative cases often
A: I did not need to.	
Q: And you didn't talk to him?	
A: I did not talk to him.	
Q: During this time, you had at least one other farmer sign what you call a contract?	

Administrative Law Case 25

Mr. Scratch v. Jabez Stone

Cross-Examination of Mr. Scratch	Comments/Notes
A: I did. Q: And his name was Mr. Stevens? A: It was. Q: On that day when you came to Mr. Stone to get his soul, you had the soul of another person in your possession, didn't you? **Claimant's Attorney:** Objection. Irrelevant. **Judge:** Overruled. 17 A: Yes, I did. Q: And that was the soul of Mr. Stevens? A: Yes, it was. Q: You kept Mr. Stevens' soul wrapped in your handkerchief? A: I did. Q: Mr. Stevens just died that very day? A: He had.	involve issues that restrict marginally relevant evidence. See *Trial Advocacy* Section 4.1 (B). 17 This statement is an admissible excited utterance or present sense impression. Advocates, during cross-examination as well as direct examination, need to be aware of hearsay objections. Opposing lawyers need to listen to the question which may contain hearsay. Cross-examiners need to be prepared to provide the judge with the applicable exception(s) if needed. See *Trial Advocacy* Section 4.8 (H) (1).

Administrative Law Case 26

Mr. Scratch v. Jabez Stone

Cross-Examination of Mr. Scratch	Comments/Notes
Q: The soul of Mr. Stevens fluttered from that handkerchief like a moth?	
A: That's true.	
Q: Mr. Jabez Stone seemed shocked when he saw the soul of Mr. Stevens?	
A: Yes, he did.	
Q: You heard the lament of Mr. Stevens?	
A: Yes, I did.	
Q: The soul of Mr. Stevens cried out for help, correct?	
Claimant's Attorney:	
Objection. Hearsay.	
Judge:	
Overruled.	
18 A: Yes.	18 The cross concludes with a strong point and a helpful fact which supports and reiterates the remedy the defense seeks. While it may have been tempting for the advocate to act aggressively and ask derisive questions, it is usually a better tactic to act professionally and ask clearly relevant questions. See *Trial Advocacy* Section 9.4 (F).
Q: When Mr. Stevens cried for help, Mr. Stone started to cry and plead and beg to get out of the deal, correct?	
A: Yes.	

Administrative Law Case 27

Mr. Scratch v. Jabez Stone	
Cross-Examination of Mr. Scratch	**Comments/Notes**

Q: You did not let him get out of it, did you?

A: I did not.

Q: You extended what you said was your contract for three more years?

A: I did.

Q: You then left and never talked to Mr. Stone again until three years later?

A: That's correct.

Q: You never contacted him again until you again came to demand his soul?

A: That is correct.

19 These leading, short, fact based questions compel the witness to agree.

Q: And he told you then that his soul was too valuable and you would never get it?

A: That's what he said.

Respondent's Lawyer:

I have no further questions.

Mr. Scratch v. Jabez Stone

Redirect Examination of Mr. Scratch	Comments/Notes
Claimant's Attorney:	
20 Q: Mr. Scratch, when you first met with Mr. Stone, please describe how he looked. A: He looked a bit frustrated, but otherwise he appeared fine. Q: Before he signed the contract, did he say to you he was desperate? A: No. Q: Did he say he was depressed? A: No. Q: After Mr. Stone signed the contract, how did he appear to you? A: Relieved. **Claimant's Attorney:** Nothing further.	20 Redirect examination provides an opportunity for questions that expand, clarify, or correct answers given on cross-examination. Non-leading questions need to be asked, although the questions can contain previous answers of the witness or others. Here only a few questions need to be asked to clarify the evidence. A risk with redirect is that the witness has not been prepared to answer the question and may not be as helpful as needed. Another risk is that the advocate will ask too many questions that repeat earlier testimony and that are objectionable. See *Trial Advocacy* Section 7.9.

Administrative Law Case 29

Mr. Scratch v. Jabez Stone

Recross Examination of Mr. Scratch	Comments/Notes
Respondent's Lawyer:	
21 Q: Well, Mr. Scratch, you did not first meet with Mr. Stone to counsel him, did you?	21 Recross-examination follows the same techniques as cross-examination: short, leading, fact based questions with the examiner insisting on responsive answers. Its scope is limited to the scope of redirect. These questions and answers reflect an effective use of recross. See *Trial Advocacy* Section 9.2 (I).
A: No.	
Q: You didn't care how he looked, or even how he felt, did you?	
A: I didn't care at all.	
Q: The only feeling you had toward Mr. Stone was that of hate, correct?	
A: That is the only feeling I have for anyone.	
Respondent's Lawyer:	
No further questions.	
Claimant's Attorney:	
I have no further questions nor witnesses, your Honor. The Claimant rests.	

Administrative Law Case 30

Mr. Scratch v. Jabez Stone

Motion to Dismiss	Comments/Notes
Respondent's Lawyer:	
22 Your Honor, Respondent moves to dismiss this case on the ground that claimant has failed to prove a prima facie case for breach of contract because there has been no showing of adequate consideration.	22 A respondent may move to dismiss a case after the claimant has rested if there is insufficient evidence to support a prima facie case. In common administrative cases, there usually is no need to bring a motion to dismiss because minimally sufficient evidence has been presented or because the judge will want to receive evidence from the respondent. In complex cases, a motion is more likely to be made and expected to be made because some issues may be resolved at that stage of the case making further evidence unnecessary. See *Trial Advocacy* Section 3.8 (C) (6).
Judge:	
Motion denied. Proceed with your case, counsel.	
Respondent's Lawyer:	
I call Mr. Jabez Stone.	
Judge:	
Mr. Stone, you are still under oath to tell the truth.	

Administrative Law Case 31

Mr. Scratch v. Jabez Stone

Direct Examination of Mr. Stone	Comments/Notes

Respondent's Attorney:

23　Q: Mr. Stone, when did you first meet the Claimant, Mr. Scratch

A: About eleven years ago.

Q: Where were you?

A: I was at home on my farm.

Q: Did you invite Mr. Scratch to your home?

A: No, I did not.

Q: What happened?

A: He just appeared and told me he could do something for me that I deserved.

Q: Where did you go?

A: I took him behind the barn.

Q: Why?

A: I was embarrassed to be seen with him.

24　Q: What happened behind the barn?

23　The direct begins with relevant questions directed to the issue in the case, which is a typical format for administrative law cases. There need not be any routine background questions needed, and administrative law judges commonly expect all questions to directly relate to the issues. These direct questions begin to establish what happened and why and introduce events, feelings, and thoughts, all relevant to the defense theories. See *Trial Advocacy* Section 7.8.

24　Evidence can be introduced to reinforce and support earlier evidence established through other witnesses on direct or cross-

---

Administrative Law Case 32

Mr. Scratch v. Jabez Stone

Direct Examination of Mr. Stone	Comments/Notes
A: He showed me a piece of paper with writing on it. Q: Mr. Stone, I'm giving you what has been received in evidence as Exhibit No. 1. Did you write any of the terms of this Exhibit? A: I did not. It was all written up when I first saw it.	examination. Previously, the Advocate had the Claimant state he drafted the terms and now has the Respondent repeat that same fact. This tactic also shows what the witnesses agree on as a basis for later explaining in summation what they disagree on. See *Trial Advocacy* Section 7.2.
25 Q: Before you signed that paper, sir, what kind of a farmer were you? A: I was a very hard worker. Q: And after you signed the paper, sir, what kind of worker were you? A: The same. I farmed just as hard.	25 These two questions establish a before and after sequence. Direct examiners have choices to make regarding the organization of the direct and when to introduce what evidence. See *Trial Advocacy* Section 7.6.
26 Q: How long had you farmed before you met Mr. Scratch? A: For 15 years. Q: How did you do? A: Not very well. Q: What do you mean?	26 These series of questions elicit answers to establish the lack of consideration defense and buttress similar evidence previously introduced.

Administrative Law Case 33

Mr. Scratch v. Jabez Stone	
Direct Examination of Mr. Stone	**Comments/Notes**
A: It seemed no matter what I did, my crops failed.	
Q: How did your neighbors do?	
A: Most did better than me. Although there were some who had failures like me.	
Q: How did your animals do?	
A: They did not fare very well.	
Q: How did your neighbors' animals fare?	
A: Most were healthy, while mine were sick.	
Q: Were you aware of any other persons whose animals did not do well?	
A: There were some, yes.	
Q: How was your family?	
A: My two children were ill, and my wife was ailing. They seemed more sickly than most other families, although I am not able to say for sure, since I spent most of my time working on the farm.	

Administrative Law Case 34

Mr. Scratch v. Jabez Stone

Direct Examination of Mr. Stone	Comments/Notes
Q: As you continued to work, did your fortunes seem to change?	
A: Yes, a bit.	
Q: Did your crops, to the best of your knowledge, seem better than others during that time?	
A: Better than some, and as good as others.	
Q: Your animals?	
A: They seemed to fare just like many animals on other farms.	
Q: Your family?	
A: They seemed to be better for a while like some other families.	
27 Q: The day before Mr. Scratch came to your house, did you say any words about selling your soul?	27 These series of questions seek to establish the defense theories of fraud and deceit. They help reveal what the witness said, thought, and felt. See *Trial Advocacy* Section 7.8 (C).
A: Yes, I yelled out some blasphemous words.	
Q: Tell us why, sir?	

Administrative Law Case 35

Mr. Scratch v. Jabez Stone

Direct Examination of Mr. Stone	Comments/Notes
A: Because I was very frustrated and very desperate. Q: On the day Mr. Scratch came to your home, did you say you wanted to sell your soul? A: Heavens, no. Q: Mr. Stone, tell us why you signed Exhibit No. 1. A: I didn't understand what the paper was. I was very much confused, unhappy, and depressed. I thought I was dreaming and told Scratch so. Q: What did Mr. Scratch say to you? A: He said I was just having a bad dream, and if I signed the paper the nightmare would end. Q: Did Mr. Scratch say anything to you about him being the devil? A: No. Q: Did he look like he does today?	

Administrative Law Case 36

Mr. Scratch v. Jabez Stone

Direct Examination of Mr. Stone	Comments/Notes
A: Yes.	
Q: Who did you think he was?	
A: I thought maybe he was the devil, but I just didn't believe it was all really happening. I believed I was dreaming.	
28 Q: Did you think over the next seven years about what had happened?	28 The direct examination questions have been relatively short and easy to understand and have been asked in a well structured and organized format. This technique makes it easier for the witness to testify and for the Judge to understand the facts. See *Trial Advocacy* Section 7.7.
A: Yes.	
Q: Tell us what you thought.	
A: I became very unhappy and further depressed because I thought maybe what had happened was true.	
Q: When did you next see the piece of paper you signed?	
A: Three years later.	
Q: How did that come about?	
A: Mr. Scratch appeared to me again and told me he came to collect on his contract.	

Administrative Law Case 37

Mr. Scratch v. Jabez Stone	
Direct Examination of Mr. Stone	**Comments/Notes**
Q: What did you say to him?	
A: I told him it was all a nightmare I was reliving.	
Q: Did something change your mind?	
A: Yes.	
Q: What?	
A: I saw something that looked like a moth fall from the handkerchief of Mr. Scratch, and I heard a small voice crying out for help.	
Q: Did you recognize the voice?	
A: Yes.	
Q: Whose voice was it?	
A: It was the voice of Mr. Stevens.	
Q: Who is he?	
A: My neighbor.	
Q: How did you react?	
A: I was shocked.	
Q: Why?	

Administrative Law Case 38

Mr. Scratch v. Jabez Stone

Direct Examination of Mr. Stone	Comments/Notes
A: Because I thought Mr. Stevens was still alive.	
Q: You learned differently?	
A: Yes.	
Q: How?	
A: At the same time I heard Mr. Stevens' voice cry out, I heard the bell toll in the church. And I knew that he was dead, that Mr. Scratch had collected his soul.	
29 Q: What happened then?	29 The direct of the Respondent concludes with a persuasive fact, similar to the conclusion of the cross-examination of the Claimant. This parallelism helps create an overall effective presentation. See *Trial Advocacy* Section 7.6.
A: I begged and pleaded for mercy. I asked Mr. Scratch to let me go, and he agreed to give me three more years. I said nothing more. I just wanted him to go away.	
Q: When did you next see Mr. Scratch?	
A: Three years later.	
Q: What did he say at that time?	
A: He asked for my soul.	

Administrative Law Case 39

Mr. Scratch v. Jabez Stone	
Direct Examination of Mr. Stone	**Comments/Notes**
Q: What did you say?	
A: That my soul was too valuable to me and he would never get it.	
Respondent's Lawyer:	
Your witness, counsel.	

Administrative Law Case 40

Mr. Scratch v. Jabez Stone

Cross Examination of Mr. Stone	Comments/Notes
Claimant's Attorney:	
30 Q: Over ten years ago, Mr. Stone, you signed a document with Mr. Scratch, isn't that true? A: Yes. Q: Mr. Stone, I have put in your hands Exhibit No. 1. You read these words before you signed them? A: Yes. Q: It is the contract you signed with Mr. Scratch, correct? A: It's the paper I signed.	30 The cross begins with the introduction of the contract, which is a persuasive piece of evidence for the Claimant. This is an example of supportive cross with the attorney for the Claimant obtaining evidence to establish the Claimant's case. See *Trial Advocacy* Section 9.1 (A).
31 Q: You read it when you signed it? A: I did. Q: You pricked your finger before you signed it? A: I did. Q: And you signed it in your blood at the bottom? A: I did.	31 The Cross-examiner allows the witness to evasively answer some questions to set up follow up questions. A witness will lose credibility if the witness refuses to provide a proper, correct answer and instead wants to add self-serving statements. See *Trial Advocacy* Section 9.3.

Administrative Law Case 41

Mr. Scratch v. Jabez Stone	
Cross Examination of Mr. Stone	**Comments/Notes**
Q: That is your signature on the bottom?	
A: Yes.	
Q: And you did sign Exhibit No. 1?	
A: Yes, I did.	
Q: You read every word?	
A: I can't recall specifically.	
Q: The words are clear?	
A: I thought it was a dream.	
Q: But you understood every word of this document?	
A: I was confused.	
Q: But you decided to sign this document?	
A: Yes.	
Q: You knew that you promised to sell your soul?	
A: That seemed like a nightmare.	

Administrative Law Case 42

Mr. Scratch v. Jabez Stone

Cross Examination of Mr. Stone	Comments/Notes
32 Q: Exhibit No. 1 states that you agree to sell your "soul to the devil in return for great good fortune." A: That's what it says. Q: The day before you signed this document you said: "I vow it's enough to make a man want to sell his soul to the devil. And I would, too, for two cents"? A: Yes, but I was frustrated. Q: You thought that Mr. Scratch was the devil when he came to you? A: I thought so. Q: He looked and acted like the devil? A: I don't know. I had never met the devil.	32 The Cross-examiner effectively and properly treats the witness with respect and compassion. A tragedy may well have occurred here, and the Respondent may appear to be the emotive victim. But the Advocate focuses on establishing facts that favor the Claimant. See *Trial Advocacy* Section 9.3 (E).
33 Q: You did not try to get out of the contract that first week? A: True.	33 Disputes commonly involve responsibility, or irresponsibility. Here the Advocate establishes the responsible choices the

Administrative Law Case 43

Mr. Scratch v. Jabez Stone

Cross Examination of Mr. Stone	Comments/Notes
Q: First month?	Respondent made which did not occur because of any alleged fraud or deceit. See *Trial Advocacy* Section 1.6 (C).
A: True.	
Q: First year?	
A: That's true.	
Q: Or for seven years, until he came to you again?	
A: That's true.	
Q: And you accepted all your good fortune?	
34 A: Yes.	34 The cross concludes with a showing of consideration the Respondent received and expected to receive. An effective cross-examination tells a story different than the story told on direct. See *Trial Advocacy* Section 9.4 (B).
Q: The day before you signed this contract, your fortune was very poor?	
A: Yes. But, it was getting better.	
Q: And after this contract was signed, your fortune improved dramatically?	
A: Yes.	
Q: Your crops flourished?	
A: Yes. I worked hard.	
Q: Your cattle became well?	

Administrative Law Case 44

Mr. Scratch v. Jabez Stone	
Cross Examination of Mr. Stone	**Comments/Notes**
A: Yes.	
Q: Your children and wife were no longer ill?	
A: Yes. I took care of them.	
Q: You were well respected?	
A: Yes.	
Q: And you prospered?	
A: Yes.	
Q: Mr. Stevens, your friend, was a successful man, correct?	
A: Yes.	
Q: And there came a time when you realized he had entered into a contract to sell his soul to Mr. Scratch?	
A: I wasn't sure, but I feared he had done so.	
Q: Mr. Stevens had great good fortune in his life?	
A: Yes.	
Q: Similar to the great good fortune you had?	

Administrative Law Case 45

Mr. Scratch v. Jabez Stone	
Cross Examination of Mr. Stone	**Comments/Notes**
35 A: Yes. **Claimant's Attorney:** I have no further questions. **Respondent's Lawyer:** And I have no more questions. The defense rests. **Claimant's Attorney:** We have no rebuttal evidence, your Honor. **Judge:** And I have no questions. You may close now.	35 Administrative law judges can and typically do ask questions at the end of direct or cross-examination, and some times during an exam by interrupting the lawyer. They need to determine the evidence that exists in order to reach a correct decision. In this case, the lawyers did a good job in presenting the testimony and we did not show the judge asking more questions in order to maintain a reasonable length for this case example. See *Trial Advocacy* Section 2.8 (E). The party with the burden usually has the option of making the last argument, and so the Respondent closes first. Administrative judges may ask the lawyers questions during summation. Summations should include answers to questions the judge might have and cover all issues the judge has asked to decide. See *Trial Advocacy* Section 2.12.

Administrative Law Case 46

Mr. Scratch v. Jabez Stone

Summation for Respondent	Comments/Notes

Respondent's Lawyer:

36   This document, this piece of paper, that Claimant Scratch calls a contract is nothing of the sort. It is invalid, it is unenforceable, it is nothing more than a worthless piece of paper.

First, this paper was based on a fraud. The plaintiff claims that because Jabez Stone signed his name, he is bound by the terms of this paper signed in blood. But Mr. Stone signed this paper based on distortion, deceit, and lies. Jabez Stone did not know what he was getting into when he signed that piece of paper.

Scratch lied to him. The devil told him it was all a bad dream. Scratch deceived him. The devil told him the nightmare would

36 This summation begins and ends with a summary of the Respondent's theory of the case. The central part of the closing lists the reasons why and how the facts establish fraud and lack of consideration. The Respondent's Lawyer does not discuss the burden of proof because while the Claimant has the burden to establish a valid contract the Respondent has the burden to prove affirmative defenses. See *Trial Advocacy* Section 11.4 (E).

The Advocate explains how the judge can issue a decision consistent with the judge's beliefs and principles. The Advocate avoids directly playing to the passions and prejudices of the judge. While the opponent is the devil and the client is a farmer facing a tragedy, the Advocate decides not to focus the argument on emotions and feelings.

Administrative Law Case 47

Mr. Scratch v. Jabez Stone

Summation for Respondent	Comments/Notes

Summation for Respondent

end if he signed the contract. Further, Mr. Stone never offered to enter into a contract. The words he uttered aloud—words said in frustration and desperation—were not an offer to enter into a contract. If they were, where would many people be?

Second, the Claimant has not proved and cannot prove that anything was provided to Mr. Stone as a result of his signing that worthless piece of paper. How do we know that Mr. Stone's misfortunes for all the earlier events were not caused by the devil himself? If this is true, then Scratch fraudulently induced Mr. Stone to sign the contract, and that makes the contract void. And even if the misfortune was not caused by Scratch, Scratch could not have done what he said he did by providing good fortune to Jabez Stone.

Comments/Notes

This summation explains how the law applies to the facts and how this process leads to only one conclusion: victory for the Respondent. See *Trial Advocacy* Section 11.5 (A).

Administrative Law Case 48

Mr. Scratch v. Jabez Stone

Summation for Respondent	Comments/Notes
Third, the Claimant did not and cannot prove there was consideration, that Mr. Stone received anything from Scratch. Mr. Stone had good fortune for the past eleven years, but that good fortune was no better than those of many farmers who lived around him, who had no contract with the devil. His cattle were no more healthy, his fields no more lush, his family in no better health and spirits, his good fortune was no better than the good fortune of many of those around him, who had not considered selling their soul to the devil. Mr. Stone's good fortune came about by his own hard work.	

Mr. Scratch v. Jabez Stone

Summation for Respondent	**Comments/Notes**
Your Honor, you must base your decision in this case on how truthfully you believe these two witnesses testified. Whose work and actions should you believe? Jabez Stone, a righteous man, a fine family man, a hard worker? Or Scratch, ah, Mr. Scratch, yes, dishonest Mr. Scratch—a deceiver, a liar, and a scallywag? Scratch, the devil, the greatest liar in this world and the next, cannot be believed.	
The law of our State recognizes that contracts like this are only enforceable if there exists clear and unmistakable consideration and if there has been no apparent fraud or deceit. For these very reasons there is no valid and enforceable contract here. There is only a very mixed up and tragic story.	

Administrative Law Case 50

Mr. Scratch v. Jabez Stone	
Summation for Respondent	**Comments/Notes**
When you review the evidence and the law, you will conclude that the Claimant has not met the burden of proving its case and this document is a worthless piece of paper. When you consider what is fair, what is right, and what is just, you will reach the right decision and find against the devil and in favor of Jabez Stone.	

Administrative Law Case 51

Mr. Scratch v. Jabez Stone

Summation for Claimant	Comments/Notes
Claimant's Attorney:	

37   A contract is a contract is a contract. Jabez Stone willingly entered into a valid contract with Mr. Scratch. The terms of this contract—read and signed by the parties—are fair, and the promises are mutual. The law of the State of Summit recognizes the rights of parties to enter into this binding agreement—and for these rights to be enforced. Your duty, Your Honor, is to enforce this contract as any other contract.

Now Mr. Stone says he did not know that Mr. Scratch was the devil, yet he took advantage of the situation. He says he did not know he was the devil with his horns and his tail, yet he wanted Mr. Scratch to give him great good fortune. He says he did not mean it when he said

37   This summation begins and ends with a summary of why the Claimant should win and explains why the Claimant must win. The appeal to law and logic not only supports a victory in this case but also suggests that our system of justice and society are well served if the Claimant wins. This appeal relies on the values and norms of the professional decision maker whose job it is to uphold the law. See *Trial Advocacy* Section 11.2.

This closing is a good example of a persuasive explanation of the facts, law, and reasons supporting a decision. The summation anticipates questions the Judge may have and answers them. And the closing identifies the difficult issues the Judge has to decide and how easily the Judge can decide them in favor of the Claimant. See *Trial Advocacy* Section 1.6 (A).

Administrative Law Case 52

Mr. Scratch v. Jabez Stone

Summation for Claimant	Comments/Notes
for two cents he would sell his soul to the devil, yet he willingly signed a contract to sell his soul. He tells you he suffered great misfortune for all the years before he signed the contract. He admits he accepted good fortune immediately following the signing of the contract, but now he wants to get out of the contract he wanted over 10 years ago. Mr. Stone did not seek to void that contract the next day after he signed it, or the next week after he signed it, nor did he seek to void it the next year, but he waited for seven years before he said a word. He did not cry out to Mr. Scratch in the early days of his good fortune saying, "Please, end the contract—take my good fortune away, I want to return to	

Administrative Law Case 53

Mr. Scratch v. Jabez Stone

Summation for Claimant	Comments/Notes
the way I was, I want to suffer like I did." He was willing to risk his soul for good fortune and when it came time to pay, he wanted out, he wanted to avoid his part of the bargain. When the seven-year contract was up he asked for an extension and Mr. Scratch gave him three more years of great good fortune. And now he claims he has no responsibility to fulfill his end of the bargain—to give Mr. Scratch what he promised to give him. We must take the words of the contract and we must see what Mr. Jabez Stone promised, what he bargained for, what he got. On that day in May, he said he would sell his soul for two cents, and he swore an oath. But he took far more than two cents. He took ten years of wonderful crops, ten years of	

Administrative Law Case 54

Mr. Scratch v. Jabez Stone

Summation for Claimant	Comments/Notes
the finest fields, ten years of the most fertile livestock, ten years of a healthy family, ten years of a good marriage, ten years of recognition and fame in the community, ten years of respect among all of those from whom he sought respect. This is more than sufficient value to establish consideration. This contract is binding and enforceable. A person does not sign a contract in his blood without understanding its significance, what it means, what its terms are. Contract law applies equally to everyone. Even though we may not like the people who live by our law, we must not avoid enforcing the law because we do not like the people. This is a country of laws—applied evenly to everyone.	

Administrative Law Case 55

Mr. Scratch v. Jabez Stone

Summation for Claimant	Comments/Notes

We have proved what we had to prove. This contract is a contract. The law is the law. And Jabez Stone must now fulfill his lawful and legal obligation under this contract. We ask you to render a decision for the Claimant.

Judge:

38   This was a well presented case. I will review the law, consider the evidence submitted, and promptly decide the case.

38   **And what is your decision and why? How effective or ineffective were the advocates. What would you have done differently to win?**

Administrative Law Case 56